Psychology
in the
Common
Cause

Psychology
in the
Common
Cause

B. R. BUGELSKI

PRAEGER

New York
Westport, Connecticut
London

Library of Congress Cataloging-in-Publication Data

Bugelski, B. R. (Bergen Richard), 1913–
    Psychology in the common cause / B.R. Bugelski.
      p.   cm.
   Bibliography: p.
   Includes index.
   ISBN 0–275–93034–3 (alk. paper)
   1. Social psychology. 2. Population psychology. 3. Economics—
psychological aspects. 4. Law—Psychology. 5. Educational
psychology. I. Title.
HM251.B785   1989
 302—dc19   88–17838

62, 644

Library of Congress Catalog Card Number: 88–17838
ISBN: 0–275–93034–3

First published in 1989

Praeger Publishers, One Madison Avenue, New York, NY   10010
A division of Greenwood Press, Inc.

Printed in the United States of America

The paper used in this book complies with the
Permanent Paper Standard issued by the National
Information Standards Organization (Z39.48–1984).

10 9 8 7 6 5 4 3 2 1

*Dedicated to everyone who thinks he knows what's
wrong with the world.*

Contents

Preface   *ix*

1.   *Basic Principles*   *1*

2.   *Clearing away Some Misconceptions*   *17*

3.   *The Problems*   *31*

4.   *An Introduction to People Problems*   *39*

5.   *Intrinsic Human Problems; or, The Trouble with People Is That They Are Human*   *43*

6.   *Social Problems: Living with Others*   *65*

7.   *An Introduction to Economic Problems*   *91*

8.   *Employment*   *101*

9.   *Money Matters*   *115*

10.   *Ideologies*   *127*

11.   *"The Law Is a Ass, a Idiot."*   *145*

12.   *Crimes and the Law*   *153*

13.	*Rights and Civil Liberties*	*169*
14.	*Schools and Learning*	*177*
15.	*The Nature of Learning*	*191*
16.	*And in Conclusion*	*199*
Bibliography		*209*
Index		*213*

Preface

Some years ago a colleague of mine and I wrote a book we called *A Handbook of Practical Psychology*. That book addressed itself to problems of individuals, such as habits, anorexia, depression. What was ignored was the alarming number of important problems facing people in groups and society in general, problems such as environmental pollution, wars, deficits, inflation, poverty, abortion, mass starvation, illiteracy, unemployment, pornography, and so on and on. Wherever one looks there appear to be problems facing the world's peoples. There are problems involving education, economics, population, the law, international relations; there are sex-related problems, moral and religious problems. Does psychology have anything to offer in connection with these? Perhaps psychology has no solutions that would please everybody, or even anybody, but it may hold some promise for a clearer perception of some of these problems. In some cases it may be that, people being what they are, they have to live with what they perceive as problems simply because they are human beings and simply being human involves accepting that some kinds of experience are inevitable. Just for starters, we will all grow old and die eventually. If this is a problem for anyone, he had better learn to live with it. It is the purpose of this book to highlight a few psychological principles that may help us live with some problems and to show that others may be found to be solvable if approached differently from currently directed efforts. This may not be the best of all possible worlds, but it is the only one we have despite our space explorers; so, before we give up on it, let us look at it anew.

In this book I have tried to look at problems that human beings create and that make life difficult for some and easy for others from a psychological point of view. The same problems can, of course, be looked at from many other viewpoints, for example, political, religious, economic, or historical. Before a psychologist or anyone else can apply a set of principles to the analysis of any problem, the problem itself must be recognized and described. Much of what is said here will amount to a description of a problem and the finding that psychologists have no special expertise to offer; but that, too, may be of value in that other approaches may have to be considered.

The problem areas to be considered are classified as those arising from the simple fact that "no man is an island," that people have come to live in groups of various kinds and dimensions, and that living with others gives rise to problems. Some of these problems are considered under the heading of population. Three other broad problem areas, those involving the law, business, and education, are dealt with in the remaining parts or chapters of the book. An introductory part serves to propose the few generally agreed-upon principles that psychologists of different backgrounds might endorse.

Obviously, not all problems that could be classified under the rubrics listed can be considered effectively by any one person as suitable for psychological inquiry. Readers may want to apply the principles described in the introductory chapters to problems they find of concern.

In preparing this book I benefited greatly from discussions with my colleagues Anthony Graziano, Edward Hovorka, and Murray Levine. They saved me from making a number of dubious statements that I was inclined to assert, but they are not responsible for any that remain. I am also indebted to James Allison of Indiana University, who called my attention to various weaknesses in my exposition in an earlier version.

Psychology
in the
Common
Cause

1
Basic Principles

In the billions of years that it has been circling the sun, a lot of things have happened on the earth. Among other things, human beings evolved to populate some of it, the habitable parts, and these human beings, being rather social animals, became organized in groups, settled in different parts of the globe, and developed various customs, traditions, arrangements for living (cultures), economic systems, and, unfortunately, governments. They did all this without the advice of psychologists for the simple reason that there were no psychologists around until 1879, and by that time virtually all social arrangements had been established. It is not likely that psychologists would have been consulted if they had been around. Most people did not pay much attention to philosophers either, although they have been around much longer. Philosophers have been important to other philosophers but not to people in general, most of whom were illiterate and still are in vast numbers in so-called primitive countries (we don't call them primitive anymore—they are "developing" or "emerging"). What being "literate" is, is itself a question. Being able to read comic books or sports pages hardly qualifies the "reader" to have opinions on other matters. Some philosophers, for example, Locke, Rousseau, and Marx, did influence some rebellious souls, but most have had little social impact. Psychologists, too, like philosophers, are of interest primarily to other psychologists, for very few, even educated people, ever read psychologists' writings. They might dip into Freud and think they are reading psychology instead of slightly titillating literature and mythology. For the most part people, educated or uneducated, are their own psychologists.

They know all about human nature—after all, they are humans, aren't they? Strangely enough, they call on medical doctors when something goes wrong with their bodies, but they never call on psychologists when something goes wrong with their society. They may call on psychologists when they are unhappy, and that makes some psychologists happier, but usually people would rather have someone else see a psychologist or psychiatrist if they don't like what that someone is doing.

Even those educated people who have taken courses in psychology have not found them too exciting or meaningful. After all, who cares about color blindness if she is not color-blind? Who cares about how nonsense syllables are learned and remembered or about how rats learn a maze or about the structures in the inner ear? Or about the thousands and thousands of facts that psychologists cram into their introductory tests? Admittedly, most of those facts are largely irrelevant to social problems, and millions of people live and die without ever hearing about them—and get along as well as those who have heard about them. On all the big, important issues that face people, psychologists have not been very helpful to their students or to society in general. Psychologists have been relegated to the same closets that are occupied by philosophers, while polticians, economists, and business people pontificate about human nature and carry out operations that affect us all on the basis of their "psychologies." Clearly, politicians know what is best for us, and if they don't, they get their advice daily from a collection of pundits writing columns for newspapers or dispensing wisdom on television. Occasionally politicians rely on experts who have "experience," that is, persons who have lived someplace or dealt with somebody and "know" what the Chinese or the Russians are really like. Professors in various fields are occasionally called on for advice, but the advice, of course, is "academic," and wiser heads such as those of other politicians are then consulted. Only rarely are psychologists consulted, and then only at lesser levels of government and about how a situation or system might be corrected or made more efficient instead of why the situation exists.

In their research psychologists have spent most of their time on what seem to be relatively minor questions and have hesitated to draw out the implications of some of the research that have profound effects on how people run their affairs. One reason for this hesitation may be the disagreements and differences among psychologists about the theoretical significance of their findings. They may agree on facts, but agreement on general principles is rare. Paradoxically, although most psychologists have not bothered to assert themselves on areas of agreement, there are certain fundamental propositions or principles on which there is rather general agreement and very little dissent. What dissent there may be is on various corollaries, extrapolations, or applications.

Quite naturally, the areas of agreement are few in number, and it is my purpose here to take these few principles on which most psychologists would agree and spell out their implications, which are rather devastating. It is perhaps for this reason that most psychologists have remained rather silent. Like the bystanders at the scene of a crime, they do not want to get involved. They don't want to rock any boats.

What are the principles on which we can find agreement?

DETERMINISM

The first principle is that of determinism as a general, all-encompassing proposition. In introductory texts the principle is often not even mentioned, but psychologists, like all other scientists, would have to stop all of their work if they did not believe that the world of nature is an orderly world in the sense that everything that happens has to happen in the way it does and could not have happened in any other way.

Average human beings, to the extent that they try to influence other people (especially parents with children, teachers with students, therapists with clients, doctors with patients) operate on the principle of determinism every day, even if they deny it if asked. They do things in certain ways because they believe those ways work, and if they do not succeed at something, they look for the cause and sometimes find it. If they cannot find the cause, they rarely believe that there was none. Sometimes, to be sure, people do look beyond nature for causes, as when the friends of a bereaved mother try to solace her by saying, "God took him" when her child was brutally murdered by some pedophile, but people who say such things are not too inclined to believe them, and it turns out to be just something to say when things get complicated.

Few psychologists have the courage to spell out the implications of determinism as B. F. Skinner (1971) did in his *Beyond Freedom and Dignity*. In this book, Skinner argues that we behave as we do because we have no alternatives. Our behavior is controlled by our nature and our reinforcement history, that is, what we have been rewarded for doing in the past. Skinner was assailed from all sides, even by some psychologists, for his effrontery in suggesting that people are not to blame for any evil they do and that, on the other hand, no one deserves credit for doing something considered good. Skinner's message was designed to shunt off our concerns about freedom and dignity. He sees these as based on mythology, as linguistic fictions, and in effect, meaningless words. He would have us turn to the real problems facing society. Skinner implied that whatever freedom and dignity were to be attained by human beings would result only from the diminution of aversive control, to which we are all subject in this world. The further implications of the principle of determinism will be spelled out when we address the problems humanity has created for itself. Note that we will not spend any time on problems created for the human race by nature, for example, earthquakes, tornadoes, volcanoes, and floods. The only solution for these problems is to live in areas that are not affected by such geographical or meteorological events.

INDIVIDUAL DIFFERENCES

The second principle on which there is general agreement is that of individual differences. So far as anything at all has been measured, it appears that no two things are alike in nature. Manufactured products may be alike to very fine tolerances of measurement, but we are not concerned here with such things as automobiles (some of which are lemons), but with such things as real lemons, no two of which are identical if measured finely enough. Add to lemons tomatoes, squirrels, robins, chimpanzees, and people, and you have the general idea. No two living creatures, including indentical twins, are alike in every respect. No two children in the same family have ever been or will ever be alike. No two people are of the same intelligence (whatever intelligence may be). Of course, two children may have the same IQ, but that is only because IQ tests do not measure minutely enough. Some psychologists suggest that we have seven different kinds of intelligence, and the likelihood of any two people being alike in all seven (or more) kinds is hardly to be considered.

What people have done with the fact of individual differences has been to ignore it, and, in some situations, to try to act by viewing or treating everyone alike as a commonly asserted operational principle. Thus parents try to treat their children alike (to their dismay at the results); teachers try to treat all pupils alike (although they cannot). Employers might try to treat workers alike, and in some respects, with union enforcement, they may appear to do so, but in slow economic periods they follow seniority rules or other formulas that result in differential treatment. To ease the problem of individual differences, humanity has invented the concept of the average man, the average temperature, the average yield per acre, the average output of anything, and so forth. The average is a mathematical creation and does not mean anything real because nothing is actually average. Most people who measure up as average do not like the finding and want to be above average in just about anything that anyone bothers to measure, except perhaps convictions for crimes.

A problem arises with averages in terms of what they really stand for. Suppose that some community has an average temperature of 32 degrees Fahrenheit over a period of years. Such an average means something; it means that it's a pretty cold place to live in some of the time. The probability is that nothing much can be done about it. One cannot easily raise external temperatures, and if anyone is to live in such a place one will have to take steps to keep from freezing (remember about half the time that temperature will be below 32). Now what about the finding that the average IQ is 100? What does this mean? We know what freezing means, but does anyone know what an IQ of 100 means? By measuring thousands of schoolchildren we know that, with an average IQ of 100, most children can barely pass through the eighth grade legitimately with an average grade of 75 or "C". Only minimal thought is required to recognize that in current educational systems most children cannot graduate from high school legitimately, and certainly not from college. The term *legitimately* refers to what passes for standard curricula in the usual schools in the United States. Yet something must be wrong, because over 75 percent of children in the United States graduate from high school and about 50 percent attend college.

In the early days of Hollywood, the movie moguls were said to believe that the average person had a mental age of 12. They were, unhappily, rather close to the truth. They produced movies that would entertain such lowbrows. Nowadays the movies are apparently designed for even lower mental ages, since most successful films deal with science fiction, horror, sex, or Godzilla. The movie moguls were encouraged in their views by the findings of World War I psychologists who lumped together the scores of uneducated draftees with those of draftees who had various levels of education. But we can raise the same question here that was raised about temperature. Can anything be done about the average IQ of 100? It is probably possible to raise the IQ of some children by rather heroic means. It would take the combined efforts of several adults per child, and rather extensive changes in social environments, to have any serious impact, and in modern cost-benefit terms it will probably never be attempted. The sources or causes of individual differences are not our immediate concern. Obviously heredity and environment are both involved. Most psychologists would agree that as far as socially significant behavior is concerned, environmental factors are preeminent. It should be admitted that because psychologists can do nothing about heredity, they are inclined to emphasize such influences as parents, teachers, other people, and environmental factors in general. The implications of individual differences will be explicated in relation to some of the problems I will treat later.

CONDITIONING

The third principle on which there is general agreement is that of conditioning. Probably no psychologist doubts that, when two stimuli are paired, some kind of association can be developed between their neural consequences so that one stimulus can bring about a reaction that is something like that originally brought about by the other. Where psychologists might differ is on details and on how much importance to attach to the principle of conditioning. The late O. Hobart Mowrer suggested (1960) that conditioning is the major factor controlling people's lives in that a great deal of conditioning takes place in connection with emotional reactions. According to Mowrer humans and others animals are, by nature, disposed to react in two primary ways: one is positive, to get more of some stimulus object or situation; the other is negative, to get away from or eliminate some stimulus object or situation. Though the details are complicated and largely unknown, Mowrer argued that animals, including humans, evolved in such a way that strong, painful stimuli are *naturally* avoided. It may be assumed that a mosquito biting one's arm will naturally evoke the response of brushing it away. Accompanying such a reaction will be some emotional reaction presumably of modest degree. A dog or alligator biting one's arm will lead to far greater physical involvement with much greater emotional content. The emotion in such cases might be suitably labeled as fear. The mere sight and sound of dogs or alligators in the future would generate fear as a result of the conditioning. The emotional reaction itself would generate stimuli for escape, avoidance, or other defensive responses such as kicking the dog or shooting the alligator if such reactions were feasible. Presumably, evolution has prepared us to indulge in such patterns of defense, avoidance, or aggression when we are in danger. The emotional response of fear, when aroused by conditioned stimuli that are otherwise neutral, is commonly labeled anxiety, and according to Mowrer, much, if not most, of our lives is spent in protecting ourselves in various ways from anxiety—or, more properly, anxieties, because these are aroused so frequently in our developing years, when multiple dangers surround us and we have not learned to cope. Henry David Thoreau (1854) sensed the ubiquity of anxiety when he wrote that most people "lead lives of quiet desperation."

On the positive side evolution has prepared us to try to get more of substances or situations that foster our survival, or perhaps the survival of the species. The species survival function may be rather blind and even denied by those who indulge in contraceptive actions or abortion, but it may underlie what is commonly called the sex drive. On a simpler level it is obvious that food is a positive stimulus substance in that normally people eat when the body generates stimuli that we call hunger. Anyone who has seen a normal, hungry baby nursing at a mother's breast has witnessed behavior that might be called trying to get more of (in this case) food. Such behavior continues until stimuli from the digestive system affect certain brain centers that apparently lead to a shutting off of such behavior. Research has demonstrated that if certain brain areas are damaged, eating behavior can continue virtually nonstop up to some limiting set-point for body fat, with resulting obesity. The original stimuli called hunger are just as negative in kind as pain stimuli, but the reactions generated can be considered positive[1] in that we look for or try to acquire something that will rid us of the stimuli instead of lashing and thrashing about, running away, or attacking objects in our environment. Mowrer chose the term *hope* to refer to the emotional reaction accompanying getting more of something. Though the term may not sound scientific, all that Mowrer meant by it was the kind of reaction that is generated in us when our bodily reactions begin to resemble those that accompany taking in food when hungry or water when thirsty, finding heat when cold, sitting down when tired, and so on. In ordinary terms we might translate hope as "feeling better." What *feeling better* means is not at all understood in scientific terms, but in general it amounts to a relaxation of the body. John B. Watson (1929), the "father" of behaviorism, used the world *love* for this relaxation in the presence of stimuli and he considered it one of the three primary emotional reactions we are all equipped with at birth. His other two were fear and anger. We will look into anger a little later in relation to aggression.

According to Mowrer, then, hope is a natural, positive, or relaxation response that is present when good things are happening to us, and this reaction can become conditioned to stimuli that accompany such a response. Thus, since as babies we are fed by our mothers, mothers become conditioned stimuli for hope and arouse the positive (relaxation) responses that food does naturally. The allegedly universal love for mothers is thus a conditioned response that is virtually guaranteed to occur in most people. There are, of course, mothers who are not loved, but that is because they also were involved in arousing fear responses in their offspring. If somebody or something else does the feeding, that somebody or something will come to be the love object, as Harry Harlow (1958) demonstrated with his monkeys and their surrogate mothers— wire constructions that held feeding bottles and provided, in some cases, warmth and cuddling material. It should be noted that the soft, cuddly surrogate mothers were preferred to the plain wire food-supplying surrogates.

Though food has been cited as the basic, unconditioned stimulus in the arousal of hope, it should be recognized that any stimuli conditioned to the arousal of feeling better as a result of any other treatment (stroking, petting, warming, rocking, and crooning) will come to arouse hope. On the human level, once language is acquired, any number of verbal items (words as stimuli) can come to arouse hope if they are paired with natural stimuli for relaxation or previously positively conditioned stimuli.

REINFORCEMENT

The next principle on which there is virtually universal agreement among psychologists, although varying in interpretation, is that of reinforcement. Actually, the principle of reinforcement is only an extension of the principle of conditioning. Ivan Pavlov (1927) originally thought of his unconditioned (natural) stimuli as reinforcers, that is, as strengtheners of associations. Reinforcement is a supposedly neutral word used to avoid what we commonly think of as rewards and punishments. It has the advantage that it may be either positive (rewards) or negative (some painful, noxious, unpleasant stimulus). The principle basically amounts to a recognition that when we are rewarded for doing something, we will tend to repeat that action given the same or similar circumstances, and when we are punished, we will tend to inhibit such behavior, at least for a while, if the punishment is long and strong enough. Some psychologists would like to extend the principle to cover what we learn—that is, they argue that we learn to do what is reinforced—but this extension is not necessary for our present purpose and is probably not correct. Reinforcers are motivators. They are the natural or unconditioned stimuli that lead us to feel better or to relax—that is, to have hope—when they appear if they are positive or to feel pain and fear if they are negative. Both positive and negative reinforcers are stimuli, and other (neutral) stimuli can be conditioned to initiate the same reactions as the natural positive or negative stimuli do. Such conditioned reinforcers are called secondary reinforcers. Thus, if the command "Stop" has been accompanied by a sharp slap on the face, it will not be necessary to repeat this combination often before an action is inhibited by the word alone. Similarly, if food is served shortly after a dinner bell is rung or "Come and get it" is shouted, the bell or the shout will arouse hope or feeling better. Food itself is a primarly reinforcer. The bell or the shout would be a conditioned or secondary reinforcer. Most of our lives are spent operating on the positive secondary reinforcement level where such items or events as paychecks, money, praise, gold stars, stock certificates, pats on the back, or medals—none of which can be eaten—motivate us into more or less continuous daily activities. On the negative side, as Mowrer would stress, many stimuli have been conditioned to arouse fear or anxiety in us, and we spend much of our time avoiding stimuli in situations that we can label negative.

The double-pronged principle of reinforcement thus underlies what used to be called pleasure and pain as all-important motives. Because these words are difficult to define, especially when we find some people "enjoying" pain, psychologists prefer to define reinforces in terms of what they make us do, namely, approach or avoid certain stimuli.

The important point about reinforcers, according to Skinner, and probably most psychologists, is that whatever we do of a positive nature is the result of prior reinforcement. We do what we have been rewarded for doing. On the negative side, we shrink from actions that were followed by punishment of one kind or another. To push the point to its extremes, as Skinner does, whatever we do (bowl, paint, write books, bet on horses, drink, take drugs, mug other people), we do it because such activities have been reinforced. And things we don't do are the result of our not having been reinforced for doing them or our never having tried them in the first place. The first time we ever do anything has to be put down to chance, to being forced to, by social pressure or to avoid doing something else.

Skinner bases his proposals for the application of psychology to social problems on positive reinforcement. He avoids any reliance on negative reinforcement as being rather useless in that research shows that somewhat restricted punishments do not result in any permanent avoidance of the punished behavior and that the punisher usually becomes a negative stimulus. Thus a punitive father could very well come to be disliked, and Skinner would rather have everyone likable. Mowrer, on the other hand, leans heavily on the fact that life is full of dangers, failures, traumas, misadventures, disappointments, and frustrations, all of which arouse anxiety and avoidance, escape, or destructive behavior. From Mowrer's point of view, much of our lives is spent avoiding more trouble than we already have.

Between Mowrer and Skinner we have enough motivators to account for anyone's activities. Note that both views are in perfect agreement with the principle of determinism, so that now we can summarize the view so far as saying that we always do what we have to do because of our history of conditioning and reinforcement. If we now note that every single individual's reinforcement history has to be unique, we are also driven to conclude that nobody can every really understand anybody else because we can never fully appreciate anyone's reinforcement history.

A word of caution here about the interpretation of the term *reinforcement*. It has been stated above that reinforcers are only conditioned stimuli that arouse appropriate emotions (positive or negative). They do not, as the term might imply, "strengthen" responses or "connections" in the nervous system or anything else. They merely affect the probability of an occurence of a response. Once a stimulus has come to arouse an emotional state, it will continue to do so unless a contrary emotional state takes over. Thus continued responding in the absence of a reward will generate fatigue, disappointment (a variant of fear), or frustration. The response will not then be weakened—it will simply cease to occur.

Pavlov (1927) called such failure of occurrence following withdrawal of a reinforcer extinction. The response was not actually extinct—it could be easily reinstated by reintroducing the reinforcing stimulus.

In many ways a positive reinforcer amounts to a payment for effort expended, a wage or salary that one works for in expectation of payment. You work for what you get. An appropriate explanation of expectation would take us too far afield for this book. Such an explanation can be found in an earlier book (Bugelski 1978) or article (Bugelski 1982). What is important to note about reinforcers is that by controlling their availability one *can* shape and control behavior in various ways; but because of the many different kinds of reinforcers affecting us throughout our lives in a basically uncontrolled environment, it is quite impossible to predict any individual's behavior without a complete knowledge of that person's reinforcement history—an obvious impossibility. Another caution: reinforcers can operate only when there is an underlying need, drive, or deprivation. Without such an underlying condition, a reinforcing stimulus will have no immediate impact on behavior. A bank teller can count out thousands of dollars and be indifferent to the fact that she has money in her hands.

When Skinner presented his arguments about the nature of humanity in his *Beyond Freedom and Dignity,* he relied on his conviction that the only available tool for effecting change in human behavior was the operation of reinforcement. For much of anyone's behavior, this is quite true. Glands and other hereditary factors affect behavior and activities. Thus a strong lad who is about six and a half feet tall can hardly avoid a basketball coach and his blandishments. He may become a basketball player even if he doesn't really care to play. Even here, however, reinforcements play their part. Which team offers the most? Some hereditary and physical factors can be altered (for good or bad) by such things as drugs, nutrition, surgery, or climate, so that we cannot argue that reinforcement is everything that counts, but it counts for most of the kinds of behavior that occur. I include here the negative sides of reinforcement: the use of threats, punishments, or deprivations of various kinds by people in a position to impose them on us. They cannot be ignored in accounting for a great deal of our activity.

What Skinner did not emphasize or spell out in any serious way is that in order to control someone else's behavior, one must be in position to present the positive or negative reinforcers, and to do this effectively one must be in charge of the person one is going to control so that the reinforcers are the correct ones, given at the correct times, in correct amounts, and so on. Outside the laboratory about the only one who is in position to do this is an animal trainer in a circus. She can control the animals' food supply, beat them, or otherwise treat them well or cruelly. She will get results either way, although one way might be more efficient or dependable. Beyond the animal trainer we might find a mother with an infant child (and no one else around) who is in position to control the reinforcement schedule. Since there is rarely no one else around, the reinforcement pattern is likely to be less than perfectly controlled. As soon as a child grows old enough to go to school, the mother (also siblings and father) begins to lose what control she may have had, and peers and teachers begin to take over. They too are less than likely to have perfect control, and the reinforcement history of the individual begins to become so varied that no one person can begin to predict what the subject will do in any given situation. Obviously, some sources of control will be stronger than others for various reasons, for example, the kinds of reinforcers, their duration, the skill with which they are administered, and competition from others. The point is that who controls whom becomes a puzzeling case of kinds of environment and the numbers and kinds of people one happens to run into. What emerges from the varied convergent and divergent sources of control is usually some sort of mixed-up person who behaves in ways we are hard to comprehend. One becomes a pickpocket, another a priest, another an Olympic class diver, another a coal miner. Some people will like wine; others will denounce it. Some will watch football on television whereas others will watch only educational programs. Others will sneer at TV as beneath their dignity. The variation in human behavior is probably impossible to catalog even if it is all based on the principle of reinforcement.

Skinner avoided the question of who is to be in charge or in control. It appears to be too dictatorial for an antidictatorial public. No one likes to be called a fascist, a Hitler, or the like. Yet that is exactly what it takes to achieve control over individuals and, with sufficient help, over populations. Even Hitler did not have complete control. There were some Germans who opposed him. After Hitler was gone, many Germans claimed that distinction—new reinforcers were now around.

The point of this, of course, is that only those in relatively complete charge of a person are in a position to reinforce that individual or groups of similar people. When it comes to dealing with populations of millions and hundreds of millions, the would-be controller has quite a task. He needs like-minded helpers by the hundreds of thousands and more. A president of the United States, with the entire Congress backing his every whim, would still not be in a position to do much if those who had to enforce legislation were not under control. Granted that ideal situation, there could be a lot of support from people in law enforcement, but unless everyone was being reinforced appropriately, there could be rebellion, resistance, lack of cooperation, or other forms of opposition. Poland represents a case of virtually complete control by the government. It can pass any laws it chooses, yet the people cannot be controlled in directions desired by the government by the reinforcements offered. The problem for the government is that the kinds of reinforcers that would work would result in the elimination of that government.

In the United States the government is not the only agency of control. Many other agencies (both business and nonbusiness groups) try to influence legislation through their lobbies, and sometimes they succeed. The president and Congress have actually little power to control events and activities of the population and find that one group or another will be disaffected by an action that would reinforce another special group. When, for example, a government wishes to control inflation, the measures taken (for example, the imposition of high interest rates) may be followed by higher unemployment and thus create new problems. When one adds international complications, for example, high tariffs or boycotts of foreign goods, new inflationary forces are put into action, creating more unemployment. Foreign wars (or domestic disturbances) result in lost lives—an undesirable state of affairs not only to those at risk but also to those who have been trained to support nonviolence. Again, the point is that it is impossible to keep everybody happy and that in fact the opposite is more probable: that is, nearly everybody will be unhappy most if not some of the time. Any completely happy person is to be congratulated and probably institutionalized. Such people would surely not be aware of what is going on about them, and if they were, they would have to be inhumane if not inhuman.

When one goes beyond one's immediate personal and family situation and thinks in world terms—with much of the world's population living from hand to mouth, if not quite literally starving, and killing one another in tribal, religious, or territorial wars—it becomes quite plain that the human species does not appear destined to have a very pleasant life experience on this earth. Perhaps for this reason much of humanity has invented a more pleasant afterlife.

The principle of reinforcement is enough for Skinner to justify his position that people constantly, always, inevitably do what they do because they have been reinforced for such behavior in the past. It might be mentioned that reinforcement need not follow on every occasion of a behavior—a person can go on doing something long after it was last reinforced and will continue to do so until some other behavior pattern is reinforced more effectively. The horse player who wins once may place many bets later and suffer many losses before she gives up, if she ever does. Sometimes she will not bet but think that some horse will win, and if it does, the reinforcement effect will be strengthened. Even if the horse comes in second, it will help. It almost won. If the chosen horse finishes last, the bettor will look for and find an explanation (the race was fixed, or her horse was bumped and lost stride, for example). The racing example is very rich. One does not have to win money. The pleasure of mixing with other people may make a player feel like one of the group, a feeling that can be idealized in many ways. After all, racing is the "sport of kings," the hobby of the very rich; it offers safe risks or adventures with only money to be lost. There may be companions one likes, parties to go to with winners, and so on. We need not concern ourselves with the possibility that "horse players always die broke"—that is a convenient fiction. Some do not if they have other sources of income. The point is that reinforcers do not have to be continuous or large or regular. Intermittent reinforcement is more powerful, as a matter of proven laboratory fact. Reinforcement in babyhood by mothers can last a lifetime. The problem here is recognizing what was reinforced by Mommy and what was not.

Perhaps the most important area where reinforcement operates, and with powerful effects, is the factory, the office—in general the workplace and the marketplace. Because of the way in which people have come to live, nearly everyone is expected to have a job, work for a living, earn one's keep. The aversive aspects of unemployment and the positive features of a paycheck keep millions of people working away at jobs of varying degrees of satisfaction but with that monetary reinforcement operating as a major motive. What is called reinforcement is actually an exchange of time and labor for money. Reinforcements always cost something, so that to think of them as rewards is grossly misleading. The laboratory rat pushes levers in exchange for food; the factory worker pushes levers and buttons in exchange for money. The MBA pushes papers. Barry Schwartz (1986) makes a persuasive case for this interpretation of reinforcement effects.

The suggestion that all of our important social and economic behavior is a result of reinforcement leaves little room for anything else. We do not act or do anything that was not reinforced in our background. We can ascribe our behavior to a sense of honor, decency, charity, thrift, nobility of character, or whatever we like, but the simple fact is that nothing like any of these is a meaningful factor in behavior. If we give to the poor, it is not a motive of charity that drives us. It is the result of having been reinforced for giving or sharing in our past. We may also give to obtain future reinforcements such as goodwill in the community or a better reputation, or because of a belief in the virtue of the cause, but that belief is a consequence of prior reinforcement.

In *Beyond Freedom and Dignity*, Skinner makes it clear that we are not free in any meaningful or serious sense of the term, nor are we entitled to any dignity. Dignity suggests that we are to be respected in some way for what we do or who we are. Because what we do and who we are is a matter of our history of reinforcement, over which we had no control, there is no way in which we are entitled to respect (or disrespect). Some people claim that respect must be earned, the implication being that we are not entitled to respect unless we were lucky enough to have been reinforced for doing what someone else would like us to do. In almost all cases, a person can be respected by some and not respected by others because of his behavior—while not meriting either reaction. President Franklin Delano Roosevelt was loved, even adored, by millions who voted for him in four successive presidential elections. Millions of Republicans voted against him and hated him violently. One would-be assassin took a shot at him. After his death some former supporters came to hate him for his alleged sellout at Yalta; others lost respect for him because of revelations about his extramarital affairs. Yet all through his life Roosevelt, like the rest of us, just did what he had been brought up to do, following a moral code that was imposed upon him just as much as his eloquence. He was not entitled to praise or blame. No one is. Such a situation is difficult to accept for those who desire praise and those who do not want to be blamed, which means most of us. What would happen to us if we never got A's in school, or medals for valor, or the first prize in beauty contests (do we every worry about the losers in such contests?). Much of life is what is called a zero-sum game. In most situations, if one wins, many others lose. In these cases there is not a simple zero sum but a lot of negatives, disappointments, crushed hopes, misery, even when the losers smile bravely and congratulate the winner.

If we can forget about freedom and dignity, the two most touted slogans of the misinformed, we might make a little progress in recognizing problems that affect large masses of mankind that do not worry about freedom and dignity and would be (momentarily) grateful for a piece of bread. Let us not spend time pitying the poor; they are not more deserving than the rich. Our pity will not help them in any way. Material help would.

Though Mowrer disagrees with Skinner about the nature of reinforcement's role (he views it as motivator rather than as a strengthener of behavior), the same net results emerge from his theorizing. People still do what they have to do on the basis of the kinds of emotional conditioning they have undergone. For Mowrer the primary emotions are fear and hope. Fear is aroused by painful or noxious stimuli, and with conditioning, new stimuli can become effective in arousing fear. A learned fear might be termed an anxiety, and it is our anxieties that propel us through most of our actions in life. Pleasurable reactions (to warmth, fondling, food, rest, and so on) become conditioned to other stimuli (Skinner's reinforcers), and these new stimuli then arouse hope. The combination of hope and fear and their varying shades or degrees (disappointment, when hope stimuli are removed; relief, when anxiety-provoking stimuli disappear) appear to Mowrer sufficient to account for most of our behavior. Our learned fears and hopes, then, constantly prod us forward or backward, in approach and avoidance of people, places, or situations. When avoidance is impossible, and where some history has effected relief or hope via aggression, we may become agressive toward our tormentors.

If we recognize that Mowrer is only providing a background against which reinforcers (as motivators) can work, we draw the same conclusion that Skinner draws. All so-called intentional behavior is controlled by external forces in the form of reinforcers. Some reinforcers can be termed positive (arousing hope for Mowrer or merely strengthening the behavior that was followed by the reinforcer for Skinner); others are negative (threatening or fear stimuli for Mowrer, painful or aversive stimuli for Skinner). Note that for Skinner a punishing stimulus is one that results in a temporary restraint in the activation of a prior behavior; it does not eliminate the action or have any meaningful effect in the long run. For Skinner punishment is a waste of time, and he would rather work on the positive virtues of reinforcers; for Mowrer a punishing stimulus will result in aversion or avoidance in future situations. Such a difference in interpretation of punitive stimulation is not of any great concern. For both theorists punishment will, if long and strong enough, halt the behavior that is being punished at least for some time. In the period following the punishment, a person might be positively reinforced for some other behavior in that stimulus situation and come to act differently in the future. Though Mowrer does not discuss freedom and dignity as forcefully as does Skinner, the net result of Mowrer's views is that the terms are rather empty of meaning; we do what we have to do because of fear and hope. There is nothing praiseworthy or blameworthy in either case.

Though Mowrer and Skinner differ in other views and areas, their differences are of no great material importance for most of human behavior, and their basic views are not challenged by the great, if not overwhelming, proportion of other psychologists, most of whom subscribe to a rather all-encompassing determinism. Psychology does not have room for willful choices or spontaneous, uncaused, innovative actions. Where these appear to occur, they are put down to random or chance variations which are themselves caused but for which a causal explanation is prevented by complexities of the moment. The principles of determinism, individual differences, conditioning, and reinforcement, which do enjoy widespread support among psychologists, can now be directed against the problems that plague human beings. As I noted earlier, some of these problems are natural because of our physiological structure. We cannot fly, for example, as we have no wings. That eliminates one form of escape from embarrassing situations. In primitive settings we might be attacked by wild animals that might be stronger than we are—there are human limitations to survival. We are beset by diseases of various kinds, and some of us eat or otherwise consume substances that the human body was not designed to accept. Other problems result from human efforts to solve other problems. Here psychology may be able to play a role.

CONTEXT

Before we approach our problem of analyzing problems created by humans, we should emphasize what might be considered another principle, that of context. In practically all areas of human affairs, there are complicating factors and interplays or interactions among our conditioned stimuli, our reinforcers, or individual differences, and our given basic human physiology. White paper looks brighter on a black background than on a gray one. A caged tiger does not arouse the basic fear reaction. We come into the world with a fear of large, unfamiliar, or noisy objects. We behave differently with different people as the result of considerable learning. The child in school may be a model of politeness and respectability. While at home she may reign as a small tyrant over some kinds of parent. In every sphere of human activity the principle of context will govern or exert an influence. A fearful soldier may fall upon a grenade to save his comrades whereas, if they were not present, he might run away in panic. Whatever is said in the remainder of this analysis, the reader should always recognize the fact of context.

NOTE

1. *Positive* here is circular in that it is derived from the behavior and not from the stimuli. We come to call things positive if they are followed by relaxation.

2

Clearing away Some Misconceptions

Psychologists spend a lot of time in introductory courses telling their students what is not so. It doesn't do much good, for after the course is over, most of the students still believe a lot of nonsense that they came into the course with. Obviously, the usual teaching techniques do not work too well. Perhaps some students' beliefs about such nonsense as extrasensory perception may be somewhat shaken, but their 18 years of exposure to parents, teachers, companions, newscasters, rock stars, and other ill-assorted influences such as movies and television have loaded them with views about themselves and humanity in general that leave them easy prey for poets, novelists, newspaper columnists and other spinners of fiction. Most people in the Western world believe they have some special purpose in existence (and if they don't know what it is, they spend a lot of time looking for it), that they are somehow better than other animals, and better than some other branches of humanity, and, perhaps worst of all, that the world owes them something, a living perhaps.

It would take us too far afield to itemize all the superstitions, ill-founded beliefs, and fallacious thinking demonstrated throughout human history. But it is necessary to spell out some of the areas of misconception that create problems for people.

The most important area of misconception arises from what has come to be called the nature-nuture controversy. What do we inherit from our ancestors in strictly genetic terms, and what about us is a function of the environments in which we grow up, including of course the people who manipulate us in one way or another? Some psychologists such as Arthur Jensen (1969) spend their time trying to assess what percentage of a person's intelligence is inherited and what percentage can be ascribed to environmental influences. The necessary research for disentangling such influences has yet to be done and poses formidable problems, the basic one being that of deciding just what intelligence might be, if there is anything worthy of such a name. It was mentioned in the last chapter that some psychologists support the notion that there are many kinds of intelligence (aesthetic, musical, athletic, spatial, numerical, linguistic, and perhaps many other kinds), and the kinds of environmental influence that might have to be measured haven't even been detailed to any serious degree. The notion that anyone could offer an explanation in heredity-environment terms for whatever differences might be found in some sample racial groups is patently absurd. Most psychologists are inclined to say that both heredity and environment are involved in practically any kind of behavior that can be specified. Certainly, in any activity—for example, running a foot race—we can recognize the role of practice, drugs, coaching, physical size, energy levels, bodily proportions, general health, and so on. A crippled child does not win 100-meter races. Whether a person even engages in such activity could be a function of either heredity or environment and probably both.

I will spend no time on assessing hereditary endowments beyond noting that nothing can be done about people's heredity—they have already inherited it. What will concern us is behavior that can be modified by manipulating the environment, by reinforcement and conditioning.

It may be useful to point out that most psychologists agree that most adult human behavior cannot be accounted for by any hypothetical instincts, that is, hereditary patterns of behavior. Though there may be some instinctive behaviors, no one has ever established that humans demonstrate any, and though some psychologists are inclined to believe that some human behavior patterns that can be labeled as sociability or temperament have an individual biological foundation, nothing much can be done about such matters, and they have little impact on major human social problems.

INSTITUTIONAL THINKING

The psychologist Floyd Allport, a self-styled behavioristic social psychologist, once wrote an article he titled "Institutional Thinking" (1947). What Allport tried to do—with little impact, for very few psychologists know or cite the article—was to demonstrate that most of our thinking amounts to practicing mythology. Mythology amounts to creating imaginary creatures and assigning them special powers and, if we believe in the mythical creatures, submitting ourselves to their machinations.

The myths that modern humans create for themselves only appear to be less imaginative than those of the early Greeks. What modern humans have done is to assign names to nonexistences and various powers to such non-entities. The most serious of such myths, for example, is that of the existence of such a thing as a government. The government is alleged to do this or that, to tell another government what to do—to attack another government, establish a new one, and so on. A moment's relfection should convince anyone that there is no, nor can there be any, such thing as a government—there can only be people who do or say such-and-such. Among other things they might say is that they "work for the government," but this can only mean that they do things other people tell them to do and pay them for doing.

Perhaps a clearer case can be made with the term *corporation*. What is a corporation? Or a company? When a company closes a plant in one town and moves to another where labor is cheaper, who closed the plant and what moved? The building did not move, although some of the furniture and machinery may have been loaded onto trucks by people. But we say the company moved or the Bethlehem Steel Corporation moved. But no one can see *a company* move. A company or corporation is a piece of paper naming certain individuals as officers and, in some countries, absolving those individuals of certain responsibilities—the so-called limited liability represented by the letters *Inc.* or *Ltd.* Note that not even the incorporation papers move. They stay in Delaware.

Perhaps an even clearer example is the committee. We are always electing committees, which presumably arrive at some recommendations. A committee can recommend that someone be fired from a job (for the "good of the corporation"). The discharged employee has no one to blame. Any member of the committee can claim that she did not vote against the employee and blame the action on "the committee". The committee, just like a company or a corporation or a government, becomes a means by which people can escape responsibility. The government raises our taxes or involves us in a war because our country was insulted or our country's interests were involved. A country can hardly be insulted or have interests. Only people can be insulted or have interests, and we may well wonder how many people in the United States had an interest in Vietnam before the government sent soldiers there. It is a strong probability that most of the people in the United States had never heard of Vietnam before "our country's interests" became involved.

On a more individual level, institutional thinking hobbles us every day. Because certain "offices" such as the post office or the law court can be serviced by interchangable individuals while the work gets done, we come to identify individuals with the names of the occupations they hold. The title becomes the agent, or, in Marshall McLuhan's words

(1967), the medium becomes the message. When our mail is late, we blame the post office instead of the letter carrier who may be goofing off. Anyone with a title, such as professor, doctor, lawyer, judge, admiral, or police officer, becomes automatically endowed with whatever mythology has developed around such people over a long period. An unscrupulous mayor appoints a politician who can deliver "the Spanish vote" or "the black vote" for a candidate for judge. The erstwhile party hack dons robes, sits on the bench, and dispenses justice, a subject he may never have considered before. He may be a lawyer, to be sure, but that proves little or nothing about his talents as a judge. A doctor who just managed to get by at the bottom of her class dispenses medicine and performs surgery, and her acts are seldom questioned except by lawyers. A second opinion is not likely to be different if the second doctor knows the first doctor's diagnosis. Whenever an action is taken by a group, it would be desirable to know who initiated the action, why others followed, and how closely the group shared the reasons generated by the leaders. What is important about such institutional thinking is to recognize that much of our behavior is controlled by the actions of individual people bearing—even masquerading under—titles that carry an excess baggage of tradition and mythology so powerful in emotional loading that we no longer recognize or realize that they are still people, and only people, who are not wiser or better than they were before they were endowed with their titles. Thus an actress marries a prince and becomes a princess; corrupt politicians get elected to Congress and must be addressed as "Honorable." When President Franklin D. Roosevelt called the Supreme Court "nine old men," he was speaking the exact truth, but many people thought he was insulting our most venerable institution.

Perhaps the most devastating of all our mythological thinking is the reification of something we call "Our Country" as if something existed that amounted to more than a stretch of earthly terrain peopled by various and sundry individuals all concerned primarily about their own affairs. We will look at this myth more closely later, (see "Patriotism and Nationalism", in chapter 6), but we should now extend the argument to what amounts to institutionalizing behavior itself, that is, to creating mechanisms that do not exist and using them to explain our own or other people's actions. Perhaps the most common of such reifications of nonthings is greed. Most people seem to act as if they believed that there is such a thing as greed and that people have more or less of it somewhere within them. Thus we hear that "money is the root of all evil." The New Testament expression was, "The love of money is the root of all evil," but in either case, the implication is that some people want more of good things than other people do or than they deserve—that is, they are greedy. Obviously, there are no measures for greed any more than there are for benevolence or altruism. A Harvard professor E. O. Wilson (1975) has written a scholarly book about the altruism of ants and other insects when he might better have simply described the behaviors. Even more common than references to greed is the daily reliance on such terms as *bad, evil, sinful*. A president of the United States referred to the Soviet Union as an "evil empire." Obviously, what he meant was that he did not approve of the behavior of certain individuals who style themselves as the politburo and pretend to represent all of the assorted millions of residents from the Oder River to the Pacific Ocean, many of them hardly aware that there is a politburo. Soviet citizens speak over 100 different languages, follow different customs, and practice different religions. Most of the residents are illiterate, uneducated, poor, and unenlightened about what goes on beyond their own little villages. To call a country evil is to multiply the error parents commit daily in telling their children that they are bad, when what they mean is that the children did something the parent did not approve of.

Terms such as *good, bad, evil, kind, moral, friendly*, and *nasty* may have some fractional merit in some context when everyone knows the context. When the terms are used to suggest that people have traits or characteristics in the same sense that they have eyes or noses, we get into trouble. We cannot study or observe kindness, for example. All we can do is note some kinds of behavior that some of us might find commendable and give it a label. Others might consider the same behavior foolish. A generous person might give Christmas turkeys to poor people she knows about or even does not know about, but except for saints, who give away all they have, generosity usually is limited, controlled by other mythologies such as "Charity begins at home." How much would one have to give and to how many different people to merit a label like *generous*? Even then, there would be no evidence that anyone possessed generosity as some little device in her brain or body that controlled her behavior. A more adequate account might be given in terms of habits she has acquired in connection with the disposal of her income or possessions. These, in general, would be limited to her own behavioral history, the kinds of people she has come to acquire sympathy for, that is, feel positive about. So with all trait terms, of which there are about 22,000 in any commonly used dictionary. They serve, as I noted above, in some contexts when nothing serious is being considered and in idle conversations. When we try to deal with problems, such terms are best put back in the dictionary, and the details of who did what to whom have to be taken into account.

Nothing but trouble arises when we spout terms such as *democracy, liberal, conservative, freedom, the Constitution, the Founding Fathers*, and so on. We will have occasion to examine terms such as these shortly, but for the moment we should recognize that East Germany calls itself the

German Democratic Republic, and that we have to deal with the People's Republic of China and with the fact that the Soviet Union has a constitution. In the last case it will be readily accepted by most anti-Soviets that it is just a piece of paper with words written on it by somebody, in this case, largely unknown. In the case of our own Constitution, it is a revered document that from the point of view of the Supreme Court (which interprets the Constitution) should be our guiding light. The members of the court seem to overlook the facts that the document appears to be rather debatable; that even the Founding Fathers knew this and added procedures by which it might be amended; and that it has been amended twenty-six times—and probably should be further amended in a great many ways if what we know about human nature were taken into account.

Not only do we have the Constitution of the United States to guide us in our daily lives, but we also have constitutions in every state. In New York State, for example, a judge held in 1984 that it was unconstitutional for a man to rape his wife, although, until he so ruled, it apparently was constitutional. But to show his judicial wisdom the judge decreed that it was also unconstitutional for a wife to rape her husband. How the latter could be done might raise some questions for our growing population of sexologists, sex therapists, and advocates of women's rights. When will the first homosexual accuse his lover of rape?

The emptiness of a great deal of our language is a truly worrisome problem, but we must get along in our current fashion with whatever vocabularies we possess. Words evolve continually, and new expressions and usages creep into the language. We use them for various purposes, sometimes to avoid communication. When Madison Avenue "runs it up the flagpole to see who salutes" we, in general, know what is implied. When the president calls taxes revenue enhancers, we still may know what is really meant, but only those who benefit from depletion allowance know what they mean by the expression. Sometimes good, strong, and serviceable words that might lead to action are perverted by substitutes, euphemisms, that mask realities and delay or prevent action. Thus a slum becomes an inner city. Something can be done about a slum, but what can you do about an inner city? Auto theft becomes unauthorized usage, drunken driving becomes DWI, old people become senior citizens, and so on. Words have their uses but also their abuses.

It would be impossible to catalog all the misuses and abuses of all the words that their users pretend mean something. A final example is offered to stand for thousands of words that are, in effect, meaningless because they do not specify concrete details. Take the noun *carelessness* or the verb *to be careful*. Every parent cautions children departing for school with the traditional "Be careful". For the most part nothing serious happens to children going to school. If something does happen, somebody, perhaps including the child, was careless. Now no psychologist has ever discovered in anyone's brain, body, personality, or anything else anything resembling carefulness or its opposite. It is a word we use when we mean that whatever happened could have been avoided. But what does happen could not be avoided—it happened. Looking for the reason why something happened is sometimes partially successful. We plug in a coffeepot on a circuit that cannot take the additional load, and the fuse blows. "How careless of me!" we say. Had we but taken a little care, namely counted all the watt loads and known what the circuit could take, we could have avoided the error. Why did we not do so? Because we were being "too careful" watching the pan of onions frying so that they would not burn, or we were distracted by the doorbell or telephone, or we were paying attention to something else that may or may not have needed the attention but called for it nevertheless. Being careful to avoid bumping into a little old lady's shopping cart, we back up into a little old man's cart. Pilots just learning to handle their plane alone sometimes forget to lower their wheels and are branded with pilot error and carelessness. Did they forget or did they fail to remember? If they failed to remember, was it because they were remembering to lower their flaps, switch gas tanks, watch for crosswinds, or pay close attention to several of a dozen things that must be taken into account in a landing? One beginning pilot was busy fighting a cockpit fire just at the moment when he would normally have lowered his wheels. The report on the subsequent accident contained the indictment "Pilot error, carelessness." (Bugelski, 1944) Nothing was done about the cause of the fire that the pilot had extinguished. Nothing ever happened because someone was careless. He did what he had to do under the circumstances.

If we watch our language, we can now proceed to look at an extension of word usage in the somewhat broader fields of opinions and beliefs.

OPINIONS, ATTITUDES, AND BELIEFS

When pollsters query the public, they presumably are inquiring about people's opinions. The assumption made is that people have opinions, and certainly common language habits support such an assumption. People frequently say, "In my opinion." The *my* implies possession. But what is that which is possessed? Where was it before it was asked for? Did it actually exist in any form? Judges frequently reserve opinions for some later date when they presumably will be announced or made public in some form. Presumably, before an opinion is pronounced, the judges do not have one. Gordon Allport (1937) suggested that opinions are really only verbal statements and as such cannot exist unitl they are uttered or written. But opinions are usually statements about positions of being for or against something. Opinions are sought or expressed in situations involving some doubt about a matter, where there is controversy, where opposite opinions might be expected. Though opinions are behavioral events in that they are verbalizations or statements, they are not, in themselves, active, productive, or consumatory events. Nothing happens as the result of an opinion. Of course, there are other ways of expressing opinions than by talking or writing. One might vote for or against something. The vote is then taken as an expression of opinion. If one abstrains, the interpretation could be that one does not have an opinion on the immediate issue. But a vote, in itself, is just an expression. It is a preliminary operation that may be followed by action of some kind later, perhaps much later, as when a law is to go into effect a year after the vote. Opinions, then, are verbal or other indications of what side one favors in some controversial matter. No action need follow. One might have the opinion that the word *Cesarean* in the term *cesarean section* does not actually refer to Caesar having been delivered by a surgical procedure but that the word really comes from the Latin *caedere*, "to cut." Opinions, then, can relate to controversies about information, the meanings of words, various symbols, worthiness of former presidents, to name but a few. In any case, opinions are always concerned with controversies, being for or against, finding something better or worse, favoring or faulting, pro and con. Opinion pollsters usually offer a range of positions with such qualifiers as *very* or *mildly*, suggesting that opinions need not be simply matters of yes or no but might include maybe.

Allport distinguished between opinions and attitudes; opinions were the expression of attitudes. Attitudes, then, were what one possessed, and opinions were statements describing one's attitudes. But then, what are attitudes? Psychologists have described attitudes in many ways, but the common ingredient in most descriptions is how someone feels about something. Some psychologists add ingredients such as what one thinks or believes, so that a definition of an attitude might read: everything one feels, thinks, and believes about something. We can assume that thinking and believing are not really different, and I will deal with them shortly, but more importantly, most definitions tend to equate attitudes with readiness to behave in some way should some situation arise that calls for action. A common, innocent example is that of a runner on the track in starting position. When the starter says, "Get ready," the runners may be standing around or stretching arms and legs, but they quickly drop to their knees and adjust their feet in starting blocks. But they are still not doing anything they might consider serious. The starter then says, "Get set," and the runners tense, push against the ground with their hands and against the starting blocks with their feet, and they are then really ready to lunge forward as soon as they hear the pistol shot. The position of being "set" is taken as an analogue of an attitude.

An attitude, then, is a readiness to act in some specific way at an appropriate signal or stimulus. It is important to note that the attitude of the runners did not exist until the starter's signals. The runners did not possess any attitudes about starting to run until their previously learned responses to the signals had been evoked.

Returning to the definition previously described as everything one feels, thinks, and believes about something, we now can see that we should include a readiness to respond, to react in a specific way, to get set at some signal if we are to appreciate what an attitude might be. Omitting the thinking and believing ingredients leaves us with an attitude as a reaction to a signal, a reaction that includes a bodily orientation or readiness accompanied by emotional components (certainly runners in a race are excited, keyed up, anxious, hopeful, fearful, and so on).

Attitudes, however, are not usually talked about in racing contexts. They are, rather, discussed in the same arenas as opinions. They become matters of interest in pro and con contexts. Instead of asking for someone's opinion about the Vietnam war, for example, we might ask, "What is your attitude to the Vietnam war?" The question, or other stimulus, might then arouse or create an attitude that would amount to an emotional reaction of a positive or negative nature and some tendency or readiness to respond in a manner tantamount to approach, avoidance, or aggressive attack, depending upon prior experience with the original stimuli symbolized by the content of the question. Actual physical, observable activity might well be inhibited or restrained because of the absence of the actual original stimulus or contexual factors—one does not reach out for or hit a missing object. The reaction might also include some imagery related to the original object, including imagery of previous reactions. Depending on the learning history and context, one might well not display any overt activity. If the subject matter of the question is unfamiliar, as might be a question about an unknown war, event, or object, the aroused attitude might amount to virtually nothing. Being asked, "How do you like sorrel soup?" for instance, might not arouse any specific response if one had never heard of such a product or substance. A correct answer might be, "I don't know." If someone should begin to drool and display the customary signs of excited delight at the mention of sorrel soup, one could then gather that an attitude of a positive nature had been aroused. There is always a question of deceit in dealing with people. They can display signs (provide opinions) of being in favor of things they oppose, and vice versa. It is not wise to accept opinions without other evidence. Again, note that attitudes do not cause anything, any more than do opinions. Attitudes, if genuine, merely indicate a state of readiness, ranging from extreme to nil, depending upon experience. If someone is in the presence of friends whom she believes to have the same attitudes, she may actually respond quite vigorously and overtly in a positive or negative manner and engage in preliminary movements of a nature preparatory to some other overt action, but such ation cannot actually occur in the absence of the original objects related to the attitude. Normally any discussion of attitudes occurs in a setting of discussion, not of action. When actual action is taking place, the subject of attitudes is no longer relevant. The action is.

We come now to beliefs. Like opinions and attitudes, beliefs do not exist in a vacuum or inside a person as possessions. When we say, "He believes in Santa Claus" or "He has the belief that . . . ," we are not referring to anything more than that the person is likely to say something in response to a question that may be asked, and that his statement will amount to an agreement or disagreement with some proposition that can be verbalized. Like opinions and attitudes, beliefs can be falsified in the sense that a human being can lie about propositions. Beliefs have the additional feature of having or not having a truth value—that is, a person may believe something that is not true or that he has no evidence for, and even evidence against. Philosophers might suggest that people believe many things that are not verbalized—for example, that the floor on which they are walking is solid and will not collapse—but such beliefs are better treated as speculative extrapolations of philosophers and might be better considered under such headings as unconscious expectancies, or as habits, or as really irrelevant to the issue at hand, which is the nature of beliefs and their role in behavior.

If we start asking people about their beliefs—in God, in ESP, in evolution, that two and two make four, and so on—all we would be doing is asking for their opinions about propositions phrased in more or less familiar ways. Some of the questions might arouse attitudes more or less mildly; others might lead to lies or provoke discussions, depending again upon context, including the reasons for the questions. Again, beliefs do not lead to any overt action and are themselves reactions to symbolic or verbal stimuli. It is simplistic to attribute the long-lasting conflict with its bombings, murders, and assorted violence between Northern Irish Protestants and Catholics merely to a difference of beliefs about religion. Many believers on each side do not resort to any violence at all and deplore that which occurs. Is the conflict due to other or additional beliefs and differences? That, again, could hardly be the case. True, the combatants hate one another and will say so if asked, but the hates do not exist unless they too are evoked by appropriate stimuli, when, like attitudes, they function as "get sets." The hater is ready to attack if new additional stimuli arouse previously learned responses. The conflict in Northern Ireland has been going on for so long now that, for the activists engaged in violent behavior, the behavior itself is habitual, learned, the proper reaction whenever a member of the opposition is observed in an unprotected situation. Any beliefs or attitudes one side has about the other are only supportive, in the sense of attitudes being states of readiness with accompanying emotions. Anyone wiring a bomb can hardly afford to indulge in religious beliefs. A man so engaged is responding in terms of learned responses to suitable stimuli. A sniper with an enemy in his sights cannot afford to indulge in religious beliefs.

If we were to say that some Irish Catholic at Mass, in church, believes that Protestants are her enemies, all we would be saying is that if the Catholic were asked if the Protestants are her enemies, she would say yes, or that she might make the whole statement, "The Protestants are my enemies," if a question or other stimulus prompted such a verbalization. Unless she were saying it to herself at any given moment instead of attending to the Mass, she would not have the belief. The belief does not exist unless it is verbalized, and, being verbalized, it does not lead to any action—the believer cannot shoot any Protestants in church. Some verbalizations, of course, are cued to action through a learning history, as when the Catholic worshipper moves her hand about in saying words related to making the sign of the cross, but such verbal-motor habits are not matters of belief. Nonbelievers can say the same words and make the same motions. Beliefs are not different from opinions and amount to the same thing, namely, verbal statements about one's positive or negative attitudes. Like opinions, beliefs are only responses to questions raised by others. Sometimes some event, for example, a noise at night, might prompt a question like, What was that? Someone might say, "I believe it was the cat." In such an instance, the word *believe* is being used loosely. The speaker could have said any number of things like "The cat," or "I think it was the cat." If he says the former, he may merely be responding in the way he responded on some previous occasion of hearing such a noise, that is, simply by naming something. We do not normally raise an issue of belief in naming situations. If he says, "I think it was the cat," he is admitting some possible doubt or uncertainty, and again the question of belief appears to be extraneous to the matter. The speaker is indicating that he is not ready to name the source of the noise.

Where do beliefs come from? How do we come to believe anything, that is, arrive at a state wherein we assert pro or con positions about controversial issues? From the fact that Jewish parents have Jewish children, Catholic parents have Catholic children, and so on, we can infer that parental training is not without its influences. Children characteristically ask, why? Children are obviously ignorant about just about everything, and any concerns they have must result in such questions. Even if they are not concerned, the parents may be, as when they say,

"Don't climb up there; you'll fall." The child falls. The parent says, "I told you so." Over thousands of occassions, a child learns that what a parent says turns out to be the case. Eventually the child learns to heed warnings, to accept the parent's statements, and to repeat them. The trust in parents can be transferred to other reliable agents: friends, teachers, and other relatives who properly predict future consequences. The child then comes to believe, that is, repeat what authority figures say even if the consequences cannot be predicted or verified in any way. A child brought up in an atmosphere where authority figures make anti-religious, racist, antifeminist, pro-Republican, or any other kinds of pro and con remark will come to accept and repeat such remarks on appropriate occasions. The child acquires a repertoire of beliefs or verbal habits.

PREJUDICE

Prejudices are supposed to be beliefs or underlying attitudes for which there is no direct, personally experienced support. A person is supposed to prejudge something (people, objects, ideas) without any reason for the judgment. Prejudices are usually thought of as against something but can just as well be for something. The implication of such a definition of prejudice is that it is proper enough to like or dislike something if one has had personal experience that was positive and favorable or negative and unfavorable. Thus, if a man has eaten clams and gotten sick, it would not be proper to say he was prejudiced if he now says, "I don't like clams." The argument here is a bit shaky in that no one has eaten all possible clams. On the more important level of race prejudice, if one has had a negative encounter with a member of another race, it would be prejudicial to dislike all other members of that race—here the evidence would be regarded as insufficient. It is when prejudices exist that are based on secondary sources—for example, being told by parents or others that some race or religion is no good or is to be despised—and one proceeds to respond toward stimuli associated with that race or religion in a negative manner that we may properly speak of prejudice as a prejudgment, although there might have been no judgment worthy of the name in that no evaluation of evidence at all had taken place.

Prejudices in the sense of negative or positive attitudes based on little or no personal experience abound. It can hardly be otherwise. No one can have contact with all members of all groups or even with some or some groups. Yet the groups will be identified by names or labels, and one can be told positive or negative things about the labeled groups by people one trusts. Such secondhand acquired attitudes will be prejudices, and one can hardly escape acquiring some, so that different people are prejudiced against or for members of other races, religions, social or economic classes, capitalism, communism, bankers, lawyers, welfare clients, old people, children, and almost anything that can be identified as a member of a class where the class name or label arouses an attitude. The very notion of eliminating prejudice is a fantasy, because all humans have only limited experience with members of much larger classes but will have to react positively or negatively to those they do encounter or are taught about by others who can affect their beliefs.

People against whom prejudice is shown will, in turn, become prejudiced against classes some of whose members they have experience with or are taught about. There are deep-seated and widespread prejudices in any society toward some subgroups of that society or other societies. In the United States, for example, the depth and breadth of prejudice against Jews, blacks, and Catholics has been long-standing, is widespread, and is probably ineradicable for a long time to come. As long as members of the Ku Klux Klan and their admirers continue to think about kikes, coons, and Catholics, members of these groups are going to encounter prejudice. The prejudice will, of course, be reciprocated. In a WASP-dominated society, immigrants from Eastern and Southern Europe, blacks, Hispanics, and Asiatics should not expect to have red carpets rolled out for them. Nor should they expect to be offered jobs if there are WASP competitors for them. Governmental efforts at equal opportunity, quotas, or affirmative action are not likely to accomplish much in the reduction of prejudice because even contact with individuals against whose class one might be prejudiced lessens the prejudice only toward those individuals one has positive contact with. Since not all contacts will be positive or extensive, even those individuals will not escape some prejudicial reactions. It is easy to identify the prejudiced person. She is the one who says, "Some of my best friends are————."

In summary, opinions and beliefs are verbal descriptions, not necessarily truthful, nor really accurate, of attitudes that amount to emotionally colored preparatory responses, usually to questions or other stimuli that identify members of some group or issue. Thus the sight of a black man in a white neighborhood may arouse a variety of attitudes in a group of white observers. If the attitudes are conditioned responses (acquired reactions) based on secondhand sources (having been told something by trusted authority figures), we may call the attitudes prejudice. Because much, if not most, of our conditioning in social situations comes from secondhand sources, all of us are prejudiced about many kinds of attitude-arousing stimuli, and there is little hope of eliminating prejudicial attitudes without control over the instructors. In short, it is human to be prejudiced, however poorly that may reflect on being human.

With these preliminary cautions about loose, really untamed language about heredity, instincts, attitudes, and prejudice out of the way, we can now turn to the kinds of problem we cannot escape, simply because of human nature.

3

The Problems

In this chapter I will list the problems humanity has made for itself. Many of the problems arise from attempts at solutions to other problems. The situation is aptly described by the expression "If it ain't one damned thing, it's another." Most of the problems are interrelated, as is suggested in the principle of context mentioned at the end of the first chapter. In many of the problems there are opposing interests, and a solution cannot be reached that will satisfy both or several parties. Hitler's attempted solution for what he considered the Jewish problem obviously did not appeal to the Jews. The problem of abortion divides people into prochoice and prolife groups. Strikers and strikebreakers look at employment problems rather differently. Political "ins" and political "outs" offer different solutions to national problems. Pro and con divisions underlie issues such as atomic weapons and atomic power, pollution, price controls, boycotts, contraception, integration, capital punishment, welfare, rent control, and virtually any problem area that can be mentioned. Any attempted solution will please only one side or neither. A solution to a problem may involve gains of some kind for one party or group and losses of some kind for others. Life becomes a zero-sum game and the losers will not relax quietly and withdraw—there are no good sports in the game of life. To the extent that the origins of some other problems can be appreciated as part of the human condition, we might be able to accept our humanity and lead less troubled lives. With a broader recognition of the principles described in the first chapter, it might even be possible to initiate some small improvements.

When problems are interrelated, as in the case of politics and economics, sports and business, sex and money, sex and religion, religion and politics, races and employment, education and politics, law and business, pollution and business, education and taxes, and so forth, there is no easy way to discuss one problem without getting involved in others. A problem such as abortion may appear to some a simple moral issue, but in countries such as India and China, with a billion people to feed, other issues become rather relevant. The multiple interests involved in virtually every matter that comes up before the United States Congress may explain the failure of that body to act quickly, efficiently, and in a completely satisfactory fashion. Somebody always objects.

It is impossible for anyone to categorize all of the kinds of problem facing the human race in any satisfactory way. Each problem spills over into other problem areas. In the present instance, four major problem areas will be described, each with a set of subproblems. Other arrangements might be considered, but the present listing appears to include more problems than anyone can hope to consider meaningfully. The four areas that will receive the bulk of this commentary are: population, economics, law, and education. The remainder of this chapter will spell out some of the subproblems under these four headings. Fuller discussions will be the burden of subsequent chapters.

POPULATION

Isolating population itself as a problem area may be a gross redundancy. Population might be considered as a heading for all human problems since without it there would be none. People can be categorized in many different ways, and each category becomes a problem area in itself. If we stopped thinking about people as belonging to different categories such as race, creed, and color, as is done in the Constitution of the United States and its amendments, and if we did not extend these by the addition of sex, sexual preference, and age, many problems would vanish. As it is, the very way we characterize people creates many problems.

In various countries throughout the world, people are divided by race, nationality, class and caste, and political affiliation. In some countries we may have as many as 40 different political parties competing for the right to run the lives of all. In the United States, the traditional Republican and Democratic parties are being splintered into far right and far left; other voters claim to be independents, liberals, conservatives, right to lifers, and other single-issue groups. Even in Communist countries, there has to be a party. Other, nonparty ways of running a government are hardly ever proposed, and the very existence of parties creates problems for the ins and outs.

The natural division of people by sex has resulted in the "war between the sexes" from the beginning of man's existence. Sex differences have provided the breeding ground for a great many problems related to marriage, divorce, prostitution, and child rearing. Sexual deviations of one kind or another also generate problems for some.

Categorizing people as children, teenagers, adults, and the elderly again results in problems. These descriptions may seem natural and innocent, but anytime a portion of the population is singled out and labeled as somehow unique or special, some members of that portion begin to organize, demand rights, form political blocs, create associations, institutions, or "Societies for the—." Politicians get into the act and adopt one or another group and act as mouthpieces. There appears to be no end to the ways in which a population can be subdivided, with each division demanding attention, special privileges, and more of the general pie.

One of the more important ways in which populations divide themselves is along lines of religious affiliation. Such alignments have been the source of major difficulties and confrontations not only in the distant past but also in a very violent present in many parts of the world. In the United States religious problems, at the moment, are not spilling over into violence, but obvious efforts are being initiated to influence education by demands for prayer in the schools and revision of textbooks by creationists. Other efforts are aimed at screening Supreme Court nominees on their views about abortion. Religions can be both problem solvers and problems creators.

For present purposes I will mention one more area of population problems, that of national and international relations, if they can be so called.

Within any country problems abound even though the varied individuals residing therein are all citizens. Problems of immigration, legal or illegal, are accompanied by racial problems, language and cultural conflicts, and class struggles. Sometimes the conflicts erupt into mob action or terrorist assaults with or without outside interference from other countries or munitions sellers. Problems of rights abound as is noted below. (See chapter 13.)

International conflicts, despite the United Nations, keep disturbing the peace of the world. At no time in history has the world enjoyed a single year without some kind of war going on someplace where citizens of one country have gone about slaughtering citizens of another in the name of Christianity, Allah, Karl Marx, or democracy. There were 271 wars between 1868 and 1986, 14 of them fought in 1986.

There is a marked disparity between the size, economic strength, and military capacity of countries. Some primitive areas are euphemistically called emerging, or developing nations though they will in all probability never emerge but be asborbed by rapacious neighbors. In many countries religious and other concerns divide groups and give rise to terrorist tactics of mutual destruction. Leaders of governments cannot walk the streets of their capital cities without armed escorts and careful screening of the areas they will visit. Some leaders fail to go to church for fear of the harm that might come to the congregation and themselves. Many people lead lives of concern over personal safety behind doors with multiple locks, chains, and dogs. In all countries people are urged to love their leaders and their countries, to be patriotic, and to sacrifice their lives for something alleged to be more precious than life. Countries are in a sorry state throughout the world, with enemies within and without. The question of how a citizen of a country could ever be an enemy of that country is never raised. As Albert Camus (1956) noted in *The Rebel*, some people will not find satisfaction whatever the nature of the arrangements might be and will attempt to overthrow the government, revolutionize it, and will then find new rebels objecting to the new arrangements.

The problems listed above as virtually inherent in being human cannot all be discussed fruitfully in terms of our limited number of principles. I will, however, attempt to deal with the areas of sex, religion and morality, and nationalism and will give only limited consideration of some of the other problems mentioned. The mere listing of the other issues tends to be overwhelming. One begins to wonder how the human race has managed to survive till now, and prospects for the future can be gloomy and chastening, especially when one observes drunken soccer fans celebrating by maiming and killing others.

ECONOMICS

Perhaps the most crucial problems are in the realm of economics. The production and distribution of goods has long been the domain of economists, who are alleged to practice a "Dismal Science." Economists have developed their own psychology based on a creature known as "economic man," who obviously does not exist. The world at various times and places goes through a variety of economic spasms known as depressions or recessions, with supposed recoveries. At present, large parts of the world are in debt to other parts of the world, with debts that can be called enormous and are probably unpayable. The creditor nations themselves may be operating with enormous budget deficits and are becoming debtor nations. The "economic man" is faced daily with problems of inflation in some countries (for example, Israel in 1984, at an annual rate of 500 percent), unemployment, various degrees of poverty, and economic threat. Slavery at one time was an official problem of governments, but now it is unofficial. (People are still tied or shackled to their jobs.) In many countries people postpone marriage for lack of separate living quarters, for which they wait for years.

In the field of production, automation and robotics threaten workers with loss of jobs whether these be white- or blue-collar forms of employment. Computers displace clerical workers by the thousands and welfare rolls rise annually in various cities, where homeless drifters sleep in doorways and eat at missions, where the concern is often more for their souls than for their bodies.

International conglomerates and cartels try to control production, prices, and consumption. Countries vie with one another in subsidizing failing industries, and they erect tariff walls against one another. Chaos probably best describes the economic world. Students worry about career prospects and prepare themselves in ignorance of what fields will be open to them after they are trained. Economists discuss all these issues as if some kinds of economic forces determined ups and downs in economies. They talk about the money supply, the market, and fiscal and monetary policies as if these were somehow divorced from people.

Countries vary in how economic matters are arranged—some favor capitalism, others some form of socialism, communism, or fascism. Some are still under the domination of self-appointed monarchs or presidents-for-life, sultans, sheiks, or military juntas. Some countries are known as welfare states whereas others preach individual rights or rugged individualism. Some try to dominate other countries as areas of national interest; others are dominated. Racial issues arise in some countries such as South Africa and give rise to economic entanglements.

The most immediate problems facing society in terms of large numbers of individuals who try to cope are the constantly rising prices and relatively high interest rates demanded by bankers, who have forgotten the word *usury*, and the risk of unemployment.

Obviously, the problems of the economic world will not be solved in a hurry, if ever or at all. Some psychological considerations may make them easier to live with for some people.

THE LAW

Because people live in groups and tend to get in each other's way, rules have been established in all societies to govern interpersonal relationships, with various degrees of satisfaction to those being ruled. Some such rules or regulations come to be known as matters of law. Our concern with the law will be limited to a few basic issues. We cannot consider the multifarious complications of commerical, corporate, or international law. Most legal activities involve many volumes of argument on specific issues. Income tax law, for example, is a special area that is covered by thousands of pages of interpretations. The basic question of why anyone should pay taxes is not covered. My treatment will concentrate on two basic types of problem: those concerning rights and responsibilities and those concerning crime, criminals, and punishment.

Somebody is always demanding rights or claiming that someone else had no right to do whatever was done. Commonly one person's rights are opposed to someone else's right. People march about, shouting, singing, demonstrating, sitting in, or otherwise demanding the right to vote, to abort, to drink, to bear arms, to practice "free speech," and even to be recognized. The government of Israel, and perhaps the people there, demand to be recognized by other people or governments. Palestinians choose not to recognize Israel, as if this were possible. Whom do they think they are bombing? We shall see that the concern for rights ranges from the rights of fetuses to the right to burial in Arlington National Cemetary and just about everything in between, including what have come to be called marital rights. Prisoners call for rights to conjugal visits from girlfriends.

A host of problems revolves around the fact that "rules were made to be broken," at least for some people, some of whom may not even know that the rules exist. Crimes range from the extortion of lunch money by children from other children to terrorist ("freedom fighter") bombings of innocent civilians, to such grand affairs as war crimes and trials of the losers by the winners. What is to be done about criminals is a continuing problem. The nature of crime and of the punishment to fit it is another basic question.

A major preoccupation in this area is the activity of criminal lawyers, whose profession exists only because rules are broken, and whose financial success depends upon the successful defense of accused people, guilty or not.

EDUCATION

According to national critics and some parents, the educational system in the United States (and elsewhere) is a mess and needs serious reconstruction. When the secretary of education announces that we are creating "a rising tide of mediocrity" in our educational efforts and faults are found in elementary schools, high schools, and colleges, we have a problem of national scope. The problems of illiteracy appear to be overwhelming despite the spending of billions of dollars on teaching children to read. Johnny appears not to be able to do simple arithmetic either. Who will build the hydrogen bombs of the future? Faults are found with schools, students, teachers, and textbooks. I will devote a short chapter to what seems to be miseducation.

SUMMARY

The problem areas described above suggest that the world is in a sorry state. There are many other problems that have not been singled out, such as those in transportation, medicine (including new areas of research and application in cloning, artifical fertilization, organ transplants, AIDS, and artificial organs), pollution, energy sources, population movements from former population centers to new sunbelt locations, the decline of cities and urban renewal with convention centers in cities no one would chooses for a convention, and public support of the arts. Such problems are grist for the mill to newspaper pundits when they run out of more pressing matters. The solution of some of these problems might bear on the solution of those that have been described earlier. We can now start looking at some of the major problems created by people and see if our four psychological principles have any promise by way of analysis and the suggestion of possible solutions that might make the problems less noxious and disturbing. Because all of the problem areas are interrelated, it hardly matters where we start. As soon as we start discussing population, we become involved with education, business, the law, poverty, race, age, slums and ghettos, and internal and external "enemies," "evil empires," and "faithful allies" on whom we cannot depend. We might as well start with people. I hope that the earlier discussion of individual differences will be recalled here.

4

An Introduction to People Problems

Problems start with people. There are some who, like Hitler, think that the solution to problems can be found in the elimination of certain people. Today's Hitlers are operating all over the world, in the Near East, the Middle East, the Far East, and the near, middle and far of all continents, some a little more successfully than others. We do not know whose turn is next in the process of the elmination of problems by the elimination of people. All that can be said for the Final Solution ambitions of modern Hitlers is that evolution will see to it.

When Alexander the Great cut the Gordian knot, he did not solve the problem. He, too, eliminated it. Some problems, to be sure, are solved to some extent by elimination. The Volstead Act solved the problem of manufacturing alcoholic liquors legally in the United States. The Twenty-first Amendment solved the problem of the Volstead Act. Violations of criminal laws are sometimes solved by elimination of the laws. If narcotics were made legally available, the problem of drug smuggling could be solved by elimination, just as the problem of illegal abortions was solved by the Supreme Court. Sometimes the elimination process is very simple and involves no more than a change of name. Slum problems are eliminated by calling slums the inner city. Clearly, an inner city cannot have problems or be one. There has to be an inner city. The problem of overcrowded mental hospitals in New York was solved by calling the patients "ready for rehabilitation in a normal environment," and the problem of unmarried couples living together without benefit of clergy was solved by invention of a phrase, *a different life-style*. The phrase was blessed with an expansiveness that allowed it to include homosexuals. We cannot omit noting that marital problems are easily solved by divorces or annulments. The last term has the magical virtue of carrying the meaning that the marriage never took place. The fact of the marriage is eliminated.

The manifold problems of children are also solved by a form of elimination. Children grow up and no longer have child problems. Their problems are now adult. But some problems are largely of an adult nature and are such that they cannot be solved by time or subterfuge. Those are the problems that are built into the simple fact that people are human beings—the problems go with the territory. We can start with the fact that we are not only human beings, we are also, of necessity, either male or female (true, some try to change the fact), and being either will result in some kinds of problem. Beyond the fact that we are of one sex or another, we are also, upon birth, immediately recognized as being a member of one or another race. Biologists are not quite sure about the reality of races, and anywhere between five and two thousand labels are pinned on members of various groupings of humans around the globe. The ordinary person is quite prepared to recognize some distinctions in skin color, hair texture, and eye formation among members of different groups, and one does not have to be a South African prime minister to identify some people as white, colored, Asiatic or Bantu. The "mixed" groups give even the South African government some difficulty since the very fact that a male of one race and a female of another can have offspring is a crucial criterion for defining species. Some geneticists observe that all modern humans have had a rather small group of original ancestors and suggest that all humans living today are relatives to one degree of another. It would, of course, be easier on humanity if the question of race were ignored and everyone were considered a member of the human race, but the fact that people do differ in skin color, for example, has created problems for some people even though such a trait, per se, is obviously irrelevant to any human interaction. A blind white person who was taken care of by a succession of nurses or aides of different races might find the arrangement quite satisfactory and find the helpers equally congenial if no one inquired about their race. There would be no more point to such inquiries than there would be to asking about the breed of a Seeing Eye dog, if one assumes competence in the dog. It is obviously something other than skin color that matters. Arabs and Jews, for example, are both Semites, but there has been no love lost between them for centuries past. A Greek in a Turkish bath might have to ask a Turk in the same steam room what he was before he could begin to hate him. White Americans have difficulty discriminating between Koreans and Japanese. These groups have no such problem and entertain mutual and instant dislikes. Presumably their ancestors were all Chinese at one time. The problems of race call for some consideration. (See "Races and Racism" in chapter 5.)

The already noted fifty-fifty distribution of people into men and women will be discussed later (see "Sex," in chapter 5), but we should note some other, less natural but rather important categories into which people have divided themselves in one way or another. The psychologist J. F. Brown (1936) suggested that we tend to think about people in terms of classes to which they belong. Among such classes are religion, occupation, nationality, race, political affiliation, economic status, and educational level, among others. Much of our thinking about people amounts to reacting to labels such as *Catholic, blue-collar,* or *socialist.* As soon as we are told that a person belongs to one or another such group, we think we know something about her even before we meet her. If we hear that she is a West Pointer, a delicatessen waitress, a banker, or a Moslem, we are prepared to react in certain specific ways. We might have a problem trying to identify such a person coming off a plane at an airport even if we had a dozen different labels for classes she belonged to. When we react in terms of class membership, we are thinking in terms of stereotypes, convenient packages of information derived from novels, movies, discussions around the family table, and so on, which may have little or no relevance to reality. If we find ourselves next to a stranger in a restaurant or standing in line at a post office, we might react to size, clothes, and physical attractiveness or lack thereof, but let someone tell us the person is a movie star or a senator and our attitude changes immediately. The person suddenly acquires charisma, which, of course, no one possesses—charisma being our own contribution from our misguided past.

Perhaps the most important class membership is that of nationality. This class is commonly overlooked in a nation where most people share the membership. Let one "Ugly American" meet another "Ugly American" abroad, however, and they are instantly good, fine people, friends. The class or nationality is rarely mentioned among people of the same membership. It is like the air we breathe, unnoticed. Let a stranger or someone known to be of some other nationality arrive, and we immediately know something about the newcomer. That what we "know" may be very wrong is rarely considered. The common knowledge we have is about alleged cultural features that are supposed to characterize most, if not all, of the members of the group. After all, each nation does shape personality and behavior through, for example, its common educational system, its common language and history, its traditions, its cuisine, and its entertainment forms, art, and literature. We can expect that some of the common cultural factors have had some impact on a member of a national class. Because of individual differences, however, we can never be sure about our knowledge. Nationality becomes important when members of different nationalities have occasion to interact. The significance of nationality will occupy us in "Patriotism and Nationalism," in chapter 6.

Though other class memberships may be important in our dealings with individuals, we cannot take all of them into account. It is true, for example, as Brown noted, that we might know a lot about a person if we knew that the individual was successful in some occupation for a period of years. After all, one does spend a large part of one's time in a trade or line of work, and certain characteristics must be acquired if one is to be successful. Our concern, however, is with somewhat broader groupings, and the last major grouping that will be discussed is that of religion. Class membership in one of the religions, the major denominations, or the hundreds of sects that have proliferated over the earth has been a major determinant of how people interact and how such interactions create problems. Religion has been both cause and cure of many problems and requires our attention. Such attention will be paid in "Religion and Morality," in chapter 6.

From the preceding discussion it can be inferred that people problems can be divied into two kinds: first, those that have a biological basis such as sex, race, age, and the use of drugs; and second, those that people make for themselves simply because they are social animals, that is, they live in groups. Here we note the importance of problems relating to cultures and subcultures, nationalism, class and caste, and religion. Chapters 5 and 6 will deal with biologically based and socially determined problems respectively.

5

Intrinsic Human Problems; or, The Trouble with People Is That They Are Human

Simply being human creates problems for the human race. Of course, the same can be said of any other species. Giraffes have problems peculiar to giraffes. Seals have seal problems. When we look at people, we see immediately that as living creatures they are male or female, young or old, big or small, active or passive, of one skin color or another, and other differentiations. Some of these differences create problems. Because all human problems begin with sex, we might well start our examination with that age-old and lifelong concern.

SEX

Evolutionary theory is concerned less with the survival of individuals than with the survival of species. In the course of evolution various species have developed different anatomical and physiological arrangements for the continuation of their kind. In the vast majority of them, the arrangement involves differences between the sexes. In much of the animal world, the sexes have periods, so-called mating seasons, so that sex becomes a "sometime thing." Females are said to go into heat (obviously a male coinage), and males become interested only when the signs of female receptivity are displayed. In chimpanzees and baboons such signs are too obvious to be unobserved by any zoo visitor. For still unknown reasons the human species does not have a regular, periodic, rutting season, and sexual behavior is, or can be, a year-round possibility. There are suggestions that the absence of a mating season is some kind of evolutionary mutation that requires frequent intercourse in order to assure fertilization because of the limited and unknown periods of female fertility. The fertile periods can be ascertained, to be sure, but the procedures are unfamiliar to most of the world's population, and even if the procedures are known, the determination of fertile periods is not quite precise.

The evolutionary requirement of frequent intercourse may have had value for the survival of the species in more primitive times, when women were pregnant about as often as possible but the offspring died off in great numbers. Even in modern times in the less developed areas of the world, frequent pregnancies are still common. In present-day China the government has seen fit to decree that no couple may have more than one child so that the population can be regulated to survival levels. With rising birth rates in developing countries, the world's population could really reach Malthusian danger levels if births are not controlled in some fashion.

Awareness of the relationship between intercourse and pregnancy may have been slow in coming, but it is now generally familiar to just about anyone interested in sexual activity. That same awareness, however, has resulted in a complex of complicated cultural entanglements that has transformed a simple, natural, physical act into a major problem area. In some allegedly primitive cultures, according to anthropologists, sexual activity amounts to a playful sport with little or no concern about the possible consequences. Fatherhood may not be taken seriously, and uncles may take over the male parental roles. In most of the world, however, both in developed and developing nations, the consequences of sexual activity and the activity itself have become intertwined with the law, morality, religion, medicine, and business. Something as natural as breathing and eating has even become an educational problem.

Child-rearing practices, for centuries, have created roles for men and women, and the obvious physical difference has been exploited by both men and women to justify a bewildering array of practices while the similarities have been obscured.

In most of the world a dominance-submission relationship has been the common parameter that formed the basis of segregation of the sexes. Over the centuries men have dominated women in virtually every phase of life save child-rearing responsibilities. In the rare female-dominant culture that existed on occasion, women were just as inconsiderate as men are in the much more common male-dominant societies. Power in the hands of either sex is a corrupting force. Why men have enjoyed the dominant role for so long is not easily answered by psychological findings. The explanation may be in masculine freedom to roam whereas women may feel more closely tied to children. The nine-month gestation period, the experience of giving birth, and the close relationship in nursing may all be factors in restricting women's freedom and may virtually dictate submission. Other factors appear less compelling. Men are generally taller, larger, hairier, heavier, and stronger than women, a differentiation by sex that is common to most animal species. In other respects, however, both sexes share the same traits to a considerable degree in what might be considered psychological variables such as intelligence, perceptual capacities, and the range of emotional and social characteristics. Both sexes share many of the same glandular secretions, but there are some differences related to progenitive equipment. In recent years studies dealing with masculinity-femininity have emphasized the androgynous similarities between men and women. The only obvious important difference is that only women can bear children and only men can sire them. Current research on cloning and genetic experimentation may alter that difference before long. For the present, however, the sexual problem centers in pregnancy and its consequences.

All over the world, from ancient times, the differences between the sexes have given rise to superstitions, mythology, romantic fiction, poetry, and, most importantly, ignorance about the sexes. Whereas the physiological facts about pregnancy are well known to obstetricians and many educated lay people, the socially important facts about sexual intercourse are obscure and mysterious to most, educated or not. Literally no one knows the facts even about such questions as how frequently sexual intercourse takes place, for example. How much incest and child abuse goes on? How many people are homosexual? No one knows the answers to these questions. The facts about one's sexual life are regarded as private, to be disclosed only to psychotherapists if one is not satisfied with one's sex life. Psychotherapists may have learned a lot about a few individuals, but these individuals are, on a percentage basis, rather rare. No one knows how many teenagers are sexually active, at what ages, how often, and with whom. Investigators such as Alfred Kinsey (1948) have learned a great deal—but, again, from a special population of volunteers. Kinsey reports, for example, that men are most active, concerned, perhaps most sexually driven at about the age of 17, whereas women are most interested at about the age of 35. Such a disparity should certainly result in problems, but the actual facts may not be too solid. Male writers of fiction like to imply that women are just as eager to participate in sexual activity as are men, but women correspondents of Ann Landers and other lonely hearts experts suggest that sex is less than a major preoccupation. No one actually has the facts at hand. That women face greater risks in sexual participation could account for some reluctance on their part regardless of any physiological or psychological needs. The risks do not deter some teenage girls, and the currently legal option of abortion as a method of birth control is chosen by millions annually. Again reliable facts and figures are not easily available.

All around the world some practices have developed that suggest that men are indeed more eager to engage in sexual activity than are women. Feminine prostitution is far more prevelant than is masculine prostitution, although that, too, exists. This may only mean that women do not have to pay for sexual adventures; too many men are ready to cooperate without additional compensation. Pornographic materials are developed primarily for a masculine market. The macho attitude is not confined to Latin America, and males around the world seem to revel in sexual conquests. The very word conquests suggests that men are more aggressive in sexual activity whereas women are alleged to play the reluctant role. The preoccupation with foreplay again suggests that women need far more arousal than do men, as does the universal joke, "Not tonight. I've got a headache." The frequency of rape also attests to aggressive masculine sexuality.

The War between the Sexes

The allegedly aggressive, sexually eager male and submissive, reluctant female have been the basis for much of the mythological thinking that prevails in this problem area. Aristophanes offers an early description of women's use of sexuality as a weapon[1] in what James Thurber came to call the "war between men and women."[2] Women have traditionally "granted favors" to deserving males or provided "services." Conjugal rights are a masculine invention.

The simple fact is that sex has been and remains an area of mystery and the unknown despite the thousands of years of sexual activity that has spawned the world's population. Surrounding this mystery customs of courtship and marriage have arisen of a great variety: polygamy in some cultures, monogamy in others, and polyandry in still others; the provision of dowries in some cultures and the purchase of wives in others. Women have been regarded as chattel, concubines, slaves, and, as in ancient Greece, potential mothers while the fathers dallied with younger men.

Over the centuries of gradual civilization, with the development of farming, male children came to be more valued by men as potential farmhands and inheritors of property. Property rights acquired sexual features, including the view that wives were property, and as such had to be protected from marauders. Males did not wear chastity belts. Along with the property aspects came religious sanctions, blessings, and proscriptions of various kinds. Sex, unless authorized, became sinful, and even illegal. Only authorized sex was approved, and the authorization consisted primarily of some sort of marriage ceremony. It has not been determined in any scientific way that monogonmous marriage or any other kind is in any sense natural. To ease some of the difficulties that a marriage relationship created, the process of divorce was invented and legalized. When a marriage involved children, a divorce created new problems. In the United States approximately half of the children now alive will spend some time with a single parent.

Psychology and Sex Problems

How do our principles of individual differences, conditioning, reinforcement, and determinism apply to problems of sex? Are they of any help? Before we can begin to consider such a question, it must be appreciated that what one person may consider a problem, another may consider a privilege, a business, a matter of earning a living, or a purely personal affair. The alleged problems may not be problems at all in the sense of something calling for a solution acceptable to all concerned. Simply listing the alleged problems may be revealing.

Prostitution. One might wonder that anyone should consider prostitution, the world's oldest profession a problem. Though the actual numbers of prostitutes is unknown, it is highly probable that most men do not regard prostitution as a problem but rather as a solution, an easy opportunity to meet needs that cannot be satisfied more easily or with fewer difficulties. From the male viewpoint any problems related to prostitution, for example the danger of being robbed, infected, or "exposed," are secondary. Women may frown on prostitution because of its competitive features. The prostitutes themselves find it a way of earning a living. Our principles do not suggest that prostitution in itself is anything but a problem created by humans. Other animals do not support the profession. It will probably continue and remain a "problem" for some time.

Homosexuality. The scientific world has not as yet discovered much about homosexuality other than that it, too, is an ancient practice. Sigmund Freud (1938) considered it a failure to develop through what he considered stages of a regular progression. Everyone, according to Freud, goes through a homosexual stage, and some become fixated before moving on to a heterosexual stage. The evidence for a Freudian interpretation is just not available, however plausible it might seem to some. We simply do not know if homosexuality is a natural, physiologically determined condition or the result of childhood rearing practices of parents. We do know that some people who are separated from members of the opposite sex for long periods—for example, sailors, prisoners, boys and girls at boarding schools—sometimes engage in homosexual affairs. Some persist in what might be considered adult civilian life. Again, homosexuality may be a problem even for some homosexuals because of cultural norms. Heterosexual women might object to male homosexuals because they are out of the marriage market. Heterosexual males should find them noncompetitors. Perhaps the only problem is the public activity of homosexuals in making various demands that no one would think of denying if they were not tied to some need for recognition of alleged gay rights. No one could consider homosexuality a problem if the homosexuals did not raise it as an issue in employment, for example. Heterosexuals do not insist on public identification as such.

In recent years the American Psychiatric Association has chosen to declassify homosexuality as a category of mental disorder. Some objections were raised about the removal as a matter of political pressure. In any case, it now appears that psychotherapists treat homosexuality not as some kind of illness but as a preferred life-style. Again, our principles do not suggest that any solutions are available or even that solutions are required. Again, a solution has been found by elimination, via the change-of-name route. Homosexuality, in both sexes, will presumably continue. It would not appear to be a hereditary condition, or it would long ago have become extinct.

Teenage Pregnancy. As I mentioned earlier, no one knows the extent of teenage (or any other age) sexual activity. What is known is that the number of teenage pregnancies is rising despite the introduction of sex education courses in public schools. The rise is to be expected with a constantly growing population, although the percentage cannot be calculated easily. The availability of birth control devices does not appear to have had any noticeable impact, and the last resort of abortion apparently is chosen often. Taxpayers will continue to express their irritation and alarm at what appears to be part of the human condition, namely, teenage interest in sex. That interest is probably going to continue regardless of any preaching, education, or parental guidance. Only extremely severe measures that would be denounced as constitutionally unacceptable could be expected to deter a natural human proclivity. Virtually all of the reinforcement techniques in Western society are geared to encourage teenage experimentation in sex, and no diminution is to be anticipated. What is apparent is a general decrease in the effectiveness of cultural and religious proscriptions that are supposed to have worked in earlier times. The indications are that support of such sanctions is decreasing. Glamorous movie stars elect to have children out of wedlock and provide inspirational examples to youngsters who are rather poorly prepared to support and rear children. The problem will grow and psychology has no prescriptions.

Pornography. For some people pornography is a problem for which they demand solutions from lawmakers. The lawmakers cannot seem to agree upon a definition, and pornographers continue to produce salacious pictures, books, magazines, films, and comic books. Some people make a living out of supplying these secondary reinforcers to those who apparently cannot or do not get enough primary reinforcement to keep them relaxed. Like prostitution, pornography will continue so long as there is a demand. Current American best-selling novels appear to call for at least one explicitly described sexual adventure even from novelists who might introduce such material with some reluctance. Four-letter words that once were excluded from dictionaries now appear commonly in respectable best-selling publications. Again, what might be called declining morality by some appears to have become more common. Psychological principles appear to have no particular application to this problem created by human beings.

Marriage, Family, and Divorce. Some animal species mate for life, and that pattern has been followed for many centuries by humans. The custom of marriage has existed so long that all over the world it is regarded as natural, proper, or correct. There are variations, of course, as in some countries where a man is allowed as many as four wives if he can afford them. In the United States, the Mormons at one time practiced polygyny, which is no longer legal. People of means now indulge in successive divorces, so that mutiple spouses are still a possibility for some. The traditional nuclear family unit of father, mother, and children is still regarded as the model arrangement, and any deviation from this pattern is regarded with some suspicion. Bachelors and spinsters are virtually called upon for explanations of such an abnormal status.

How marriage came to become the model for human living arrangements is lost in history. Presumably, the birth and helplessness of children had something to do with the cohabitation of a man with a woman. The myth of the American Indian woman catching up with the rest of the tribe on the march after pausing to give birth may be just that. The pregnant woman needed someone around for some time before and after delivery. Men somehow came to play that role.

In modern times the traditional pattern has become rather unstable. Divorces now are becoming as common as marriages. The participation of women in the industrial and business world, especially during and after World War II, has enabled them to support themselves and has given rise to excuses for both parties to break marriage vows. Men do not have to concern themselves about the survival of a deserted working wife and women no longer have to feel dependent upon men for support. Men and women who cannot get along with each other can indulge in fanciful thinking that they could get along either alone or with someone else. Though some marriages may be mistakes, it is likely that people who make such mistakes will continue to do so. Conditioning principles suggest that anyone who is attracted to one kind of person enough to get married will seek out a similar person in the future should the marriage turn sour.

At the present time (1988) marriage patterns are undergoing changes.

Couples sometimes live together without benefit of clergy or judges. Such live-in companions sometimes formalize the arrangement with some kind of marriage ceremony; frequently enough they do not. The major problem couples face is the old one of pregnancy and children. Child support is commonly left to mothers while fathers leave, having accomplished their evolutionary mission. Psychologists are not of much help in marital problems and do not do much more than survey statistics. Individual differences appear to become multiplied when one man and one woman try living together, and psychologists have arrived at no principles that would advise anyone to marry or not to marry. George Bernard Shaw may have been quite astute when he noted that, in either case, "you'll regret it."

With advances in genetic engineering, the male role in procreation may diminish to virtually zero, and women may become increasingly dominant in decisions not only about sexual activity but also about such matters as the sex of future children and even whether or not they need to or care to participate in the gestation of fetuses. Our principles cannot carry us far in this realm.

Summary. The simple difference between the sexes lead to enormous social consequences. The relationships among economics, religion, education, and living arrangements are obvious. It is equally obvious that nothing is being done about the interrelated problems that holds any promise of anything but a breakdown in traditional social structures. We cannot anticipate what the present trends will bring about some 20 years from now any more than the impact of television entertainment could have been anticipated.

RACE AND RACISM

The heading for this section includes one more or less irrelevant and unimportant term and one far more significant. All human beings are descended from common ancestors and are not only members of the same species but are also related (at least as cousins 50 times removed) to every other living human. Some well-meaning people like to say there is only one race, the human race. It is more correct to say that all humans belong to one species. A species comprises individuals who can mate and procreate, that is, have fertile offspring. Within a species there can be subgroups residing under different climatic conditions that foster the development of characteristics that are adpative to those conditions, for example, withstanding decreases or increases in body temperature. Individuals inheriting mutant genes of a favorable nature may survive and reproduce more effectively than those not so fortunate. Long periods of relative isolation from other groups has apparently resulted in the development of groups of people differing in some physical characteristics

such as skin pigmentation, weight–skin surface area ratio, and suscep-
tibility or resistance to some diseases. Other differences such as those
of hair color and texture and some facial features (eye color, lip formation) also distinguish some groups from others.

When groups of people are identifiable through some easily distin-
guishable characteristic such as skin color, the term *race* may have some
utility if there is any need to distinguish one group from another. Note
that the racial difference itself could hardly be the basis of the need. The
color of any person's skin could not matter in any situation of consequence and might concern only dermatologists—and even they might
have no interest in the color per se. Many groups, however, can be
distinguished from one another by nonphysical features such as language, clothing preference, housing style, religious practices, geographical location, and other nonphysiological features, and some such groups
are sometimes called races. When the term *race* is applied to such a
group, it loses any biological significance and becomes a legal, political,
social, or cultural term and not only loses utility but creates problems.

In common practice the term *race* is usually used to refer to large
groups that have occupied certain territories of the earth for many generations and through intermarriage have acquired gene pools that show
up in some obvious physical features such as skull formation, skin color,
hair color and texture, or facial hair. Among such large groups there are
some that are referred to primarily on the basis of skin color: hence the
yellow race, the black race, redskins, and whites. Red skins are probably
seen only on beaches favored by whites. Because of out-group sexual
interactions through conquests, slavery, or other relationships, a considerable amount of mixing of gene pools has occurred over the centuries, so that a great range of individual differences has developed
within the broader groups, and any meaningful biological classification
of people into races is difficult, if not impossible. Race, then, is not a
useful scientific term.

As an example of the kinds of problem that can result, we can cite
the long enmity between the Israelis and the Palestinians. These groups
are commonly referred to as Semites or people of the Semitic race—
persumably on the basis of a common origin as descendants of Shem,
the eldest son of Noah. The conflict between the two groups makes
them mutually anti-Semitic and thus cannot be based on any original
racial differences but simply on cultural differences—in this instance a
mixture of religious, economic, and territorial factors. The Arab-Israeli
wars of the last 40 years are not racial wars. For that to be the case, it
would be necessary to show that a group of people, the Jews, for example, has some common "racial" characteristics; the visitor to Israel
might have a problem when he encountered Russian, German, Spanish,
Italian, African, and even Chinese Jews. About the only thing the citizens
of Israel have in common is that they call themselves Jews. Only a

minority is dedicated to a specific religion or culture. Israelis comprise a nation, not a religion or a race.

In the United States at the present time, one is free to call oneself a member of any race one chooses. Two black parents, for example, can call their children white on their birth certificates regardless of the skin color of either parents or children. In some cases both parents and children might be recognized as white regardless of their ancestry if their skin color was not obviously darker than that of the average white person. At one time in the state of Louisiana, anyone who had a black ancestor, however far back, might be legally defined as black. As recently as 1970 anyone with 1/32 of black ancestry was considered black. At present the legal procedures in Louisiana allow any parent to register a child as white; ancestry is ignored. Only the United States Census Bureau and affirmative action programs ask for a person's race; such answers are required for statistical purposes, but one can list one's race as one pleases.

The fact that biologically fit members of different races can have fertile offspring, and frequently do, suggests that race as such is not the real source of interracial difficulties.

Whether or not we include interracial (mixed ancestry) persons, the range of "racial" characteristics is so great within any one group as to make absolute distinctions between races quite impossible. Though group averages in any one characteristic may be apparent, if not obvious, the differences between groups in any one trait may have multiple causes.

As I mentioned in connection with Arabs and Israelis, there may be many other factors that create difficulties when members of different groups come in contact. Under "Patriotism and Nationalism" in chapter 6, I will consider the causes of intergroup conflicts in more detail. At this point I suggest that such conflicts are more properly seen as efforts to increase or protect one's economic interests and cultural values, for example, religious convictions, institutions, language. The fear of the unknown is also a formidable factor in extragroup relationships.

The second term in the heading of this section, *racism*, is of far more serious concern than the irrelevant term race. Racism refers to negative attitudes (and actions) on the part of members of one group toward other groups. The underlying animosity is based on faulty assumptions about the natural, innate inferiority of the hated group. The enemy is of a lesser breed.

The term *racism* is likely to prompt imagery of conflicts between blacks and whites in the United States or South Africa, but it is equally appropriate to describe conflicts between other groups where skin color is not a factor, as in the case of anti-Semitism, the caste conflicts in India, conflicts between Islamic sects, or the Catholic-Protestant troubles in

Northern Ireland. In none of these groups can the "enemy" be identified by skin color or other biological features. In black-white racism the color only makes it easier. Hitler's Nazis had difficulty in identifying Jews. They had to check birth certificates, in some cases for several generations.

It should be recognized that wherever racism exists, it exists on both sides because racism is essentially a culture clash in which members of different cultures, feeling an identity with other members of their culture, respond defensively to any attack (or inferred threat) on any member of the group as an attack upon themselves. The attacks, physical or otherwise, are expressions of various fears, envies, or desires to protect interests.

Seymour Sarason (1973) stresses the importance of history in culture conflicts of a racist nature. Cultures that have survived for centuries impose certain characteristics and values upon their members. In some cultures the characteristics can become sources of difficulty when, for whatever reasons, that culture comes into contact with another that values its own, different characteristics. In both cases the cultural differences took centuries to generate and are unlikely to disappear for similar time periods even if drastic measures are employed to extinguish them. No culture will quietly surrender its values. On the contrary, the supporters of that culture will do anything possible to preserve them. Sarason sees no early end to conflicts that are based on long-existing cultural values.

What must be recognized in racist conflicts is the readiness with which members of a given culture assume the superiority of their own ways, beliefs, arts, skills, and values and the corresponding inferiority of any other culture. Members of one group will deride members of another as of lower intelligence, indolent, immoral, and generally inferior; and, what is worse, they will assert that this inferiority is biologically based, "in the blood" of the despised group. When constitutional inferiority is assumed, there is little, if any, hope that racism will disappear. When "scientists" find interracial differences in IQ scores and draw conclusions about genetic differences, they fuel the fires of racism. They might do better by recognizing that any standards of superiority or inferiority are arbitrary abstractions created by members of a culture and are hardly applicable to other cultures.

Segregation, Desegregation, and Integration

In many areas of the earth, there are two or more different racial groups living in relatively close proximity. Sometimes such groups live in some sort of harmony, but if they are not equally matched in numbers or political power, conflicts develop and one group tries to dominate another. This is so even where racial differences are not the main distinction—even tribal differences, as in Zimbabwe, or religious distinctions, as in India, Northern Ireland, and Lebanon (and historically in England and Scotland) can result in difficulties. In the United States, one race outnumbers others and may seek to dominate or at least reserve certain perquisites to itself.

A dominant racial group might attempt to establish legal distinctions in privileges or rights, for example, in voting, transportation, school facilities, or form of government. When one group is legally excluded from any activity or privilege, the term *segregation* applies. In some cases no laws are passed to establish segregation, but economic factors force some people to live in less desirable areas of a city, and these areas may become ghettos without any official action. Children living there may attend so-called neighborhood schools and find themselves in a building with no representatives of another race present. Such de facto segregation can be just as potent in its effects as segregation by law.

In some circumstances a minority group may develop enough power to obtain some recognition and alleviation of its situation through the enactment of desegregation laws. Desegregation, when enacted, simply means that there is no legal reason for anyone to be segregated. In such small matters as the part of a bus in which one may sit, a member of a formerly segregated group may now sit where she pleases. In other areas, for example, schooling and employment, difficulties may arise and the new legal freedom may be rather meaningless.

In many instances the difficulties with desegregation are a function of numbers. A small minority group can be accomodated more easily than can a large one. In the case of education, a school district will have only a certain fixed number of schools. To permit people to attend the school of their choice could result in the overcrowding of some schools and underutilization of others. Distance from home to school involves costs of transportation. The problem becomes complicated when desegregation becomes interpreted as integration. Leaders of minority groups begin to talk about "racial balance," which in turn amounts to seeing to it that the students in a given school are enrolled by racial classification in some kind of proportion to their numbers in that area. No one knows what a satisfactory mix of races might be, but proportional representation would mean that some areas of a country might have to have large numbers of a minority group and small numbers of a majority group. Where long-standing animosities exist, a former majority group may begin to leave an area or send its children to alternative schools, thereby creating additional problems. The notion of integration includes the implication that different racial groups will somehow mix and mingle together in other aspects of life besides the education of children. This notion might have some plausibility if the members of the separate races had no desire to maintain some kind of racial identity—to stick together, to form political blocs, to preserve some kinds of custom, or cultural inheritance—and value their differences for whatever reasons. The problem is readily recognized in the arena of housing. If a black person buys a house in a white neighborhood, some of the white residents immediately suspect that other neighbors will also sell to blacks and their property values will drop. The history of the practice has been that other blacks try to join their friends in the white neighborhood, and the integrative operation dies aborning. There is apparently a conflict of interests in that in a desegregated society people want the freedom to live where they choose and also want to be able to choose their neigbors. The two freedoms clash wherever prejudices exist on either side.

Assimilation

The ultimate form of integration would be a mixture of all races or groups with distinctive labels into one social structure where no groups held themselves apart as better than others in any way. Assimilation of racial groups calls for intermarriage or mixed mating on a broad scale, and obviously several generations are required for any meaningful mix. Any efforts at instant integration, to say nothing of assimilation, are not likely to succeed. Desegregation is a first step, and even that is followed by difficulties in that some perquisites are lost by a dominant group whenever another group gains any rights or privileges.

In South Africa, where the whites are a minority but control the economic and political life, the whites are fearful not only of the loss of power but of the loss of everything else they hold dear, including their lives. The sheer numbers of the surrounding black population bodes possible extinction of the white residents, especially in the light of the history of race relations in that area. In the United States, where the population statistics are reversed, desegration is more feasible. The simple conclusion is that dominant groups will continue to try to dominate and will surrender only as much as they are forced to.

AGING

As I stated in the preface, aging is not a problem that psychologists can do much about. As long as one lives, one will age, decline in many ways, and eventually die. There is a limit to how long life can be extended and a great question about the possible pleasures of living in a state of continuing decline in sensory, motor, and intellectual capacities.

There are no strong data about the relationship between age and competence at any age, but there are indications that athletes, for example, tend to peak at about age 26. Some can continue effective performance long after that, but there are no 60-year-old baseball players on major league teams. Satchel Paige may have been one. There are no 40-year-old tennis or boxing champions. Of course some people play tennis at 80, but not at Wimbledon. In other areas, for example, business, science, medicine, and literature, some people continue to operate into their 70s and 80s, but in most cases it is impossible to determine how effective they are. A painting by Grandma Moses may be highly esteemed in some circles, but when the critics call it primitive, they may be trying to say something. Most scientific achievements are effected by people who are not yet in their 40s. They may carry on, of course, with the help of their reputations, and can even be fruitful, but sooner or later they find that they cannot keep up with younger people following in their footsteps. Some obstinately refuse to raise their feet to leave footprints and act as if they were indispensable. If they are politicians, for example, there is no way to demonstrate that anyone else would be better. Too many variables are involved for any clear-cut conclusion that a different president, for example, would have been "better."

The real psychological problem in aging relates to the attitudes of younger people who find old people a problem. Young adults with aging parents who are no longer independently productive and involved in affairs that do not require attention from the children become concerned about what should be done to or with the old people, who may need some kind of care.

The fact of aging is beset with medical puzzles, economic and business issues, and moral or ethical questions. We will not discuss the medical problems here but will leave them to medical experts. But we can look at the other kinds to problem even if there are no solutions. Psychologists are not very helpful in these areas. In the economic world old people sooner or later become unable to meet the needs of a job. They retire or are eased out. They are no longer producers and function only as consumers of goods and services, mostly the latter, especially in the medical area. They are, of course, a source of profit for doctors, nurses, hospitals, and retirement homes, although many quickly run out of funds and become a burden on relatives or taxpayers. Relatively few have savings, pensions, properties, and the like and can afford highly personalized medical services that keep physicians from serving others.

Statistically, we are informed, life (existence) expectancy is increasing, and there is a growing population of old people: about 20 percent of the citizens of the United States are expected to be over 65 in the year 2000. Actually life expectancy has not changed over the centuries as far as the individual is concerned. He will not live any longer than any other human has if he is not murdered, does not have an accident, and does not contract some debilitating disease. Some people have managed to live to a 100 or more all through recorded history (the limit seems higher because of the advances in labor-saving technology, nutrition, and medical care). No one should plan on living to 100. The discovery of penicillin has saved uncounted numbers of people who would have died of pneumonia. Some medical advances merely keep people breathing long after they normally would have stopped. Whether they should continue celebrating birthdays after they are unable to eat birthday cake or blow out the candles is a question people are afraid to ask. A governor of Colorado suggested that people who were no longer able to function on their own had a duty to die. He was referring to chronically hospitalized people who were kept alive by intravenous feeding, mechanical aids for breathing, circulation, and excretion and who had no likelihood of surviving if these devices were removed. The governor's hint was not warmly received by those old enough to consider themselves prospects for such care. If breathing and heartbeats are criteria of life, people can be kept alive forever by mechanical devices or replacement of organs from those who die accidentally.

In the 1930s Tiffany Thayer (a science fiction writer) published a fanciful novel (*Dr. Arnoldi*) with the premise that one day people stopped dying. They could not be killed by any measures, even being ground up into hamburger (the product would pulsate). The problems created by the fact that people would not die were overwhelming and can be left to the imagination of those who cannot read the novel. The simple fact, however, is that people do die, some even before birth, some in infancy, others in childhood, and on through the years. It is when they survive to their 70s and 80s that some become a problem not only to themselves but also to others. The longer they live, the less efficient they become in their senses, muscles, and intellectual capacities, and some reach a second childhood so well described by Shakespeare: "Sans teeth, sans eyes, sans taste, sans everything."[3]

Not all aging people become problem cases even in their 80s and 90s. Only about 5 percent of the aged are afflicted with Alzheimer's disease. Many others can take care of themselves and enjoy life, even if they are slower and less efficient. It appears that those who were intellectually alive in earlier years can continue to function at satisfactory (at least to them) levels. Some can even please others, as Arthur Rubinstein did even in his ninetieth year. Will and Ariel Durant continued their historical publications well into their 80s.

When people do reach a stage of diminished capacity and require care to continue to exist, they become a problem. The question is then raised, What should be done about them? The simple response of *nothing* is rejected out of hand by most people. But no generally satisfying answer is forthcoming. Some answers are proposed by business people who run old age homes. They are glad to have the problem. They will even provide hobby rooms where old people can create ceramic ashtrays and listen to high school girls singing Christmas carols. They will even provide bus trips to places the current residents never cared to visit when they were independent individuals. Various religious groups operate similar establishments where the motive is not profit but the salvation of souls. Sooner or later, however, the residents develop serious medical problems and are sent off to hospitals to die, if the ambulance arrives in time.

The enormous costs of caring for the old soon reduce survivors to penury. No one has considered the possibility of providing just the amount of care that can be paid for with a social security income—the actual amount of care that would be needed to house and feed and clothe a person (a no-frills residence) does not appear to be financially infeasible on that level. Apparently, people are not content with minimal survival facilities for the helpless old.

On the ethical-moral side the problem strikes directly at the children of old people who are themselves already getting old. They may have children and grandchildren of their own and are now faced with the additional problem of taking care of their aging parents. In former times in what was known as the extended family, an aging grandfather or grandmother lived with the now adult children with varying degrees of tolerance or pleasure and could sometimes be useful with baby-sitting or other small chores. They were taken care of as suited the caretakers until they died. It was considered the normal pattern for children to accept the situation, especially the oldest child, frequently the oldest daughter. Commonly the problem did not last long if exceptional medical attention was not provided or available. As the extended family disappeared and the practice of living in small apartments or flats developed, the difficulties of taking care of incompetent oldsters increased. Young people began to worry about their future—they saw themselves as becoming burdened by their parents and began to wonder about what they could do. The cultural practices in many countries included the inculcation in children of emotionally loaded conditioning to the effect that parents were to be loved, respected, and honored, however little they might merit such attention. Love for a mother was supposed to be natural, instinctive, a proper compensation for the ordeals of childbirth and all the sacrifices the mother had made in the drudgery of child care. Mothers did not even have to say, "After all I have done for you" to load their children with guilt. The introduction of social security has sproved to be one of the most significant therapeutic measures ever invented in that it relieved children, at least to a degree, of the financial burden of supporting parents. But the aging population have other than financial problems—they need care in various forms, all time-consuming, undesirable, and unattractive obligations.

The problem of taking care of parents is unknown in the rest of the animal kingdom. Animal parents take care of their young until they are able to shift for themselves and then see to it that they leave the nest or other habitat. The parent-child relationship no longer exists. Animals do not take care of aging parents. Only humans have created the parent-child problem with a role reversal that is not always developed successfully or resolved in a satisfactory manner. Children may well be considered the responsibility of parents, but reversing the responsibility does not appear to have any natural, that is biological, basis. No culture has developed satisfactory (to all concerned) procedures for handling the problems of the older members who need care to survive. Psychiatric casebooks are full of examples where a young adult sacrificed his or her own life prospects because a parent needed help. Evolution is not concerned with the survival of people beyond their procreative years. It is a problem created by human beings, and it has no satisfactory solution.

The problem is even more complicated if children die off before the parents, leaving their aging parents without any immediate source of help. Those adults who do not have children are in the same situation. Some take to the streets and sleep in doorways and join the homeless people, about whom no one seems to care. The problem becomes exacerbated when politicians and other social pillars mouth slogans about the sanctity of life and when other sentimental values are raised in relation to older, no longer productive people. Psychologists, for their part, are rather less than helpful as they turn their skills to studying old people—finding out how much they remember or can learn, as if their time for learning is not past. They might better turn their efforts to relieving children of guilt feelings and teaching them that parents are not the responsibility of children.

The problem of aging and an increasing older population is a comparatively recent one. In Bismarck's Germany a form of social security was introduced for a limited number of people who survived to the age of 65. Because relatively few people did so, government pensions were feasible. When President Franklin Roosevelt proposed a social security program in the 1930s, the same age was still considered practical. In the 1980s social security became a major item of expense in the federal budget. The growing number of senior citizens has become an unforeseen social problem. The older population began to be a serious voting bloc with new demands and a strong reluctance to support any tax programs, for example, school taxes, that no longer concerned them.

Aging is an example of a new social problem for which no culture has developed suitable solutions. It is analogous to the problems faced by the atomic energy developers, who are unable to guarantee the safety of their operation, or by the gene-splicing biologists, who do not know what might happen as a consequence of some of their experiments. One problem with aging is that it is not faced early enough by enough people to develop possible solutions. One does not feel oneself growing older until rather late in life, when it becomes rather difficult to plan for declining years. It is time for psychologists and other social scientists to start thinking about how people should be prepared to avoid becoming a problem for others to solve.

DRUGS AND DRUG ADDICTION

The use of drugs by humans is probably as old as humanity in that drugs are (except for some synthesized products) constituents of various plant forms ingested in one way or another by both people and other animals with some reinforcing consequences. The term *drug abuse* has somehow become accepted to describe addiction or psychological dependence on certain substances, although how a drug can be abused may be questioned. It is the users who abuse themselves. *Misuse* or *overuse* might be more suitable terms.

As I have just suggested, drugs can be constituents of such commonly consumed products as coffee, tea, cocoa, and cola drinks, which contain caffeine, tobacco, marijuana, and alcohol in its various forms (wine, beer, whiskey, Geritol). Humans use drugs in their food and in medicines (tranquilizers and aspirin are used in enormous quantities), and though often addicted to such substances, people do not think of themselves as abusers, only as users.

When abuse is mentioned, the occasion is likely to involve someone's frequent or overuse of opium-derived drugs such as morphine, heroine, and codeine, or cocaine or marijuana.

Efforts to reduce the use of some drugs are frequently directed at suppliers of the substances, police agents conducting periodic raids on pushers and producers. A tolerant public views the users as innocent victims of a criminal enemy—except in the cases of alcohol and tobacco, whose purveyors support magazines, newspapers, and television networks with their advertisements of wine and beer (the U.S. government has outlawed hard liquor and cigarette advertisements on television but not in the press and has forced cigarette manufacturers to print warning messages on packages). It should be noted also that governments support tobacco producers with exclusive licenses. Brewing or fermenting, distributing, and selling alcoholic beverages make up a large business, and governments do not like to see businesses fail, especially when legislators are supported by powerful lobbyists. Senators from tobacco states know where the votes are.

The fact of public tolerance is evidenced by the support of "victims," who are treated in emergency rooms, in rehabilitation programs, in counseling sessions, and so on, all at public expense. A great deal of police and medical personnel time is spent in caring for the victims, and only pushers are blamed. The drug users (once called dope fiends) are now described as having a chemical dependency. The public has demonstrated its acceptance of determinism is not blaming the victims.

That there would be no producers or pushers if there were no market may be recognized but not eagerly pursued. Parents of schoolchildren who are caught with drugs will blame the schools for permitting pushers to get to their innocents—the immediate question is, Where did you get it? instead of the more appropriate question, Why did you use it? Governmental efforts at apprehending pushers are rather weak and ineffective, for the market is growing. The pushers will prevail as long as there is a market. It is the users who are the problem and who create the additional problem of crimes committed to get the money for the purchase of illegal, and therefore expensive, drugs. A partial reduction in crime might be the result of legalizing any drug anyone cared to buy, since prices might drop considerably unless the suppliers were able to form OPEC-like cartels. Even if drugs were cheap, however, other problems would remain. Perhaps more people would overdose at lower prices. The demand law of economics states that consumption increases as price decreases (see Allison 1983).

There is probably nothing psychologists can suggest to eliminate or reduce drug consumption or misuse that is not already being done in educational efforts. How much time can educators devote to a subject that is not a general concern in the sense that only a relatively few schoolchildren actually become serious victims? Many high school children do drink some alcohol and try marijuana or cocaine, but, as yet, drug usage is not epidemic in nature.

To the question of why drugs are used, the answer appears simple, but the remedy is complex. People use drugs for only one reason: drugs are powerful reinforcers. In the period during which some drugs are effective, they bring about a sense of relaxation, an easing of tensions, or a high similar to that some joggers experience during their daily runs. Other drugs make people who are otherwise unhappy, disturbed, nervous, or miserable feel better than they were before taking the drug. Just as a "nice cup of tea" eases some more gentle folk, a drag on a cigarette or marijuana joint is followed by a sense of gratification or satisfaction, the typical consequence of a reinforcer. Drugs either stimulate or depress the nervous system. In either case the user finds the effect reinforcing in terms of his prior condition. Prior conditions vary with the individual, but they have in common a lack of reinforcement from other activities or inactivity. To put it another way, if the drug user had anything better to do she would not be using drugs at the time of doing something better. The trouble arises because many, if not most, people suffer from the impossibility of attaining reinforcing effects from their usual activities or circumstances.

It should be appreciated that drug use is not a racial or ghetto problem. Drugs are commonly used all over the world by all classes of people— the rich, the poor, the young, the old, males, females, the educated, and the ignorant. Some people merely experiment with something novel; others use drugs recreationally for a while without becoming addicted. For some, drug usage is a flirtation with potential danger, an adventure in an otherwise dull life. Others use drugs as an expression of their contempt for authority (parents, or other lawmakers). Children see drug usage as a sign of maturity and peer respect. In most cases the drugs that happen to be popular at any given time do not solve the user's problems, and the use declines or ceases. Some people, of course, become addicted, and new problems are created.

Drug usage can be assumed to arise from frustration, dissatisfaction with one's status, whatever that may be. The Wall Street broker, with his promotion worries, the unemployed ghetto resident, the unpopular adolescent, the failing student, anyone with problems can seek relief and hope to find it in drugs.

Not everyone can be as talented, successful, brilliant, popular, or energetic as he might like to be. Success is always relative, and goads for greater "satisfaction" are always present. The anxious student fearing tomorrow's examination burns tonight's midnight oil and may resort to aids beyond that of the lamp. The Olympic aspirant may accept help from her coach in terms of steroids and other supports such as "uppers." The host at the social gathering will try to break the ice with ice cubes floating in various kinds of liquid. Once one obtains reinforcement from an action, that action will be more likely on subsequent similar occasions, and in the case of addictive drugs, it can be not only more likely but also more necessary. In a culture where success is the Holy Grail, many will look to achieve some variety of success. Since there is only a little room at the top, there will always be failures, dropouts, and losers, and for them drug reinforcement can be the avenue to solace.

It should also be noted that some drugs of a stimulating kind give the user the impression that he is more effective in whatever he is doing— for example, pitching a baseball or hitting it, playing better jazz than he has been able to produce before, being sharper, wittier, or somehow better—and he may sometimes find this to be true possibly for other reasons. Children can be induced to try a drug because they can be goaded into believing that it is an adult thing to do. It is a way of expressing rebellion against childhood, not always a happy stage of life. In any event, persistent use will result in addiction or psychological dependence, both of which will be likely to bring on inefficiency and inadequacy.

When so many people are indulging in drugs, we can expect all sorts of individual differences in tolerance, effectiveness of the drugs, accidental overdoses, dangerous experimental mixtures, infections from unsterilized equipment, and other misadventures.

We can conclude that drugs are substitutes for other kinds of reinforcement for some people and will continue to be used and "abused" by those who do not get enough reinforcement by other means, some of which may not be of any great moral virtue either. If a government is successful in eliminating a drug, some people will find new substitutes that may be more dangerous.

The efforts to eliminate the problem of drug abuse either by prevention of imports and synthetic manufacture or through education are not likely to be successful. Too many already educated people use drugs, many uneducated dropouts do not care to be educated, and the costs involved in preventing importation or manufacture are prohibitive. The difficulty lies in the fact that the reasons for drug use are not being addressed. To prevent drug usage, it is necessary to prevent frustration, an impossible goal.

NOTES

1. Aristophanes, *Lysistrata*.

2. James Thurber, "The War between Men and Women," *Men, Women, and Dogs* (New York: Bantam, 1946).

3. William Shakespeare, *As You Like It*, 2. 7. 139.

6

Social Problems: Living with Others

With the problems that affect us as individual human beings behind us, we can now proceed to examine the problems that arise when individuals come together—our social and antisocial behaviors. The problems that will occupy us in this chapter are worldwide and involve us all, regardless of the particular groups with which we are associated. The problems to be discussed are those arising from religion, culture, nationalism, and social class.

RELIGION AND MORALITY

Because religion appears to have been a factor throughout mankind's existence, as evidenced by primitive burial customs, we had best start with that subject. It should be pointed out that every human has some orientation toward or about supernatural or metaphysical issues. Even atheists have their religious orientations based on their disbeliefs, which are only other kinds of belief. Orthodox communists may decry other forms of religion, but they too have their faith—a faith in the messianic victory of history. We turn, then, to religion and its inseparable companion, morality.

Over the centuries during which human beings have lived as social animals, individuals have questioned their own nature, their reasons for existence, the nature of death, the possibility of an afterlife, and the apparently haphazard individual fortunes of people. Some live to a ripe old age and others die in infancy or during childbirth. Some live through wars and others die in training. Some get rich and others stay poor or lose their fortunes. Some are born with silver spoons in their mouths

and others will need braces. The world seems to be permeated by unlimited unfairness. Enough of such misadventures and paradoxes occur
to or are witnessed by everyone to raise the question, Why? Answers
have been provided by various prophets, seers, philosophers, vision-
aries, and others who might have been regarded as knowing better than
the questioners. Sometimes the answers were systematized in the form
of a religion, and religions have flourished for thousands of years among
the followers (and their descendants) of Moses, Buddha, Zoroaster,
Christ, and Mohammed, along with the systems that hold sway in Japan,
India, and Africa. Most of the religions had an appeal for ordinary
people. The poor and the hungry, the wretched and the misbegotton
could find solace and comfort in the beliefs propounded. Though most
religions were founded on a belief in some supernatural being(s) with
one or many gods and goddesses and offered some promise of an afterlife
(heaven or reincarnation), they also usually addressed themselves to
mundane affairs and spoke for some kind of order that ought to be
followed by the believers. Again, most religions proposed guides for
orderly behavior among individuals and in one form or another advocated some form of the Golden Rule.

Will and Ariel Durant were impressed enough by the positive virtues
of religion to emphasize them in every one of their 11 volumes of *The
Story of Civilization*. On the whole they felt religion does more good than
harm.

There may be no socially critical problems with religion as such—
people believe and will continue to believe many things, and beliefs are
innocuous in themselves. What has happened throughout the history
of humanity, however, is that religions have divided people and have
been used by political leaders to divide them even more, to engage in
destructive actions, in war, torture, execution, and other nefarious activities specifically forbidden by the formal doctrines of the religions
involved. Both the Bible and the Koran proclaim, "Thou shalt not kill."
Injunctions against murder may not be based only on religious principles. Communist (atheistic) regimes also enact laws dealing with murder
and other crimes that are considered sinful in countries that endorse
some religious orientation.

We cannot attempt to trace the origins of the various religions that
claim adherents in all parts of the world. Many current religions were
established so long ago that their roots are difficult for historians to
uncover. In modern times the various religions have in some cases modified or adjusted their doctrines and practices to scientific or technological
changes and social movements. We can assume that virtually all religions
arose out of ignorance of nature and its ways. The fact of death must
have been a mysterious puzzle for ancient and primitive people. It is
still an unacceptable kind of event for most people, and modern believers
in spiritualism keep trying to communicate with the departed.

However the different religions did arise, it appears clear enough that today's children raise the same questions their ancient ancestors did: questions about why people exist, where they came from, where they go when they die. And modern parents answer the questions with the only answers they have, those that were passed on to them by their parents and their schools. It is no mystery that Jewish parents have Jewish children or that Seventh Day Adventist parents have Seventh Day Adventist children. The early childhood training includes varying degrees of ritual, ceremony, or education relating to the religious beliefs of the parents. The conditioning of children to respond along certain lines to certain religious stimuli is standard operating procedure in most households. Children become accustomed to attending religious exercises on Saturday or Sunday and practices conducted in an atmosphere that facilitates the conditioning of specific responses. Virtually everyone is familiar with the environments in which children learn to become Catholics, Protestants, or Moslems. Along with the kinds of information that children acquire about supernatural matters, there are various moral or ethical views that are impressed upon them and that they are expected to express in appropriate circumstances. How strongly moral precepts are accepted by the children varies with individuals. It appears to be basic to all religions that people are assumed to be naturally or innately bad or evil and that they must be taught to be good. The Christian doctrine of sin may reflect such a view. Freud developed his entire system on the basis of a conflict between the Id (natural or instinctive urges of a selfish nature) and the Superego, the conscience, or proper moral guidelines of a civilized society.

Moral and ethnical training of children is again an individual matter. Though some religions spell out some guidelines (for example, the Ten Commandments, the Seven Deadly Sins), not all parents are successful teachers; some do not even try, and many do not practice what they preach, thus creating doubts and uncetainties in the children. Some are taught not to lie or steal, but the training may be rather situation-specific. Children may not lie about some things and not steal some things. By the time they are adults, about 50 percent of them commit adultery. There are no exact figures. Probably 100 percent will lie about something, and stealing (for example, falsifying income tax returns) may depend upon many circumstances. Too many pillars of the community, from stock exchange presidents and bankers to members of Congress and corporation presidents, have been exposed as frauds, cheats, thieves, and all of the rest of the catalog of crimes, sins, and varieties of immorality for anyone to be confident about the effectiveness of moral training.

Psychology cannot provide any moral imperatives, any more than can physics. Physicists, however, can inform us about what would happen if atomic missiles were exploded in various numbers on any terrain, and it is quite clear that only a few such bombs could destroy the entire planet Earth with all its living creatures except for the cockroaches. Along such lines, psychologists can also tell with some accuracy what happens when people get angry, for example, or frightened, and to what lengths people can go given enough stimulation for either reaction.

During World War II, for example, it is obvious that a great many Germans spent a lot of time exterminating Jews and members of other nationalities, along with many people who were handicapped in one way or another and thus less than perfect in Nazi eyes. The barbarism of the Nazis on such a mass scale far exceeded any barbarism ever before displayed in human history, although there has never been a time when people were not tortured, brutalized, and killed, perhaps with less sophisticated procedures. Torture is officially practiced in many countries today. It cannot even be argued that the exterminators were personally injured by, frustrated by, or angry at their victims. Most of them claimed that they were only following orders. The same claim is made by pilots and bombardiers who create fire storms over cities and destroy thousands of people they never even knew existed. We can assume that some people follow orders because of fear of what would happen to them if they did not. Others can be talked into or trained to perform such final dispositions as a personally acceptable part of their patriotic obligations. Some even like to follow orders or give them (see Milgram 1974).

On a more individual level, some people are at ease while functioning as hangmen or executioners knowing that they have the strong support of thousands of their fellows. Capital punishment is favored by large segments of any population for various (even trivial) reasons. Some assume that it is a deterrent to potential criminals; some think of it as cheaper than supporting a convict for life; others support it for religious reasons (an eye for an eye), but many others with different religious training are appalled at the prospect of anyone being killed for any reason. They may oppose capital punishment in various ways yet, at the same time, be prepared to join the armed forces in time of national crisis and exterminate millions of enemies. Some who oppose capital punishment march in parades or demonstrations in favor of abortion, not stopping to reflect that eliminating a convicted killer might be a rather different operation from that of killing an innocent though yet unborn potential human who has, as yet, not sinned.

Both abortion and capital punishment presumably derive from fears. Some pregnant women may fear having a baby for many reasons—from simple fear of the process of delivery to various socially based fears (humiliation if the baby is not born under customary socially approved circumstances, for example, out of wedlock), or for economic reasons.

The fear of criminal attack is enough to justify to some people the support of capital punishment; such fears are probably contaminated with religious and other moral training involving concepts of retribution or revenge, which originate in fears themselves.

In different countries and cultures, varying customs prevail about contraception, abortion, and capital punishment. Clearly, there is no natural or innate predisposition to behave in any specific way about these issues, and people will keep on doing what they are doing with occasional changes as new conditions develop. In the United States one judge offered convicted rapists the option of castration or life imprisonment as punishment. His own upbringing dictated such a Solomonic decision. Immediately outcries of rage came from various sources denouncing butchery, inhumaneness, and so on. The rapists themselves were dubious about their choice; some surgeons announced that they would not perform such operations. Unfortunately, morality has no biological foundation except in a rather negative sense. People will continue to do what they think is best if it is in their power to do so. The Darwinian struggle for survival will dictate morality for individuals just as the fear of strangers will continue to feed prejudices of various kinds. The thin veneer of civilization is just that, *thin*, despite the claims for some hereditary genes for altruism, which appear to find little expression as one views the wide range of crimes and corruption and senseless killings, some individual and some organized by death squads, some through terrorist bombings, and some through bombings ordered by governmental leaders who denounce terrorists.

Throughout the centuries there have been individuals who, for their own reasons (that is, because of their backgrounds), did behave and urged others to behave in more peaceful, friendly, cooperative, and helpful ways. In some cases they worked under the influence of religious beliefs that promised rewards in heaven for those who behaved in what was described as a desirable way; for some the carrot of heaven was supplemented with the stick of hell. Others, like Socrates, were led to their life-styles and views through what was described as an exercise of reason. There have been many advocates of the Golden Rule, stated either positively or negatively (that is, do unto others, or do not do unto others). In most cases of such do-gooders, the rules they prescribed were just too difficult for others to live by. Their personal sacrifices may have been admired, but they were seldom emulated. The complexities of civilization get in the way. Very few people can get what they want when they want it, and the competition for goods, needed or not, leads to push, shove, and if that is not enough, then kill. Leaders of organized religions sometimes preach annihilation of infidels, and religious wars have bloodied the pages of history, even under the doctrine of peace on earth, goodwill to men. So long as some people do not have the means of survival in peaceful ways, morality will play a secondary role in human interactions.

As I mentioned earlier, there may be no problem with respect to religious beliefs themselves. Many beliefs pertain to an afterlife that cannot be proved false. Many views about the nature of the mind or of the soul cannot be tested by scientific procedures. No material tests can be performed on nonmaterial entities. In condititoning terms, beliefs about an after life cannot be extinguished. They may be replaced by other beliefs that may be equally untestable. It is not the beliefs themselves that matter but the behavior of the believers, who freequently enough use the beliefs of others as an opening wedge to arouse emotional reactions that can trigger other behaviors. The James Jones mass suicide in Guyana in 1978 indicates the extremes to which believers can be led. Followers of Mohammed may indulge in suicidal bombings to hasten their arrival in heaven. The victims of the religious beliefs of others might find great cause for alarm.

On a different level problems may arise when citizens of no religious affiliation or of a different one suspect that a religious practice has political overtones that in their opinion foreshadow problems. Thus a Christmas creche on city property arouses the ire of some excitable people enough to raise the issue of the separation of church and state. When a president of the United States advocates school prayer, he again excites some devotees of a sacred constitution to rally against "an establishment of religion." Other zealots fight against textbooks describing evolution, and still others support or fight against sex education or "adult" bookstores. The motives of people who raise religious or moral questions in other contexts should be questioned. Some may be quite sincere; others may be looking for political or other kinds of support from the dissatisfied.

Most people manage to keep their religious beliefs quietly separated from their daily affairs. They go to church or temple on appropriate days and enjoy religious holidays, and some even do good works in the name of their affiliation, whatever their private motives may be. Until people all over the world learn to do the same, we can expect charismatic religious leaders to exploit the views of followers. The United States Supreme Court illustrates, perhaps, a suitable arrangement. It opens its public sessions with a prayer and then proceeds to ignore any supernatural principles.

CULTURES AND SUBCULTURES

In many countries an original, native population has been annihilated or subjugated by invaders who have taken over the territory and become a dominant group, leaving the surviving original inhabitants, for example, American Indians, in an inferior status. This was the common pattern in the conquest of North, Central, and South America and Africa by Europeans. In time, new arrivals may be acepted as immigrants, most of them at first accepting low status, doing the manual work that the original invaders are no longer inclined to do now that some of them are in a position to employ someone else. Thus millions of Germans, Chinese, Swedes, Italians, Poles, Jews from various countries, Puerto Ricans, and Mexicans, along with dozens of other groups, settled in the United States to begin a new life. These immigrants brought with them their own languages, folklore, music, dances, cuisine—in short their culture or way of life. Because in most cases they could not speak English, they settled in communities where earlier immigrants from their old country had already established themselves to some degree. Without such communities they could not communicate with anyone, find jobs, housing, or even food. In most cases they had no money for hotel accommodations and translators. They did not come as tourists.

By settling in communities of their "own kind," they could survive even without learning to speak English. They could and did establish businesses, newspapers, insurance companies, schools, churches, community centers, clubs, and other organizations and lived out their lives in their own ghettos. Many of the immigrants were young men escaping military service in their own countries; others were unable to make satisfactory progress for various reasons, for example, because a family farm had been subdivided so often that no one could make a living from his share. The young men would marry women immigrants who could not find employment or husbands in the old country after the men left. Children from these marriages would be second-generation and pretty much second-class citizens and would be brought up in the ghettos of their parents as young bilinguals as the schools and other contacts outside the home fostered the new language.

Each hyphen-American ghetto was an island in a sea containing similar islands, with an obscure mainland somewhere out on the horizon. The islands of hyphen-Americans amounted to subcultures, and the dominant culture (that of the original invaders and their descendants) looked (down) upon them as a necessary evil, "foreigners" who worked the farms, mines, and mills, built railroads, tunnels, and subway systems, served in the homes, and otherwise made themselves useful. Though immigrant groups were thought of as foreign for a long time, their descendants born in the United States had to be recognized as citizens. The fact of citizenship, however, did not eliminate the apparent need for a label, and one was found—*minority* became the tab by which groups were distinguished. The label is not meaningful, of course, unless there is a majority, but there appears to be no majority except for such distinctions as that between blacks and whites. Even within black groups there are minorities of one kind or another, and within the white majority there are now dozens of minority groups. Everyone is a member of some minority group as far as national ancestry is concerned. When one considers the individual characteristics of people, one is left with the conclusion that everyone is a "majority of one." When Thoreau used these words, he had a different distinction in mind, but it is just as applicable to the status of any resident in the United States. It has to be added that everyone is also a minority of one.

The members of the subcultures in the United States made some progress, generally improving their standard of living over the years, and their children began to make inroads into the dominant culture as it began to lose ground in terms of numbers because of declining birth rates as well as the sheer number of immigrants, some of whom had to be employed to handle the rest. The immigrants gradually began to dominate some areas politically and economically.

Immigrants who arrived after the Civil and Spanish-American wars had strong ties to their homelands and found the local American mores not always to their liking. They tried to instill their original values and customs in their children, to foster some kind of love or loyalty to the old country, which the children could not acquire with anything like the parental strength. Parents would struggle to keep the language alive, to pass on their culture, to foster in-group marriage, to keep some kind of cohesion within the group. Fraternal, church, and choral socieites and every kind of organization that depended upon new recruits for survival tried to keep the group together, to keep up an identity that was not totally American. So long as one stayed within the group—for example, if one did not attend high school where members of other groups would be encountered—problems of identity would not arise. One did not know that one was poor or non-Americn if one stayed within the ghetto.

Slowly, with the years, one ghetto after another began to break up, to disintegrate; new immigrants from other sources began to invade formerly Irish, Jewish, or Italian neighborhoods. The breakup of the ghettos was largely a matter of space. The original neighborhood could not provide living quarters for all the children when they grew up, and they had to move out to new housing. As the original immigrants died off, their homes were taken over by new arrivals, often from different cultures. One ghetto replaced another.

The exit of the second- and third-generation subculture members out of their ghettos did not amount to assimilation with the dominant culture in any meaningful sense. Often enough the moves were new and improved ghettos; some suburbs would be predominately Polish, Jewish, or Italian, for example. Some sociologists and politicians began talking about a melting pot, with the implication that some entirely new and presumably better, enriched kind of product would result from the in-teractions of members of various subcultures with the dominant culture. What really happened was that the members of the subculture indeed associated with or came in contact with members of other subcultures and, in order, to communicate or cooperate in any venture, they had to lose, eliminate, or supress some of their own subcultural features. Eng-lish became their common language, and the prevailing pattern of eco-nomic activity became their common ways, but nobody contributed any new ingredient to the melting pot. The brew turned out to be mostly water without any flavor having been contributed by anybody. It is of course true that some small items from one or another subculture have been adopted by members of other subcultures and sometimes even by the dominant culture. Nearly everyone has eaten pizza, for example. To what extent pizza eating has enriched American culture might be a question. A Polish-American popular singer once introduced a couple of lines of Polish into a song that enjoyed some popularity, and some Italian words are included in popular songs, but the value of such ad-ditions to the culture is rather debatable. It is not as if pizza and a few foreign words have been adopted into the American culture—rather they are recognized as foreign and not something that has been assimilated into the general pattern. As the subculture groups tended to increase their contacts, intermarriages increased, which would again result in the loss of specific cultural features. Children of such intermarriages would not learn either of the old languages of their parents and would not find their lives doubly enriched. There would instead be a net loss, an emp-tiness, for neither parent might want to impose his background at the expense of the other. The effort would instead amount to an attempt to rear the children as "not different" from the others around them.

One obvious reason for the failure of the melting pot to create some novel dish of some alleged "higher culture" is that the contributors were not strong. The immigrants who came to the United States were not especially well versed in their own old cultures. They were, for the most part, uneducated peasants or laborers who spoke dialects of their basic languages. They knew little about the art or literature or music of their own countries. Sicilian peasants would not be familiar with Dante, Tasso, Verdi, or Raphael. Few of them would have heard of Galileo, Machiavelli, or Botticelli. Most had never been to Rome or even more than a few miles from their villages before they came to the United States. How could they even pretend to inculcate some Italian culture in their children? At best they could teach them a few folk songs, dances, and religious customs. The same, of course, was true of other subcul-tures. Jewish parents would see to it that their children could read Hebrew, and many did learn to pronounce words from Hebrew script, but few would know what they were reading so proficiently. Jewish children in the United States could not know at first hand the meaning of pogroms, persecution, or raw anti-Semitism.

The assumption underlyiung the concept of assimilation is that there is an American culture to which someone can be assimilated. To some extent this was true up to about 1850 or so, when most of the Americn population was of English stock, with a modicum of education; there were the beginnings of an American literature, with rather little in the way of art or music, a mostly Protestant religion and morality. Indians and slaves and their ways did not count for much or were downgraded as primitive or savage. Following the Civil War the great westward expansion of the United States, with increasing industrialization calling for immigrant labor, the great growth of the cities, the mechanization of farming, and other technological introductions such as the telephone, electricity, and the automobile all created a vast change in the ways of living in the United States. The extent and rapidity of the changes precluded any definition or identification of what might be called a culture. It is difficult to analyze a culture that does not stand still for a few centuries.

The concept of subcultures really requires the examination of what a culture amounts to. Commonly people talking about cultures have in mind notions about fine arts, music, literature, intellectual interests, traditions, customs, religious orientation and so on. One speaks of the culture of China, France, or Italy, as if it were something standard and uniform characterizing all Chinese, Frenchmen, or Italians. In actuality very few people in any country are aware of much more than their own interests and special problems. They vary by occupation, language patterns, education, economic levels, and narrow local concerns. With changing times and new technologies, life-styles and patterns change in unpredictable ways. Even the language changes over the years. Not much else stays the same. Political events, international conflicts, technological changes, methods of transportation and of the distribution of goods (for example, supermarkets) all have their impact. The construction of a highway may change entire neighborhoods. Foreign competition may result in the closing of local factories, and the loss of jobs forces some people to migrate to other sections of the country where they may be surprised by how people live. Culture is not a stable, unchanging entity that maintains an identity for any great period of time. The cultures of Eastern European countries are quite different from what they were prior to almost 50 years of Soviet domination.

Culture does not consist of attending the opera. In any country few people can afford to do so or care to spend their time in that fashion. Many prefer football. Only a few people visit museums of art, history, or science—they may prefer to visit a local tavern or play pinochle. Others prefer bridge or poker. In short, the term *culture* means so much that it means very little. If we identify it with a way of living, there are so many ways in which individuals live that it defies description in any realistic manner. The term might be useful in describing a small population on an isolated island. With large populations one has to resort to statistics and talk about the percentages of people who attend what kinds of movie and of what age groups they consist. How many read books? A best-seller, for example, may be such with only a tiny fraction of the population even aware of its exsitence. With 250 million people in a country, a book can be a best-seller with fewer than 100,000 copies sold. That would amount to less than one-half of 1 percent of the population. One cannot talk meaningfully about the culture of any country. It is possible only to speak of subcultures and the subgroups of the subcultures because the subcultures themselves are scarcely uniform in any characteristics. The new class of Soviet rulers, for example, does not live as the old nobility did, but it tries to, and it certainly does not live as the workers or peasants do. Every culture has its subclasses, which are divided in numerous ways—in the way they eat, work, play, in their housing, dress, and intellectual and aesthetic interests and levels.

In the constantly changing scene involving patterns of living, various forces exert their influence on people in convergent ways that do tend to create some uniformity. Manufacturers of clothing with their annually changing styles attempt to make last year's styles obsolete and hope to dress everyone alike in this year's styles. Television networks copy one another in producing shows that they hope everyone will watch and become addicted to. Food producers or packagers try to control dietary habits and kitchen practices with prepackaged, precooked dishes. The newspapers in one-newspaper cities try to control public opinion by restricting viewpoints. Home building contractors create communities of uniform houses, and automobile manufacturers restrict the number of choices to a few. Despite the efforts of some to create a uniform population of consumers, individuals remain individuals and try to make themselves distinctive, if not unique. Many try to identify with whatever they describe as the "beautiful people." In some cases they point with pride to their origins; in other cases they try to hide their origins. In the case of black people, the origins cannot be hidden easily, and some effort is made to suggest that "black is beautiful."

Though some may try to hide their origins, this is not easy. Names, physical characteristics, and perhaps residential areas sometimes suggest origins. Members of a group may be curious about the origins of people who are not members because they think they may know something about a person if they know her "nationality." Most people have some stereotypical knowledge about members of other groups and use this information or misinformation in their dealings with others.

Some people become so concerned with their identify that they spend time trying to trace their roots, their family trees, or to learn about about the cultures from which they sprang. It is not always an easy operation, and few people have time to spend becoming familiar with an older culture when they are so busy trying to adjust to their present one. The old culture in the meantime has changed into something quite different from what it might have been. Communist takeovers of Eastern Europe, for example, have changed the culture of many countries from which immigrants to the United States arrived 100 years ago. Can descendants of immigrants develop a fondness or a partial dedication to something that no longer exists and that, when it did exist, had nothing much to do with the immigrants? Of course, an intellectual curiosity can be developed about anything, and pursuit of such curiosity can be individually rewarding. A problem arises, however, when values are attached to one's interests and the interests of others are denigrated. When the subject of one's affections is not a concrete reality but consists mostly of fantasy and fiction, one had best be careful.

PATRIOTISM AND NATIONALISM

Long before anything resembling what we now call nations, people lived in small groups in relatively localized communities somewhat like the small villages we still find in rural areas of the United States, and indeed, around the world, where a few families eke out existences within shouting distances of one another when the wind is right. In ancient America such groups were called tribes; in Scotland they were clans, and in other places, such as the modern Appalachians, they were merely families like the Hatfields and the McCoys.

When a family increased in size beyond the immediate compass of a father, mother, and their children, by addition of grandchildren, intermarriage with other families, acceptance of strangers, and otherwise, it appears that inevitably formal relationships would emerge or develop resulting in some form of local government. The relationships might be simple ones of dominance-submission, leadership, specialization of function in terms of special skills, distribution of labor and so one. Men might do the hunting and fishing, fighting, and farming while women might do the work around the living quarters such as cooking, making clothing, and taking care of children and other small animals. Different groups, depending upon environmental constraints and facilities, arranged their living relationships differently—men were usually, though not always dominant. Some societies were matriarchal, others patriarchal. In either case, some individual assumed the role of chief, headmaster, or whatever title might designate the person who seemed to have most to say about what the group would do.

Some groups prospered; others died off because of unfavorable environmental circumstances. Others fell victim to onslaughts by other groups. Some groups settled down in what appeared to be favorable locations; others led a nomadic existence following migrating animals or leading animals such as sheep to different locations with the change of season. Such nomadic groups ranging in size from several families down to single individuals still exist in some parts of the world. Nomadic groups remained small. Nonnomadic groups expanded to cover a large territory, and their shelters, whether tepees, caves, pueblos, or cabins, formed villages, and in effect, small towns, then cities, and finally metropolis-size groupings or city-states.

In every instance group living required some kind of organization, some understanding of one anothers' activities, some recognition of the existence of others, and some estimate of what others were likely to do under various circumstances. At a basic minimum, no two people could occupy the same spot on the earth, and any two people could decide to fight for it or share it at different times, or one could give up any interest in the spot. To battle one another about everything would become boring, futile, unsuccessful for some, and generally unsatisfying for losers. After enough encounters and misunderstandings, successes and losses, certain arrangements must have been reached and recognized as acceptable and tolerable, if not necessarily desirable, for all concerned. The arrangements, if they survived, became customs, mores, routines, and traditions.

Group life required relatively permanent arrangements and understandings of who was to do what and when. In small groups nothing further was needed, but as groups grew larger and newcomers were added, the arrangements had to be taught, enforced, and directed to avoid the turmoil of starting all over again with each new arrival. Someone had to play the role of instructor and/or enforcer, and the role of leader or leaders arose. As with groups of gorillas, we can surmise that the oldest, biggest, and strongest individuals took charge and ran the groups until they were deposed by younger, bigger, and stronger newcomers. In human families the strength variable might be overcome by cunning or special skills that fostered survival to old age, and, in general, the older people would (because they had survived) have become more knowledgeable, simply through experience, and might be tolerated as leaders or rulers.

As groups grew still larger, the leadership role became more complex. Intergroup as well as intragroup problems arose and required solution. Leadership could become a full-time preoccupation leaving no time for personal breadwinning. Groups had to develop arrangements for taking care of the leader's personal needs. The first taxes amounted to such operations as feeding and housing the leaders. Such needs appear to have no end and could easily lead to corruption, as the world has learned over the centuries. Though absolute power might not corrupt all leaders absolutely, there is little doubt tht most leaders did little to avoid more support than was necessary for mere survival. Commonly enough they took steps to pass the reins of power to their children. Congress and other legislators tend to show little reluctance about raising their own salaries to whatever level they think they can get away with. It is even safe for members of Congress to speak against prospective raises because they know this speech will have no effect other than to raise suspicions about their motivation. It is the rare member of Congress who does not become a millionaire.

In some cases the expanding needs of rulers or leaders led them to look at their neighbors as additional sources of need satisfiers. They then began to develop ways to get their followers to help them take over new territories and add more people to their taxable sources. In short, some leaders became warlords. The term is now commonly applied to leaders of small bands of outlaws in remote areas of large countries such as China, but the simple fact is that all leaders of governments are war-lords—commanders in chief of the armed forces. Some just do not feel the need to add to their territories; some even object to the practice of other warlords who are not even threatening them but appear to have designs on their own neighbors. Some modern warlords would like to be regarded as peace lords, but most of them seem to think that peace is something that has to be imposed on some other warlord by threats or actual attack. Some warlords are not strong enough to do anything about adding to their tax base or may have too many intraterritorial problems to be concerned about foreign affairs, and any acquisitive urges must be suppressed or lie dormant. But there appears to be an insatiable need to impose one's own form of government on the rest of the world, however reluctant the rest of the world might be to accept that rule. The Soviet Union is notorious for its affirmed policy of communizing the earth. "Workers of the world, unite" was not a limited appeal to the workers of Britain, France, or Germany. Karl Marx saw a need for all countries to be run in the same way. Trotsky and Stalin had their falling out on the issue of international communism or one-country socialism. Trotsky seems to have won. Communist countries such as Cuba try to export their revolution. Capitalist countries such as the United States try to export democracy. Problems arise when the term *democracy* is applied to such places as the German Democratic Republic or China.

The attempt by one country to export its form of government to others is an extension of a warlord's (and his immediate supporters') effort to increase the size of his own domain. It may not lead directly to personal, material satisfaction but it might help secure one's borders and lead to other satisfactions. The leaders in the Kremlin may hate the Poles and would shed no tears if they all died from some plague, but they like to have an additional several hundred miles of battlefield terrain that is not the Soviet Union. To keep Poland under control is assumed to add to the security of the Soviet Union. The material benefits of looting Poland are a secondary benefit. The Brezhnev Doctrine amounted to a program of assisting any Communist group that can take over a government regardless of the wishes of the people governed.

Warlords do not necessarily engage in wars on a daily basis. They may have as much territory as they can handle or may not have the resources to engage in new conquests by force, or their enemies may be too strong to attack with impunity. The underlying desire to control more people and land may be dormant at times. Shakespeare expressed it best through Henry V, who shouted, "No King of England, if not King of France."[1] The present queen of England may have no designs on France and may wish that France just did not exist—and the feelings are probably mutual in the ruling circles of France—but the urges to control and not to be controlled persist at levels in all ruling classes and in all rulers from dictators, politburos, and presidents down to governors, mayors, and fathers and mothers. There may be some people who like to be managed, but they are not easily found.

The original motivation for invading a neighbor's territory could well be the promise of more personal and material gain for the invaders. The warlord could promise land, goods, and other real or imagined profits to anyone who would participate. If positive gain was not sufficient, other values could be invoked—the enemy could be described as dangerous, with designs on the properties and lives of the people. Even this might not be sufficient to arouse a populace, and it might become necessary to raise an army by other means. That problem took a long time to solve, but it was finally solved by some leaders through the magic of an appeal to nonmaterial forces. At first the appeal was through religion—crusades were mounted to attack the infidel, to rescue the Holy Land. One did not yet fight for king and country, but for God. It was not too difficult to transfer the loyalty to and love of God to loyalty to and love of those who led their armies in wars for God's sake. The Divine Right of Kings developed from their activities on behalf of God, who obviously would bestow His blessings on such benefactors and their followers, and by derivation on the territory in which they lived.

It should be noted that no one is born with a sense of patriotism or love of country, motherland, fatherland, or any other kind of land. Some lands such as the polar regions or the Sahara Desert might be a little difficult to love, but almost everyone who survives a few years in any environment develops an affinity, a fondness, a liking for that environment—after all, he has survived there; it has been his security blanket. Adults often suffer nostalgia as they recall their childhood homes and locales even if they lived in shacks in isolated mining towns, log cabins, or dirt houses on windswept prairies. One identifies with—that is, becomes conditioned to feel positive about—an environment in which one eats, sleeps, and is free from danger. One even develops a fondness for a favorite chair, place at the table, and side of the bed. Any interference with one's special niches in an environment are resented and repulsed if possible. Among some animals and some birds, protectionism over a particular space or area is especially noticeable and is called territoriality. Dogs and cats mark their territories and often defend them successfully even against more powerful invaders who stray into them. Not all cats or dogs are territorial, however, and it is hardly a universal pattern even for animals. Humans express their fondness for a piece of ground by other means: fences, leases, walls, and locked doors. These are not instinctive patterns but the natural outcomes of positive emotional conditioning to places where one enjoys satisfaction and security. When a property fails to provide satisfaction, it is ignored or sold or otherwise disposed of. When an area fails to provide security and sustenance, people leave it—witness the departure of the downtrodden masses, the peasantry of Europe, Asia, and Latin America, and the migrations of farmers, peasants, and villagers to the larger cities of Brazil, Mexico, the United States, the Soviet Union—in fact any country that has cities.

The conditioning of pleasant emotions can extend beyond one's immediate childhood home to frequently visited places in the surrounding neighborhood, and one gradually comes to feel comfortable in familiar surroundings—local parks, campsites, swimming pools or swimming holes, skating rinks, and baseball diamonds. One comes to identify with a community, which usually carries a label that distinguishes it from other communities. Simple association transfers the positive emotional conditioning to the label. One's community is always on this side of the tracks, although, as one grows up, one may discover that it is really on the other side. One will still feel positively about one's old stamping grounds, the old homestead, or the old home town. When circumstances force some change, as when a successful businesswoman moves to another section of town, she may still enjoy going back to the old neighborhood to shop, to go to church, to participate in festivities, and otherwise keep ties alive. Successful people who were born and brought up poor commonly say that they did not know they were poor.

As people age, go to school, read newspapers, watch TV, and otherwise expand their horizons, they learn that their community is not the whole world, that the people in it have ties, however loose, with other communities, and that the boy in Maine has something in common with the boy in Hawaii or Texas. They are all Americans, they all sing "My Country, T'is of thee," salute the same flag, and celebrate the same holidays, and when they recite "one nation, indivisible . . . ," they are probably stating the mispronounced truth, but they are gradually becoming conditioned to respond positively to words like *country* and *motherland* because of the identification with the singing or chanting group, which includes some friends. The activity itself may be enjoyable, for it is usually performed in an atmosphere of approval by teachers or other adults who reinforce the performance with praise.

The feelings of mutuality or commonalty among residents of Maine and Texas are probably rather thin, and when a girl from Maine visits Texas, Alabama, or Colorado, she may feel strange and not completely at ease. The language is still English, but not quite the same as in Maine, and the food is a little different—after all, grits with eggs, when everyone knows it's ham or bacon and potatoes that go with eggs. And even if everything is pleasant, upon returning, the girl still feels good to be back home.

The press, in its insatiable desire for more circulation and the benefits thereof, encourages the notion that scattered suburbs are all part of Greater Walla Walla or Greater New York, and any government, anxious for all of the votes or a mandate, insists that we are all one, that we "belong" to one country, to one family. (Governor Mario Cuomo of New York likes to say that residents of New York State are all one big happy family. He does not like to face the fact that families are getting smaller and smaller.)

From the moment we enter the school system, supported by local, state, and federal funds, we are encouraged to love something we have little awareness of, namely our country, be it *la belle France,* or America the beautiful. A child becomes a little patriot, an American, before he realizes what a town or village is and before he has any conception of the world. When he crosses a border into a neighboring foreign country, as Americans do when they cross into Canada, nothing seems to change—the grass is still green, instead of yellow or red as a map might suggest, trees have leaves, streets are paved, houses have roofs, and there is nothing (except customs and immigration posts) to show that a line on a map has been crossed. What is a country?

Everyone knows what a country is. It is a place on a map with a different color from that of surrounding countries. Were there countries before there were maps? Ancient maps tend to be a little vague about borders except for islands. Britain may be a country except that it seems to some of the residents that it consists actually of four countries. At one time a large part of a world map was colored red to represent Britain. Was all that red one country? Well, no, some parts were colonies, which bordered on colonies of other countries and amounted to what the explorers and settlers could wrest from the natives.

Poland was once the largest part of Europe, stretching from the Baltic to the Black Sea, and included most of the Ukraine. Rather rapidly it ceased to exist, being gobbled up by its neighbors in 1771, 1733, and

1795. In 1919 it became a country again, with new borders. By 1939 it ceased to exist again, only to revive again with new borders in 1945. Millions of people were moved from east to west, the western part consisting of former German territory. The eastern part became part of the Soviet empire. Apprently the land itself is not a country.

Some countries such as Israel and Lebanon were created by the simple process of other countries giving up mandates; others such as India and Kenya ceased to be colonies and became countries. What a country represents besides some lines on a map has never really been determined. Within a given country—say, Lebanon—there may be several languages, several religions, several racial groups, and no apparent common interests. Zambia includes two tribal groups that cannot get along with each other, and South Africa has a population the majority of which plays no role in government except to obey unaceptable rules. In another 50 years the United States may be a Spanish-speaking country with a rather different style of living and with pockets of Caucasians holding out for rights and privileges like those that Puerto Rican, Cuban, and Mexican residents now struggle to attain. Residents of Miami may have little in common with Iowans or Nebraskans, but they are all Americans who love their country, or at least the children will be Americans as they survive and go through the educational system. But what it is, was, or will be, to be an American is difficult if not impossible to describe and will not be attempted here.

In Switzerland three groups of people, French, German, and Italian, speaking their own languages, and having little in common other than that they are Swiss, survive and prosper because it is convenient for wealthy foreigners to have a safe place for their bank accounts and to have a nice place to meet for international conferences. The Swiss, of course, will deny this canard. They too, love their country.

In most countries the rulers make every effort to condition what amounts to loyalty to the country's name so that, should it become desirable or useful, the residents can be called upon to support the rulers' decisions, including that of going to war. In many countries rulers demand military service of all young people for a few years. In other countries rulers rely on a draft procedure if its voluntary army is inadequate for some need. In most countries military service is accepted, if reluctantly, because the alternatives are undesirable. In nearly all cases some young people find the prospect of military service unattractive, and some go so far as to desert their own countries for others that will not require such service. Motives for leaving vary. Some young people believe that they have a conscience that precludes the use of force against others. Others simply would rather not go into situations that might result in bodily harm or interference with other plans. Some claim that it is more patriotic to refuse to fight when their country is engaged in an adventure that they don't find to be in their country's *true* best interests.

The effort to instill patriotism commonly works to a considerable extent and almost automatically. One's own home and immediate neighborhood are not enough for most people's range of identification or ego needs. They identify serially with their schools, towns, states, and countries, or even with the "West," whatever that is, since it seems to include Japan. Some people identify with something called the Third World, which suggests that there are two others, and still others align themselves with nonaligned countries. It appears that belonging has become a powerful human motive for some people; others tend to be more limited or confused about where their loyalties belong. The Northern Irish seem to be divided along lines of religion, wealth, jobs, and the control thereof, as well as country of origin, however distant in the past that origin may have been.

A curious example of loyalty arises in professional sport. Los Angeles supports and roots for the Rams or the Dodgers (who came from Brooklyn) even if none of the players previously lived in Los Angeles or even in California, or the United States for that matter. The owner of the team may buy a Cuban or Dominican ball player, and the player instantly becomes an Angelino, a Dodger, a local treasure, if he is any good. If his lawyers are clever, he may have no loyalty to the team and leave as soon as he has a better offer, but the fans can be counted on to be loyal to anyone in the Dodger uniform. The fans despair when their team loses to Houston or Philadelphia and get excited when it wins a ballgame, as if it mattered to anyone but the players, who care only because their salaries are a function of winning. The enthusiasm for professional teams is an outgrowth of similar enthusiasms for high school and Little League teams, where the players have some closer identity with a community. School spirit itself is a function of winning, and principals despair of the lack of the spirit when the fans are few in number, which usually is the case for a losing team. Everyone loves a winner because the winner is part of the identity of the fans and they find it more pleasant to be identified with winners than with losers.

People refer to "our town" or to "my home town" and think of themselves as Texans, or whatever, even though they own no property there or are on welfare in another state. The immediate "patriotism" for one's own kitchen expands to wider and wider areas until one is ready to die for the good old high school or college. (The student fans sing, "As the backs go tearing by/On their way to do or die" and later, "for God, for Country, and for Yale"—the arrangement of values in the latter motto is interesting, for the values of the students might be in reverse order.)

Samuel Johnson allegedly said, "Patriotism is the last refuge of a scoundrel." He may not have been entirely correct. Not all scoundrels are patriotic, and certainly not all patriots are scoundrels. What he meant, of course, was that when rulers can find no other motivation to encourge their subjects to make scrifices, they call on patriotism as a last resort. They might have to resort to a draft and force. Not all of the subjects will be equally patriotic, and some may interpret their patriotism as somehow not related to what the rulers are doing. Thus draft resisters during the Vietnam War could argue that the patriotic thing to do in order to display the true values of their country was to resist the war and even support the enemy, waving North Vietnamese flags, spilling red ink on the Pentagon, and so on. Some of them may have felt very patriotic in engaging in these activities.

Certainly patriotism is very convenient for rulers; they can demand submission and sacrifices in the name of patriotism. President Kennedy at his inaugural exhorted the people, "Ask not what your country can do for you; ask what you can do for your country." The words had a ringing appeal for those who were charmed by Kennedy, but to those who stopped to examine them they appear rather hollow. Clearly any taxpaying citizen should question what her country is doing to her or for her, and one should obviously raise the question, How can anyone do anything for a fictional construction like a country. If Kennedy meant something else by his remarks, he did not explain his meaning. If he meant that one should look after one's fellows or help clean up pollution in the streets, he could have said so. If, on the other hand, he meant, "Listen to me and do what I tell you," that would, of course be another matter, and if he did mean that, he would not say it.

Throughout history the various nations on the globe have found it difficult to leave their neighbors alone, and there has never been a time in recorded history when some group of people was not engaged in trying to annihilate another group. In recent and current times, ignoring the great World Wars, we have had a lot of bloodletting conflicts in many parts of the world, and today huge armies are standing ready on their national borders to repel prospective invaders. Nations such as East Germany and West Germany may well become embroiled in conflict on the orders of their rulers, when the people on each side of the border would probably rather have no wall between them. They will, however, march and shoot when told to do so. It will be a patriotic duty. In most of the wars that have occurred in the past, the actual participants (and even the generals who sat well behind the lines) had no personl quarrel with the people they were killing—it could be a matter of kill or be killed, or, as in more modern wars, releasing death-dealing forces on people far below or far away who were not even known to exist. Dropping a bomb on London or Berlin could not be considered killing—how can one kill London or any other target. One only *hits* targets. In wars where religion is a motivating force, one might well come to hate anyone on the other side, for religious patriotism seems to bring out the worst in people. In communist-capitalist clashes the same kind of emotional patriotism operates because any support of either economic system is hardly a consequence of rational conclusions arrived at by years of study. Communism is a substitute religion for those who believe in it and will be fought against as such not by supporters of capitalism but by anticommunists who are just as religious. Capitalism itself is a religion for only a few devout millionaires and some conservative economists. Anticommunism can be a powerful religion especially as it is linked to an antiatheist postulate.

Even before there were nations, there were wars between smaller collections of people. The city-states of Greece and Italy apparently felt the need to destroy one another, and before that, one tribe or another would take a fancy to another's goods or terrain. Eliminating nations would not eliminate wars, but it might reduce their scope and duration. In any case no one is going to abolish the national boundaries of all nations in the foreseeable future. In time the boundaries of many will be changed. Colonial India is now three nations and may become four or five or more. With the surrender of colonies after World War II, many new nations came into existence without any special reason. They immediately joined the United Nations and started making demands. Little groupings with as few as 100,000 people began to act like major powers when small cities in the United States with larger populations could get no attention from the federal government.

In some colonies warring tribes, previously held together or kept apart by the colonial powers, now saw the opportunity to get at each other again. Many countries, such as those in Central America and some in Africa, contain native populations who live in abject poverty, with little or no awareness of the fact that they belong to a nation, and who have no loyalty to small ruling classes of landowners who run the countries and amount to the nations. In all so-called countries people have different status—they are workers, bosses, managers, rulers, politicians, idle rich, or idle poor—and the people so labeled have little or nothing in common, although they might all watch the same television shows, sports, or bullfights. In some countries, as in India, the classes are formalized as castes; in other countries the caste system is less clear and there is some possibility of movement—a worker can become unemployed and become one of the idle poor. Some poor people get rich, but only their grandchildren are recognized by "the 400" if they are still rich. It is quite a trick to make people of different status all feel part of one big family, but to some degree the trick works, and people take pride in being German or French, or whatever.

In the United States many people, according to pollsters, have no real awareness of the Constitution or the Bill of Rights and would vote against many if not all of the rights they are endowed with by the Constitution. Most people do not vote, and a president who gets only one-fourth of the possible votes considers himself blessed with a mandate. The non-voters may, in some cases, stay away from the polls because their votes are meaningless as far as their personal welfare is concerned. Politicians will continue to vote for laws favoring the financial contributors who have supported them. Milk producers throw money at politicians of any stripe and are rewarded by subsidies that make them prosper. Taxpayers pay for both the milk and the politicians. There may be some honest politicians but they are hard to identify. One does not know when the next honorable politician will be exposed. The corruption is sometimes blatant, as when Congress passes a bill allowing cities to sell public buildings to private citizens, who then lease the buildings back to the cities because they have no other use for them. They buy the buildings in order to take tax deductions on grounds of depreciation, business expenses, and the like. The cities take advantage of these opportunities to ease their problems of raising taxes to support the buildings. The taxpayer now is working not only for the government but also for the private owners, who do not pay their share. Politicians are neither better nor worse than other professionals. Some may, indeed, be saints, but few remain poor, and their financial supporters expect results.

Patriotism can be a big help when a foreign neighbor who plans to exploit you threatens to invade your country. You join up to fight him off. Such defensive or "just" wars are greatly facilitated by patriotism. Clearly, almost all people could be worse off than they are, and if everyone around them is ready to help protect the nation, it can be of major value. To the extent that identifying oneself with a nation brings personal comfort, again patriotism can be rewarding. When such patriotism turns to chauvinism, there is less to be said for it. The problem with patriotism is that people in other countries are also patriotic, and it looks as if one has to put up with it.

CLASS AND CASTE—SUBSETS OF NATIONALISM

Perhaps the thing most wrong with the world is the notion that some people are better than others and that, by virtue of the ssumed superiority, they are entitled to privileges that include respect, power, and favors, to say nothing of monetary awards. The grossest example, of course, is seen in hereditary monarchies, where a royal family and its offshoots (the nobility) feel entitled to the best of everything regardless of the cost or the deprivation that automatically is enforced on those who provide. At present there are only a few royal rulers around, and they appear to be a perishing breed, but similar arrangements come to exist in so-called democracies where imperial presidencies develop and obviously in many countries where upstart sergeants remove former upstart sergeants, make themselves presidents-for-life, strive to ensure the succession of their own children, and become ruling monarchs. The royal house in Britain has the good taste to recognize that it does not rule, that it serves only as a tourist attraction and a stabilizing force, like the royal families in the Scandinavian countries, but the very notion of royalty is taken to mean that some humans are somehow different, better, or "entitled."

In the United States, former presidents have managed somehow to be "entitled" to retinues of guards, handsome pensions, even car washes at public expense. For former President Gerald Ford to have the tax-payers pay $4.95 for a car wash in view of his living style appears a bit much. Yet the populace merely reads the news and groans. It accepts the notion that someone is entitled to little perquisites like oriental rugs in offices and secretrial staffs typing memoirs while the country sinks into depressions, recessions, and absurd deficits.

In many instances distinctions or differences are attributed to heredity, and if the claim is accepted, those with an inferior heredity also accept a lower status. It took a hundred years after the Civil War for blacks to begin to argue that their skin color was "beautiful" instead of being of some lower grade. They had accepted, more or less quietly, that their skin color automatically placed them in a lower caste, as in the caste system in India, which classifies millions of people into groups of more or less privilege.

Now, some hereditary distinctions do provide advantages for some people in certain activities. An eight-foot-tall basketball player can score a lot of points by merely standing next to the basket and pushing the ball through the hoop. Does this make him better than anyone else? It certainly does—in basketball. Even beyond physical sports, heredity is responsible for a lot of differences among people. Some people learn faster than others, some are more attractive than others to members of some cultures, some are faster or stronger, see farther, or hear higher tones than others. These distinctions are immediately seized on as proof of superiority, of betterness, and a scale of values develops (with some reliability in a given culture but of no known validity), and the notion of someone being better than someone else pervades the human race. Even where heredity is not a factor, people will find their grass is greener (therefore better, and therefore they are better) or their cars are bigger or get more mileage—the search for distinction is unending, and every-one tries or is encouraged to try to be considered better than everyone else.

The concept of "better than" is essentially empty. It cannot be meas-ured by a stopwatch or a ruler or any other objective scale. One can be bigger, stronger, faster, thinner, or fatter, but no one can be better than anyone else. It has become the grand illusion and extends to families, cities, nations, even hemispheres. If other worlds are discovered, it will extend to them.

The idea of "better" has invaded the sphere of morals. Children are good, bad, or somewhere in between. "That's a good girl" is the universal expression that is uttered when a girl pleases us. That man is "evil" or "no good," we say when we are displeased with his behavior. The very foundation of our legal system is formed by what pleases or displeases us or those with the power to make laws. People are praised or blamed because they are considered to be good or bad (all people are responsible for their behavior), and we concentrate on rewarding or punishing people because we cannot reward or punish the behavior itself. Thus, instead of preventing bad behavior, we try to develop or create good boys and girls by a variety of meaningless measures (preaching, example, threats, and punishment), but none of these appears to work, and none can. Everyone does what she has to do at a given moment, and in effect she does what pleases her or seems better or best to do at the time. The action may displease someone else, who will call the same act bad. A hoodlum who shoots a police officer will be praised by his hoodlum buddies and cursed by the police.

It is probably safe to say that some behavior is bad or worse than other behaviors if it results in actual loss or harm to someone else. This may not be the only criterion, however, and exceptions are close at hand. An injury in a football game beyond a minor scrape—for example, a damaged knee—is certainly displeasing to the owner of the knee, but it can be regarded as unintentional, the result of a risk freely taken, and usually compensated for in some way. The risks are presumably more or less equal for all of the players. When someone is robbed, she may regard the loss as unpleasant if she can ill afford it. The robber may have needed his ill-gotten gains desperately. Who robbed whom might be an interesting question. A Robin Hood robbing the Sheriff of Nottingham is one thing. A robbing hood assaulting a nun while robbing a church poor box to buy drugs might be regarded as something else. Is the behavior bad? Is the drug addict bad or just sick, in need of care and rehabilitation? Mowrer would have called him "dis-eased."

In any case it can be argued that some behaviors are generally undesirable, that is, most people do not engage in them and do not approve or, on the contrary, regard them as improper, but the transfer of the label *bad* from the behavior to the person may not be warranted. The same person, in different circumstances might not behave in the undesirable way. We can assume that no baby is born evil, bad, or unworthy, regardless of the social status of her parents. To assume that her birth should destine her for life to live like her parents (whether slaves or kings) is out of order. And, as the baby grows into adulthood, her current status (employment, eductional level, clothing, habits, and behaviors) must be appraised in terms of what opportunities her environment provided for alternatives (presumably none), so that there can be no occasion for referring to her as better or worse than anyone else. The old adage "There but for the grace of God go I" might form a reasonable basis for regarding all others.

In most democratic countries the notion of classes is frowned upon officially, but the historical vestiges are still prevalent. People do regard themselves as belonging to classes—lower, middle, and upper, at least, with most assuming that they are somewhere in a middle class, whatever that may be. The distribution of income in a country such as the United States may not justify any strong distinctions. There are a relatively few very wealthy people, and the rest drop off from reasonably satisfied to miserable. Poverty levels are adjusted with inflation, so that nowadays a family of four with an income of $10,000 per year is classified as poor. At one time such an income would have put one into a high middle class. The class distinctions based on income are not very meaningful, for many poor people on welfare may heat their homes better than those who support them through taxes. They may watch the same television shows, shop at the same stores, run up credit charges, and in other ways obscure differences in income. The very wealthy are in a class by themselves, but some of them also watch the same television shows as their less financially stable neighbors. Often enough, rich people starve themselves on diets while the poor eat more, if not "better," food.

We have seen that nationalism leads to international problems and that the existence of subgroups within nations (classes, castes, minorities) leads to intranational problems. A perfect solution to these problems would call for the elimination of all the distinctions that groups have created and came to value, cherish, and nourish: there would have to be one religion or no religion, one nation or no nations, one race or no races, one language or no languages. Such choices are clearly unacceptable to most people on earth. The Soviet Union is presumably dedicated to the concept of one world-nation. Its anthem proclaims, "The International Soviet shall be the human race," and its official atheism indicates that its ruling party has opted for the no religion choice, but the large number of minorities, languages, and religions within its own boundaries, along with the class distinctions that the Yugoslav writer Milovan Djilas has described, suggest that the international soviet is losing rather than gaining ground despite some gains in "backward" countries.

Within the Soviet bloc the separate nations follow various economic systems, and in China, for example, communists are encouraging capitalism, creating new problems. In former Northern Rhodesia tribes that once united against white rule are now trying to exterminate one another.

In general, then, so long as one person or one group regards himself or itseslf as better than others, the general level of human happiness will suffer. The crimes, assaults, tortures, poverty, wars, revolutions, violence of all kinds will continue. Countries will come and go, be divided and reunited; empires will rise and fall; some people will grow fat and others will starve. There is no reason to expect that the human race will enjoy any fate better than that of the dinosaurs.

NOTES

1. William Shakespeare, *Henry V*, 2. 2. 193.

7

An Introduction to Economic Problems

Economic problems are perhaps the most significant and ubiquitous concerns of mankind. They underlie or participate in almost all of the kinds of problems people face—problems concerning law and crime, drugs, education, sex (especially marriage and divorce), racial discrimination, personal welfare (jobs and careers), and international relationships, among many others. Everything costs something. There is no free lunch. We cannot examine all of the interrelationships that prevail, and we must be content with looking at some in which our psychological principles appear to be pertinent.

The theory of evolution teaches us that it is the business of every living creature to survive and reproduce, and for some creatures that business is a struggle, the struggle for existence. Some creatures do not or cannot struggle successfully enough and are eliminated in one way or another. Among humans some individuals decide that the struggle is not worth the prize and commit suicide, an occurrence not commonly observed among other species. The form of the struggle has varied over the centuries as man passed through the stages of hunting, gathering, herding, farming, cottage industry, the industrial revolution and mass production, into today's age of information, robots, and computer control over the means of production and distribution.

In the course of the changes in the way humans earn their living, it became convenient to devise methods of exchange, with barter giving way to various symbols of value. To handle transfers of ownership, it was convenient to devise some kinds of universal unit by which the value of objects or services could be measured, and money was invented as the medium of exchange. Today no one complains about money as a unit of exchange. True, actual cash is a nuisance to many enterprises because it has to be translated into numbers in ledgers and other forms of business accounts, but money as a measure of value is one of humanity's most practical and useful inventions. Of course, one cannot measure value as readily as one measures length with a ruler. How much a work of art is worth might be a problem. What is the value of a finger, an arm, a life? A person's time? But, for practical purposes in most exchanges, money is the medium of choice—far more practical than the measures of salt used by the Romans.

Although money is, in its function, only an innocent medium of exchange, it has acquired different images for different people. Long ago, Timothy [1] pronounced, "The love of money is the root of all evil," and surely much crime and evildoing is related to money. On the other hand, Publilius Syrus, somewhat earlier (about the time of Caesar) told us, "Money alone sets the world in motion." Today we hear the same thing in the common expression "Money makes the world go around." For psychologists money is a secondary reinforcer, something associated with a primary satisfaction such as food and other sources of direct gratification.

The trouble with money is not with its function but with the simple fact tht not everyone has the same amount of it in the same way that people have two legs, two eyes, and one nose in common with everyone else. Some people have more money than they can possibly spend in ordinary transactions, and others do not have enough to buy the necessities of existence. In the struggle for existence, some are less well prepared than others, as Darwin observed in his discussions of the survival of the fittest. The survival of humans today depends not on size, strength, or sharpness of teeth and claws, but on having some minimum amount of monetary income to pay for necessities.

In the animal world it is assumed by psychologists that lions and elephants and even chimpanzees do not worry about tomorrow's dinner. They appear to be concerned only with today's. Humans, on the other hand, tend to worry not only about their next meal but also about meals 50 years ahead, about meals for their children when they grow up and about meals for their grandchildren. There are many exceptions, of course, but most humans are future-oriented and try to prepare for it if they can. Some animals do bury bones or store food but such squirreling away is put down to instinct and not to anticipation of the future.

It is in this context of the anticipation of the need for money in the future that virtually all economic activity is conducuted. Producers of material goods cannot simply pull them out of the air. They have to build plants, acquire machines, hire employees, and develop means of production and distribution in anticipation of payments in the distant future. Farmers must plow their fields and plant their seed in the spring for harvests in the fall. Even motion picture producers think about next year's Oscar-winning potential of a story not yet written but being worked on by some promising writer. The wage earner must wait till the end of the week before she receives her allotment of the medium of exchange and must then consider the monthly payments for rent, automobile insurance, fall school clothing for her children, and the like. Even providers of services have to anticipate how and when they can provide services and if they will be wanted in the future. A professional football player likes the idea of a four-year contract (with renegotiation options should he come to appear more valuable). In a broader context governments prepare for possible wars in terms of developing weapons that will not come on line for ten or more years.

It is concern over the future that leads to a host of economic problems and their side effects (for example, overpopulation, crime, strikes, boycotts, trade barriers, and runs on banks, and solutions are not readily at hand because every solution satisfactory to some will be found unsatisfactory to others. It may be that some people are never satisfied, but it seems more correct to say that many people are not satisfied sometime.

In a small but fascinating book, *The Rebel*, Albert Camus (1956) described the nature of revolutions. According to Camus, no matter what form a government takes, no matter how goods are produced and distributed, there will always be those who are dissatisfied with the status quo and who will preach, agitate, argue, debate, and try to enlist followers who will overthrow the existing system in favor of some system-to-be that is never really defined with any precision. Commonly enough such revolutionaries are not personally deprived or wanting comforts of life, although they may disdain them. They speak in slogans such as *the stateless state* or *dictatorship of the proletariat* or, indeed, liberty, equality, fraternity. If they succeed in their revolution and proceed to reorganize society in a form more to their liking, they find sooner or later that they have not created Utopia, that there are some who will find the New Order not to their liking and will proceed to foment a new revolution.

Camus is particularly concerned over revolutionaries who promise great benefits to humanity in the years to come, for generations yet unborn; people are asked to face misery and suffering in order to build a better world with little or no prospect of living long enough to enjoy the new world. Camus himself preferred to improve his immediate circumstances, to point out faults that could be fixed, *to rebel* (not to revolt) against current injustice of whatever form so that more of his contemporaries could live a little better. No one can be sure that generations yet unborn will like what they are born into.

Whatever the nature of the society, then, it can be expected that there will be dissatisfaction and that dissatisfaction can be traced to the fear of the future, a fear that is shared rather generally but less perhaps by those who hve more of the world's goods than by those who have less. An immedite problem arises in that people cannot know for sure how much of the world's goods they should have, need, or want in order to be able to assure control of the future. No one ever appears to have enough. Many millionaires keep on making money (in some cases they cannot even help making money simply from interest on what they already have) far beyond their possible needs or even those of their grandchildren. Probably no one really worries about the needs of great-grandchildren, for few people get old enough to have them. We have the example of extremely wealthy people appearing in television advertisements for what must be, for them, a pittance. Do they only want to see themselves on the tube? We might ask, Have they no pride? Some wealthy people do scorn invitations to advertise sanitary napkins and are selective about what they are associated with, but opportunities to earn more money are not often rebuffed if it's "an offer you can't refuse."

Wherever psychologists look in any society, they observe differences of all kinds. Some are obvious—in size, in clothing, in attractiveness (which would be based on different values, criteria, or standards in different communities), and in accommodations for living. There are communities, for example, the Amish, in which the differences might be less obvious or noticeable, but closer scrutiny would result in the observation of some differences. Even in housing developments, for example, Levittowns, where all or most of the houses are built to fit some standard cost, there will be differences in paint, decor, lawns, and even in house construction, with some with doors on the left and some with doors on the right. After a few years in such prefabricated areas, greater differences will emerge as house owners add awnings, shutters, porches, lean-tos, or garages. Many of the differences that are observable reflect income or relative wealth. People can be described as rich, filthy rich, poor, poverty-striken, middle-class, and so on. How do such differences arise?

At any given moment in history, the relative wealth of any individual might be explainable—she inherited it, found it, stole it, worked for it and saved it, or made wise or lucky investments. Other explanations include such notions as being smart or intelligent, talented, or shrewd. These explanations are somewhat more difficult to assess or accept. The American psychologist Edward L. Thorndike (1932), in formulting his theory of learning, liked to express his findings in terms of "trial and error and chance success," which can be translated to mean that if a man tries and tries and works hard, he may make some or many errors but eventually will stumble on the right answer to problems, if he is lucky. Of course, if he does not try, he will get nowhere and even if he does try, he may get nowhere if he is not lucky. Talking about luck may be as empty as talking about shrewdness or talent, but Thorndike meant by luck only chance, that accident or simply blind reaching and groping might produce a satisfactory solution to a problem. From Thorndike's viewpoint, those who learn something learn only because they tried, made an effort, and hit upon solutions to problems by chance. Success in economic terms can be accounted for in the same way—one works hard, tries, makes mistakes, is in the right place at the right time for no good reason, and is lucky sometimes that things work out to one's advantage. Armand Hammer (1987) describes his financial success in just such terms. The poor, on the other hand, either do not try hard enough, are not lucky, or both. The philosophy of "rugged individualism"[2] is as much a guide for Hammer as it was for Thorndike.

In the economic world we might accept a considerable impact of trial and error and chance success. Many people do try one thing or another; some keep trying, and things over which they have no control do have impacts that may ruin them or make them wealthy. Certainly the pioneers who ventured out into unknown territory and claimed it for themselves tried. Some were lucky in that the land they claimed had oil or other valuables in it. Others arrived first at what became important river junctions, lakefronts, or more fertile land. Some families lived in poverty on land that, generations later, was needed by a railroad company or for a superhighway or supermarket. Many of today's wealthy families started out poor. Somewhere along the line there were people who worked, tried, were lucky, or assisted their luck by their own efforts, sometimes in what might be called immoral, unethical, or even illegal and criminal ways. Crime is not a novelty of the twentieth century.

Another factor that has to be considered is that of personal characteristics: strength, energy, sheer size, the capacity to dominate others and, with their help, dominate more and more. Some people become leaders, attract followers, and with their help manage to acquire material goods, control over the work of others and, in effect, tax them for personal gain. This is the observed history of the human race—self-appointed monarchs, warlords, dictators, captains of industry, presidents-for-life. The exploitation of others by those in a position to exploit is as old as history. Slavery was not a seventeenth-century idea. The democracy of Greece and the empire of Rome were founded on slave labor. Of course, once control over land and the means of production and distribution has been established, it becomes more difficult for those at the bottom to rise to the top or even out of their lower-level status. Opportunities become restricted. Not everyone can become wealthy and powerful. "For ye have the poor always with you"[3] remains a pertinent observation.

What is interesting about wealth is that generally, except for periods of natural disaster or war, when everyone may be stricken in some area of the earth, there is enough wealth, however unequally distributed, for most people to survive and, in most cases, reproduce, with the poor reproducing more rapidly. The world's population has continued to grow from the beginning of humanity's emergence. Goods and services have always been produced and paid for in one way or another.

The problems of economics can be thought of as problems of production and distribution of goods, and economists concern themselves with the intricacies involved in such activities. Adam Smith (1776) described how the world's wealth had been acquired and distributed up to his time. The picture drawn by Smith was that of private ownership wherein some people acquire capital (money, tools, land, machines, work animals) and produce goods, which are then sold at a profit, if possible. Other people, without capital, sell their services and work for wages, which they can then freely spend on whatever the money will buy. In the case of slaves, no money was provided, but food, clothing, and shelter served as the compensation for their toil. Those who made profits and spent them redistributed their gains. Eventually even the lowest-paid person would obtain some money. This is the "trickle-down" theory. In Smith's view, an "invisible hand" spread the wealth.

Milton Friedman, a present-day Adam Smith, sees no marked differences in the way in which the world's economy is run from the time of Smith. He even endorses the "invisible hand" in that every step of manufacturing or producing something involves expenditure of money along the way, so that many people get some of it, some more, some less, but since no one can take his money with him, it eventually "trickles down" to the last person involved in the production and its accompanying transactions. Thus, as Friedman (1980) describes the production of a lead pencil, he finds money changing hands at many stages (lumbermen, miners, manufacturers, sales managers, transporters, store clerks, and so forth), so that when one buys a pencil, one is paying perhaps hundreds of people, who get varying shares of one's dime. Friedman might endorse Thorndike's analysis. Some people work harder than others, they try more steadily, and maybe they "luck out." Others may try, perhaps not so steadily, or they are not so lucky. They fail. There is nothing wrong with failure. One can always try something else that one is better at. The same view is applied to international traffic and trade. Some countries are better at something than are others. Brazil and Colombia grow better coffee and produce more cocaine than the United States. We are better at other things, perhaps making computers. We should sell computers to Brazil and buy its coffee. Troubles do arise if Brazil doesn't want computers and we still want its coffee—there is an imbalance of trade. At the present time, the United States has what appears to be a huge imbalance of trade because for various reasons other countries do not buy from us but keep selling us their products.

Friedman endorses a laissez-faire policy of letting anyone try anything regardless of the outcome. What Friedman does not approve of is any interference from government to support inefficient or incompetent producers who cannot make it on their own.

Other economists, for example, John Kenneth Galbraith (1975), tend to be softer on the weaklings, the failures, the unfortunates, and think that government should step in with a more visible hand than that of Adam Smith and provide jobs, backups, and various forms of support for those whose troubles Galbraith would hope were temporary. Friedman sees this kind of governmental interference with a free-market economy as preventing progress, supporting inefficiency, and generally leading only to greater economic trouble. Friedman supports the right of some to fail. They should try something else at which they might be more successful.

Regardless of economic theory, the interesting point, as I mentioned above, is that there always has been enough wealth to keep the population alive and multiplying or at least growing. China, with a supposedly backward economy, now has over a billion people and is trying to keep families down to a one-child norm. Mexico is enjoying a population boom and an economic bust. In some countries, such as India, children have long beeen looked on as a form of social security and slave labor. The introduction of social security in the United States has led to vast changes in styles of living: fewer children, fewer marriages, working women, different modes of housing (condominiums, apartments, trailers), to name but a few. The traditional extended family is rapidly disappearing, but the population continues to grow, although more slowly.

Regardless of the kind of country, the economic system, or the means of production and distribution, the fact that the population keeps growing when much of it amounts to people who produce nothing edible or material (the young, the unemployed, the retired, the entertainers, the underworld) can only mean that the world's wealth in material goods, including food, can be produced by a relatively small number of workers or producers. In the United States at the time of its formation, most of the adult male population was comprised of farmers. Today less than 2 percent of Americans are engaged in farming, yet we feed all Americans and can feed much of the rest of the world. With machines and modern methods of production, one person can produce what formerly took dozens if not hundreds. Today the Panama Canal could be dug in a few weeks with what by comparison would be a few people operating giant earth movers and using modern explosives. Even in more primitive times, one man could produce more than he and his immedite family could use. Karl Marx emphasized this in his hypothesis of surplus value. Any business or enterprise that employs workers operates on the assumption that any worker will produce more than she actually needs for herself or, in more meaningful language, every worker producers more than she is paid for. Her work adds value to whatever article she is engaged in producing. Obviously, no one would hire a worker if she would not produce more than she was paid for.

The difference between what a worker is paid and what the employer gets for the product is the source of most of the trouble between labor and management. Both sides want more. The employer pays as little as he must to keep the worker working. The worker wants more of the value added by her work. As of now, no one has yet discovered what a fair wage would be. In the parable of the vineyard, Jesus seems to imply that a fair wage is whatever is agreed on between worker and employer—a contract is involved and should be honored.[4] It is arriving at a contract that is the problem. At no time in history has anyone determined what amount of profit an employer should properly retain or attempt to attain. During World War II the United States set up a policy under which employers (management, owners) would be paid for all of the costs of production, including labor, plus 10 percent. What made 10 percent a correct profit margin was never spelled out or explained. It probably appeared to be a nice round number subject to easy computation. Many utilities (light, heat, and power companies) offer dividends to stock owners in the region of 10 percent and manage to stay in business by keeping their costs at a level that will provide such dividends. Other businesses, conglomerates, buy up companies that make a 10 percent or so profit but want their newly purchased companies to improve their efficiency to a 15 percent profit level or they sell them off (benefiting by "losses" that can be claimed in tax write-offs). A regular profit of 10–20 percent might be satisfactory for many employers or inventors, but the ups and downs of economic activity frequently prevent any profit at all or cause occasional bankruptcies. Businesses operate on the principle that bad years must be compensated for by good years and that to stay in business one must make as much profit as possible, whenever possible. Consequently any standard such as 20 percent can be only a ballpark figure. It is, then, not a wise policy to abide by a standard profit percentage, and the only intelligent position, according to business people, is to charge as much as possible for their products or services, regardless of the amount, hence the expression to *charge what the traffic will bear*, a statement of what economists describe as the law of supply and demand. This law is stated variously in economic texts, but it amounts to saying that if a product or service is in low supply, it will be more valuable than if it were in great supply, and consequently, the owners of such product can charge higher prices. What is more, they (or others) will strive to produce more to sell at these higher prices. On the other hand, if the price appears too high, demand will fall off and the price appears too high, demand will fall off and the prices will fall to a point where demand will equal supply. Demand, it must be understood, is defined as the capacity to pay for something, and not as the desire, want, or need for the product. Thus, if a loaf of bread costs a dollar and people are buying as much as is produced, demand is equal to supply. If the price rises, people will stop buying as much, and the price will fall or production will drop off because the demand has decreased. Economists are quite aware of the looseness or generality of the law and recognize that many factors prevent the stability of prices represented by an equilibrium between supply and demand. Governments tend to interfere with the working of the law, whether they be capitalist or Communist in proclamation. In capitalist countries prices may be supported by governmental purchase and storage if the demand is not there, or by tariffs, taxes, or other governmental manipulations. Producers can arbitrarily restrict supplies, as do diamond producers, who find themselves satisfied with a small demand at high prices. Some producers prefer to destroy supplies rather than lower prices, and, of course, monopolies, cartels, or understandings among producers can keep prices at desired levels by preventing competition, which might allow some producers to accept a lower profit.

The law of supply and demand need not concern us, since it deals not with any real person's action but with the behavior of some hypothetical "economic man," who is indeed a man of many parts. Producers know that "economic man" consists of various buying publics some of whom buy one type of commodity and not another. Thus teenagers buy rock records and attend horror movies. The buyers of drugs are quite a separate public from the nonbuyers; senior citizens represent a great market for medical supplies; children do not buy houses, and so on. Nor is there anything equivalent to awareness of supply and demand by the "economic man," or the real one, for that matter. No one knows what the supply of anything is or will be. One does not haggle in the marketplace, despite some appearances to the contrary. The purchser of a car pays either what the dealer intends to get or more. Prices are set not by actual demand but by anticipated demand. Often much time passes between the setting of or decision about a price and the actual placement of a product on the market—the anticipated demand may have vanished or increased. Rapid changes cannot be implemented in an active economy. Prices are frequently changed in supermarkets for example, long after the products were ordered and displayed with no real awareness of what the demand would be. In general, the law of supply and demand may represent a reasonably accurate picture of long-run activities, but it is commonly in contradiction to the unlawful (not illegal) behavior of people. Despite the looseness of the law of supply and demand, there is some evidence that it does apply to individual buyers (see Vernon Smith, 1978). More people will buy at cheaper prices.

In the broad area of economics, people are concerned with all sorts of individual and personal problems, but most people when queried report that their chief economic problems and those of the nation they inhabit are primarily three in number, namely, unemployment, deficits, and inflation. We can turn to these problems as samples of the perennial human tragicomedy. We will look at the psychological aspects of these problems and leave it to the economists to worry about their interactions.

NOTES

1. Timothy 6:10.
2. This is another name for Social Darwinism.
3. Matthew 26:11.
4. Matthew 20:1—16.

8

Employment

EMPLOYMENT AND UNEMPLOYMENT

Every month the government supplies the news media with figures describing the employment and unemployment status of the citizens. So many millions of people are working and so many millions are not. Both sets of figures are misleading and lead to various kinds of action and reaction. What the government means by *unemployment* actually refers to the number of people receiving unemployment benefits or who say they are looking for work. It does not include people serving in the armed forces, for example, and if there were a draft, the unemployment figures would suddenly be reduced because members of the armed forces are not considered to be looking for work. They are considered to be at work, employed by the government, and receiving some kind of compensation. They are ineligible to take on other employment. High school dropouts (teenagers) are counted as unemployed although why they should be employed is perhaps a good question. Considering the training required for some jobs, how old and how qualified should a person be before being considered unemployed?

People who are retired are not counted as either unemployed or employed, although they may be working, part-time or full-time at unlisted jobs, but they are not looking for work. Nor are people who do not depend on salaries or wages from legitimate employers for their income. The latter group includes the rich, college students, hoboes, and semi-self-employed members of the underworld engaged in the drug traffic, prostitution, gambling operations, and the like. A pimp or pornographer cannot be considered unemployed if he is not looking for work. The most absurd and pathetic omissions from the ranks of the unemployed are those who have given up looking for work because they could find none. If they are not looking, they are not unemployed as far as government statistics are concerned. No one knows how many people are employed either, for the same reasons as I listed above. Gangsters are not counted. Apparently no one knows or cares to compute how many crooks, burglars, muggers, prostitutes, drug pushers, numbers runners, and other varieties of criminals manage to stay alive without being on any lists the governmental statisticians pursue. They pay no social security taxes.

The definition of employment as being on someone's payroll is not too accurate, for many such people are not working either. The government itself employs numerous "no-show" people on padded congressional payrolls. State, city, and county governments are notorious for creating jobs that are filled by people who do no work because they have deputies under them who do the work allegedly covered by the title. A city treasurer may drop in at his office on occasion to have his deputy assure him that all is well. A county attorney will hire other lawyers to handle county legal matters, and consultants will absorb a nice part of a government's budget at any level. Various professionals (actors, songwriters, surgeons, mountain-climbing guides) may not be listed as unemployed when they are not working or as employed when they are.

A minor point should be noted—some people moonlight and get two salaries, sometimes using an alias for the second job or being paid in cash, with no record of the second employment to interest or annoy anyone.

Whatever the numbers, and in different countries the source of the numbers may vary, some people are looking for work and do not have any visible means of support. They may be receiving financial aid from relatives or welfare agencies or relying on savings or unemployment compensation but would prefer to have a job and be counted as among the employed. Some may have given up the search; others never did search and do not care to; some don't know how to search; and some would accept only certain kinds of employment. President Reagan once referred to long columns of classified ads in newspapers as showing that there were plenty of jobs available. He may not actually have read the ads—most of them required qualifications that only a few people who already had jobs could meet, or they were simple come-ons for magazine solicitation and other jobs that no one should be allowed to work at, such as telephoning people with offers to waterproof their cellars, cover their walls with aluminum, or to sell them diamonds or Florida swampland.

People with experience in some line may be inclined to seek jobs in that line when the jobs do not exist. They cannot bring themselves to consider occupations they feel are somehow beneath them; a steelworker might not think of dishwashing as a proper job, and humpback labor picking lettuce heads in the fields might strike him as repellent. Any decrease in wages in some preferred or available job is sure to be resented, at least for a while. Such people consider themselves overqualified; in other cases prospective employers might consider some applicants overqualified and troublesome.

It should also be noted that some people are counted as employed when they have taken a job at much lower wages than they received in a former job that had been lost. They may be employed, but they may keep hoping for a return to former jobs (and higher pay) that no longer exist. They, in fact, have dropped into a lower category of worker and illustrate the adage that the "poor get poorer."

Whatever the actual number of unemployed may be, it appears that the number has been growing since about 1950, not only in the United States, but in Britain, France, West Germany, and Japan. There are ups and downs, of course, but the trend is unmistakable (*New York Times,* Nov. 30, 1986).

It is possible that there just are not enough jobs to do whatever work is necessary. If unemployment is to be reduced, jobs will have to be manufactured in unnecessary activities. Many jobs today are rather pointless and socially useless even if they provide incomes for some. Every reader will have her own nominees (advertising, the stock exchange, television soap operas, political appointments), and door-to-door salesmen of magazines might be rather generally cited.

WORK OR SLAVERY?

Any person who works for wages (a "wage-slave") or a salary or is self-employed thinks of himself as having chosen or having been chosen for his means of earning a living and may even be quite content about it. The newcomer to the labor market or the unemployed person looking for work is, in her own opinion, offering her services, her brains, or her brawn to prospective employers, and again, she may feel quite pleased with herself, especially if there are several opportunities and she has a choice of jobs. She thinks of herself as choosing freely, but once she has chosen, she is merely selling herself into slavery instead of being sold into it by some owner. She is now beholden to her employer. If self-employed, she is beholden or her work for a certain number of hours per day, week, or other period, and if she fails to meet these demands on her time, she will suffer for it, not in terms of a whip, as she would have in the cotton fields of slavery in the old days, but in terms of loss of income, which in turn means loss of whatever she uses money to

buy. The reference to slavery, according to Galbraith (1987) is "not al-
together hyperbole."

Many people love their work, either at once or after a while; they get
used to the routines involved and eventually feel that what they are
doing is proper, even desirable, perhaps important. After many years,
some people shrink from retiring because they have no suitable alternate
patterns, just as some long-term convicts shrink from being released
from prison. They like to feel useful, perhaps indispensable, refusing
to recognize that sooner or later they will not be able to get to the job.
The job itself may disappear with new technology or business reversals,
and the worker finds himself adrift.

The only difference between free employment and slavery is that with
the latter, one had a guarantee of support so long as the owners had
the means. The owners had some responsibility toward their slaves. Of
course, they could sell them if there were buyers. With free employment,
employers are free to sell out, move jobs to another country, or change
their arrangements so that the employees are no longer needed. The
employers have no responsibility beyond what moral qualms they might
suffer.

Actually, employers are not much freer to do as they please than are
employees. They too must face the inevitable end of their days and, in
the meantime, the troubles with unions, wayward or unproductive employees, complaints of partners or shareholders, governmental regulations, competitors who can freeze them out of the market, and other
ills too numerous to count. Thousands of employers go bankrupt every
year, sometimes through no direct fault of their own.

Whereas the old slave owners dictated the mode of housing, quantity
and quality of food, and the kinds of clothing their slaves could wear,
modern employers do the same through not only the wage scales they
control but also through their managerial practices. The employees must
wear the appropriate blue collar or gray flannel suit, narrow lapels or
wide, safety shoes or the latest corporate-style, hairstyles as dictated by
the current stylists; they must live in "proper" neighborhoods, belong
to the appropriate clubs, and so forth. Some employers expect employees
to be married to their jobs, devoted to the company (which may dismiss
them with no concern about loyalty), and travel for days or weeks at a
time regardless of family concerns. Wives and husbands are separated
at inconvenient periods, and employees are moved about, just as members of the armed forces get their orders to report elsewhere on a specified date. At one time only priests were given 24 hours to move to
another parish. Today company executives can be moved to Shanghai
or Houston from New York or Chicago without concern over children's
schools or other personal ties. The company comes first. The white-
collar slave may enjoy and revel in her status and perquisites, but she

is no less a slave than if she were bought from another owner instead of having been bought in what is cheerfully referred to as the open market.

In pre–Civil War days some slaves lived extremely well, if their owners chose to indulge them, and could dismiss notions of freedom as irrelevant niceties that would extinguish their perquisites. Most slaves suffered quietly, as do most modern employees.

WORK AND EMPLOYMENT

In the modern world getting and keeping a job is considered a primary need. An occupation is apparently the chief preoccupation of most people. The standard question children are asked by relatives and family acquaintances is, What are you going to be when you grow up? "Older" is not an acceptable answer. Education is largely dedicated to fitting students to some kind of employment. Anyone of an employable age who is not working is regarded as a ne'er-do-well, or, at best, unfortunate.

Unemployment is considered a problem instead of the goal of humanity. Of course, given the necessity for most people to buy food, clothing, and shelter, some source of income or wealth is a correlated requirement. If people raised their own food, made their own clothing from the wool of their own sheep, and burned wood in huts or log cabins they constructed for themselves, there would be no need for money or employment. Employment is a rather unpleasant burden that most people in modern societies have to subject themselves to in order to survive. It is part of an arrangement where someone, as employer, offers money in exchange for someone else's services.

In prehistoric times it was necessary to hunt or fish or gather fruits, roots, nuts, and berries in order to survive. This activity might not have had much regularity to it. One moved when one got hungry, and it probably took centuries before human beings began to plan for tomorrow's meals. When they learned to farm, some more planning and regularity was forced upon them. Raising cows for milk required milking them at regular intervals. Slowly the daily grind came into being. People rose with the rooster and worked till sundown, and perhaps later, depending upon needs. With the development of specialized skills, work became both diversified and specialized, so that a system of exchange developed. Only relatively recently in human history did the practice of exchanging work for the medium of exchange develop.

In modern times we have arrived at the situation where, if you have not inherited money from ancestors, you have to acquire it in some other way. For most people that other way is to sell their time and energy to an employer. The employer, in order to be an employer and stay in business, requires that an employee report at a certain time to a certain place (regardless of how inconvenient it may be) and stay for a certain time and do certain things. From the efforts or labor of employees the employer herself makes money, some of which she returns to them. Obviously, workers are expected to produce more than they are paid, or there would be no point to their employment. How much they are paid has always been a problem. It is probably safe to say that people have never been paid what they were worth. Either the employer made a mistake and paid them too much (and eventually went out of business), or she paid them too little and got wealthy while the workers got poorer or stayed the same. The surplus value proposition is always the sticking point in labor-management relations. Unions always demand more money (or better conditions—which means more money as far as the employer is concerned). the employer always wants to reduce her labor costs, and consequently there is no peace—never has been, and never will be, as long as someone works for someone else. There may be temporary or relative satisfaction on both sides, but the issue is not resolvable. It is always settled in terms of power. Lester Thurow (1985) describes the war between workers and owners (managers) in these words: "Labor and capital are natural adversaries much as the viper and the mongoose."

In the conditions described above, it should be quite clear that there is nothing natural about working for someone else. As for working for oneself, it is a matter of necessity for some, but it may not require setting alarm clocks, traveling in morning and evening rush hours, reporting to the same place day after day, winter and summer, doing the same thing over and over again.

Psychologists have not discovered in any species, including humans, any drive, instinct, or other inborn demand or craving for work. At best it might be said that there may be some natural tendency to move around. Some psychologists are willing to admit a "drive for exercise" or an "exploratory drive," but such drives, if any, are easily satisfied with relatively little expenditure of energy.

It is true that after many years of following a routine, some will come to accept it as natural and not fight what has become a powerful habit. Some managerial types may continue working into their 70s and 80s because they don't trust anyone else, regard themselves as indispensable, don't know what they would do with themselves if they didn't work, and so on. But about 70 percent of the work force retires at 62, when social security becomes available and other income is expected from pensions or savings. The other 30 percent may not be able to afford to retire for various reasons. the question remains, Does anyone really want to work? Certainly, the corporate executive who is forced to retire at 65 does not look for a ditch-digging job so that he can fulfill his drive to work. He might seek another executive position because he likes power, not because he likes work. Traditionally labor unions have demanded shorter work days and work weeks. Public service employees fight for longer vacations, sick days, personal days, and many take advantage of early retirement opportunities.

Some psychologists emphasize great individual differences with respect to an interest in working at a job. McGregor (1960), for example, divides people into two types. Theory X people are lazy loafers (grasshoppers, who think the world owes them a living). Theory Y people are energetic ("eager beavers" or ants, who are happy only when they are busy). Though human adults display a range of differences in their approach to work, there is no evidence that these differences are inherent. People do what they have to do depending upon their reinforcement history and circumstances. Some are driven to work because of aversive conditions; others will have learned to accept and even enjoy some employment activities. Even some children of the wealthy can be made to feel somehow irresponsible, and they venture into politics, the art world, philanthropy, or other outlets to avoid the opprobrium that is associated with doing nothing.

In psychological terms work creates a drive that demands rest, and except when the physical or mental activity is somehow rewarding in itself, no one works very long, because the drive to rest develops quickly and inhibits further activity. Clark Hull (1943) ascribed "extinction" of habits to what he called "conditioned inhibition." Any expenditure of energy or work would result in fatigue and lead to rest. Because rest following fatigue could be thought of an reinforcement, one could presumably learn *not to work* as a consequence of working without reinforcement. Working is, by nature, a negative drive-producing activity akin to pain, and might therefore be considered naturally undesirable.

Though Hull's notion of learning not to work might apply to the extinction situation (no reinforcing consequences), the drive for rest has to be recognized in such arrangements as coffee breaks, lunch periods, and control of production line speeds and total hours of work. The drive for rest is also countered to some degree by the conflicting need for compensation. One may not feel like working but knows that wages will suffer. If no one is in a position to enforce all-out energy expenditure, every worker will settle down to some convenient pace that can be maintained for some appropriate periods of time (Bugelski, 1941). Even laboratory rats will settle for a work schedule that provides a stisfactory return in the form of food pellets (Allison, 1983) and will not work at a higher rate that would increase the payoff. Here, again, we must reckon with how great the need for food is—how long a rat has been deprived. In general, it can be presumed that no one works any harder than is necessry.

The opposition to work is perhaps best displayed in what are called labor-saving machines. The wheel was invented because it was too hard to push things that did not roll. The washing machine and the electric iron, any tool or machine, saved a great deal of labor. It may be that when women washed clothes in the nearest stream and did it as a group, certain social compensations made the work tolerable, in fact even enjoyable for some, but the electric washing machine gained universal acceptance by anyone who could afford one. Manual workers usually object to the introduction of labor-saving machines in their places of employment, but it is not becuse the machine will save them effort. It is simply because the machine threatens their jobs, as it clearly does. Some economists cheerfully proclaim that machines result in only temporary unemployment as new markets open and new jobs are created, but that does not solace the displaced worker who has no other marketable skills and who may remain unemployed forever. the world situation is now arriving at the point where some people will never get a job and will spend their lives on some form of dole. Their children may never hold jobs. Those who still have jobs and pay taxes look down upon those on welfare. They try to make it appear mean, nasty, dishonest, and corrupt, but that is clearly only a form of rationalization of their own miserable situation. They too would prefer not to work.

The problem with welfare is that it is never enough. Governments try to make sure that it is never as good as a working wage—to encourge people to get off welfare and go to work. The situation is, of course, ridiculous when every employer who is in position to do so is looking for labor-saving devices so that he does not have to hire more workers. It is a simple fact that, given technical advances, for example, robots, fewer and fewer people will have to be employed to produce the same amount of saleable goods. The only way to keep everybody working is to resort or return to primitive methods of production or to expand so-called service occuptions. One can, of course, insist that people on welfare do work like shoveling snow or pulling weeds in public parks, but this does not solve the problem of where the welfare money comes from, namely the taxes of those still employed. Employed workers will not cheerfully share their jobs by insisting on fewer hours per person unless wgaes are kept up—instead, they ask for overtime. Employers would rather pay overtime than rehire laid-off workers because it is cheaper to do so. Every additional worker costs more in terms of both government-imposed costs and union benefits or perquisites.

To make the lot of the worker bearable, a whole system of rationalizations has been developed, starting with the admonition to Adam that he must now toil and earn his living by the "sweat of his brow," to the present Protestant work ethic, which is by no means exclusively Protestant. People are encouraged from childhood on to think about getting a job, a profession, preferably, to work hard and save money so that they can eventually retire and not have to work. The fact that the un-employed enjoy the privilege of not working prior to retirement is galling to some still working. Though there may be nothing dishonorable about work, there is nothing obviously honorable about it either.

The simple fact is that all of the work that needs to be done can be done by fewer and fewer people as technological advances are made. Scientists concerned with artifical intelligence (see Fjermedal 1986) and robotics now predict that in a few years there may be little or no need for humans to work at production or clerical jobs. They see computers programming themselves and building robots that can reproduce them-selves and do any kind of work that humans can do. Albus (1976), for example, thinks that the United States can become a nation of million-aires with robtos doing all of the necessary work and providing large incomes for everybody. The only problem would be that of arranging for the distribution of profits. Albus regards work as degrading and demeaning and looks forward to the time when everyone can enjoy perpetual leisure during which other human values might be enhanced. Unless jobs are simply manufactured merely to keep people busy for no reason related to human nature, there will be increasing unemploy-ment and more and more free or leisure time. How that leisure time is spent bears some consideration.

BREAD AND CIRCUSES

It appears that at all times and in all places, mankind has found time and energy for entertainment of some kind or another. When the prac-tical realities are met (and even sometimes when they are not, as in rain dances during droughts) people have spent their leisure, that is, un-employed time, in rites, rituals, ceremonials, sports, and games of one kind or another. The entertainment industry in the United States is one of the largest, and much time and money is spent in attracting people to theaters, sports arenas, music halls, parks, and convention centers than in any other activity. Thousands of fans flock to football stadia (it has become an all-season sport) and drink beer or sit before their tele-vision sets on Saturdays, Sundays, and Monday nights. The other days are filled with baseball, hockey, bowling, basketball, and for the affluent, polo and golf, not to mention tennis and soccer. For the intellectually inclined there is chess, backgammon, bridge, or crossword puzzles. Some people devote their lives to sports, to becoming Olympic medal winners or professional athletes. In Roman times they might have been gladiators.

That all such activity (including reading novels or poetry) is not re-garded as serious by most people is reflected in the common expression

"It's only a game," usually said to a loser, who is, equally usually, unhappy.

Whence comes this insatiable desire for participating or watching people engaging in essentially unproductive activity? What possible difference can it make to spectators who wins a tennis match (unless they have bet money on the outcome)? Do the spectators hope to improve their own game by watching?

Huge sums of money are spent to support philharmonic orchestras, museums of art, folk festivals, and arts and crafts that are of no obvious practical value. The value always has to be explained. Why aren't the people who spend their time cutting lacy figures out of paper not out in the fields hoeing their corn?

Clearly, when there is time for entertainment, there must have been enough time for some to attend to the practical needs of food, shelter, and clothing, and some people are left with time on their hands. Unlike bees or ants, people are not programmed to work at food gathering from dawn to dusk. Those who do work at an occupation that calls for exertion may argue about winding down or needing a break, but they do not just sit and rest—they go to bars, clubs, or show places and sometimes exert more energy in cheering, stomping, and yelling, than they do at their regular employment.

The problem involved is two-sided. On the one hand, there is the factor of free, spare, or ample time to be filled and no requirement that it be filled productively in material terms. On the other hand, there are the entrepreneurs, the participants who make their living out of the entertainment operation. The owner of a football team may or may not have any interest in the game itself; it may only be a way to make money to be spent in yachting or whatever form of recreation she may have come to describe as her favorite pastime (note the term *pastime*—it is in itself revealing). Motion picture moguls often indicate that they do not care what kind of films they produce so long as they draw a paying audience. Others assert an art-for-art's-sake stand and lose money while bemoaning a benighted public that does not come to enjoy.

Between the fact that time must be filled by something and the fact that some people make it their business to fill other people's time, there are many other factors to consider.

Possibly the chief psychological factors determining the way in which free time is employed are both social and individual. For many complicated reasons a given culture may foster competitive group activities with a military or quasi-military orientation. People can be cajoled or coerced into group activities on a large or small scale with uniforms, drills, marches, all of which involve auxiliary industrial activities—band and music suppliers, uniform makers, instructors, organizers, and the like. The emphasis may be on physical fitness, including health, on mass loyalties, veneration of leaders, to name but a few. Other cultures may foster individual or small-group (teams) efforts with a strong element of competitiveness among individuals even where a team effort is primary. In baseball a team may win or lose, but each player is carefully monitored for individual statistics. The players on the same team compete with one another for number of hits, putouts, and successfully stolen bases. In a bowling league teams compete, but again, individual performances determine the outcome. Competitiveness is rampant throughout some cultures where, from kindergarten on, children compete for grades, prizes, and recognition of one kind or another, aided and abetted by parents who try to make their children all-around athletes, scholars, artists, and musicians, as well as popular.

In a competitive society no one can be best in everything, and the more diverse activities that can be devised, the more opportunity there is for more people to be best at something. The Olympic Games now include a large number of sports invented to increase the number of participants and spectators. Of course, there will be efforts on the part of those good at one thing to denigrate the virtues or values of other activities, though why a first-rate violinist should be regarded as somehow better than a first-rate tiddlywinks player is moot. There may be higher levels of income for top-flight basketball players than for excellent football players, but certainly the activities of either kind of athlete are of no intrinsic or practical value to observers.

Some interpreters (Lorenz, 1965) would like to believe that underlying all competitive activities, whether in sports, games, business, or education, there is an inherent aggression drive that motivates people to compete and win—winning amounts to conquering the enemy. This analysis is probably too simple to account for all of the competitiveness we witness daily even among siblings, where aggressiveness may be clearly visible to observers who make the aggressiveness assumption. But the aggressiveness may be only an artifact or modus operandi that covers a more basic drive state, namely fear and anxiety about one's own status, now and in the future. From infancy on we literally do not know where our next meal is coming from. Children eating lunch may ask, "What are we having for dinner tonight?" And as they grow, they learn more or less effectively about the need to plan for future needs and find strategies for problems about to come. Will my teacher like me? What do I have to do to be liked so that I will avoid trouble that comes from not being liked? Should I plan on college? Will I get in? Will I get a job? Will I have enough money to buy x? The stream of questions is endless and supplies a daily quota of anxieties for even the best adjusted and comfortable among us. We are not only constantly in competitive situations and constantly goaded to win, but we also find that with winning we have at lest momentary relief (satisfaction) that helps sustain us until the next battle situation.

As we gradually find our place in society and accept our lot as not among the best in the competition (there can be only one president of anything at a given time), we begin to accept observer status to some extent and get vicarious satisfaction out of backing the real competitors. There is some satisfaction, and even some rewards are possible for backing winners. Rewards can come in many forms—we can bet and win, or we can demonstrate to others that we have better judgement in that we backed the winners, or, if we back them enough, they may appoint us to a more favored position. Even if we get no immediate and personal gains of a material sort, just being on the winning side is better than being on the losing side. It shows we are wise in choosing the side, or lucky to be on the winners' side, or that we are part of something better than someone else. Professional football or baseball players may not care a fig about what team they play for, but Yankee fans or Green Bay Packers fans will feel better when "their" team wins than when it loses.

In addition to any personal satisfaction from winning or losing, the observer, being part of a crowd, can feel that he is accepted, "one of us," not a loner or outsider. The social satisfaction can also be rewarding because it assuages any feelings or rejection or abnormality. People who join clubs or participate in activities involving groups—for example, bridge games or bingo—can find an identity with others and get various kinds of satisfaction from such activity even if they do not profit financially. Losing at poker has its compensations in camaraderie. One can mention last night's poker game to other acquaintances to demonstrate that one is accepted someplace and by some people.

It has been suggested above that participation in sports, games, entertainments, and the like has rewarding aspects and need not be put down to any innate aggressiveness or desire to compete. The motivations and satisfactions may be quite diverse, and for many people it "kills time," as watching television does for millions. The fact that so much time is devoted to essentially unproductive activities indicates that most of mankind in much of the world enjoys a surplus of time and has to find ways to waste, pass, or kill it. Such a surplus becomes a problem for society only if it is not due to unemployment, with the accompanying feature of lack of funds to spend on entertainment. So long as a society can afford to entertain itself, there is nothing wrong with most of the ways in which people fill their leisure time. As I indicated before, there is no reason why someone should do nothing at all to pass the time between birth and death, both inevitable for anyone who happens to be alive. It does not really matter what an individual does with her time unless she is hurting someone else by her actions. There is a possibility that many kinds of recreational activity for some are hurting others in some small way as individuals. The connections might be hard to trace, however, and only the cumulative effects can be discussed. If all the money spent on entertainment in the United States were given to a poor country, for example, the poor country might become rich and start entertaining its own citizens, who would no longer have to work and spend time looking for subsistence.

The simple message of this section is that what is called work or employment is usually identified with having a job, a position, or a career, in which the activities involved have very little to do with work. Work is something to be avoided, something someone else should do. It is obvious that most of the truly necessary work that has to be done to provide food, clothing, and shelter can be done by a small percentage of the people with a small percentage of their waking hours. All the other activities that are identified as work or employment are artificial, manufactured ways of gaining money, prestige, and power. The virtues of most kinds of employment might well be questioned. Perhaps the greatest virtue of most employment is that it keeps people off the streets. This is not a novel observation. In the seventeenth century, John Gaunt wrote,

> Moreover, if all these things were truly clearly and truly known (which I have but guessed at) it would appear, how small a part of the People work upon necessary Labours and Callings, vis—how many Women and Children do just nothing, only learning to spend what others get? how many are mere Volup-turies, and as it were meer Gamesters by Trade? how many live by puzzling poor people with unintelligible notions in Divinity, and Philosophie? how many be persuading credulous, delicate, and Litigious Persons, that their Bodies, or Estates are out of Tune and in danger/how many be fighting as Soldiers/how many by Trade of meer pleasures, or Ornaments? and how many in a way of lazie attendance &c. upon others? And on the other side, how few are employed in raising, and working necessary food and covering? and of the speculative men, how few do truly studie Nature, and Things?[1]

NOTE

1. Quoted in Daniel J. Boorstin, *The Discoverers* (New York: Random House, 1983).

9

Money Matters

INFLATION

Along with unemployment, the problem most often cited by people queried about the economy is that of inflation. Like unemployment, inflation is regarded as a problem that could be solved if only somebody, someplace, would do something about it.

Technically inflation is defined as a rise in prices when supplies are limited and money or credit has increased, so that available goods can be sold at higher prices. In 1923 in post–World War I Germany, the government printed money about as fast as possible, but there were few or no goods to be had. Such a state of affairs might be described as runaway inflation. In less drastic times governments do not print money without restraint and goods are more readily available. According to economists, the law of supply and demand tends to keep a balance between supplies and prices, and the rate of inflation should fluctuate around zero. Actually, since the introduction of money as a medium of exchange, prices have been rising on everything that has been offered for sale. Will and Ariel Durant in their *Story of Civilization* have occasion in each of the 11 volumes to calculate the cost of goods over the centuries and find that nearly everything costs more than it did. Any person over the age of 50 will recall that things "used to be cheaper," and only adolescents can regard today's prices as normal. The dollar has demonstrated a constant history of decreasing value, and in 1985 it was worth about 15 cents in 1935 terms. If we consider the dollar of 1885 and recognize that a fine dinner in a top-rated restaurant then cost about

$0.75, we can see that the 1985 dollar is worth about $0.05 or less in 1885 terms.

If incomes rise along with prices, individuals do not suffer, except in their memories of lower prices. They forget or do not keep recalling the lower wages along with thee lower prices of bygone days. Problems do arise, however, in that prices generally rise faster than or sooner than wages, and purchasers become disgruntled.

The real harm in inflation comes when prices are arbitrarily raised by monopolies such as OPEC (extorting countries) far beyond any increase in general income, even though the technical definition of inflation does not hold in that there is no real diminution of supplies. The supplies are merely not available at earlier prices. Poor countries without oil cannot solve their problem by printing money because their exchange units may not be acceptable. Countries with acceptable currencies may choose to try other methods of combatting the price rise, for example, conservation or the development of alternate fuels.

When people complain about inflation, they are really complaining about rising prices. They find that goods are available in what seems like endless supply and see their own income as inadequate. It does not appear to them that there is more money and credit around that permits price-setters to raise prices. Their own income always appears to be insufficient; they are never paid what they are worth; other people are overpaid, and so on.

The fact that more money and credit are available does not, of course, justify rising prices. Prices do not rise by themselves. They are set by people in a position to do so. The problem of inflation, then, is that people with goods or services to sell always seem to want more money. If their supplies do dwindle, they feel entitled to charge more. A popular athlete or other entertainer cannot be everywhere at once and entertain all day. There is a limit to her supply of services, and if the demand increases, she can ask for more compensation. But there is no logical or physical reason why the owner of some limited supplies or service should charge more than previously. Why should the last apple in the world cost more than the first? For economists prices rise when supplies dwindle and there is money around. Economists do not deal with the people who raise the prices and write as if the lack of supplies in itself causes the price to rise. But prices rise even when supplies are unlimited. The "penny postcard" now costs 15 cents. Does the post office sense a shortage of paper? Is there a greater demand for postcards?

Why have prices of goods and services risen over the centuries? True, there have been period of deflation, and prices have fluctuated from time to time. The prices of some newly marketed product may drop off after initial demand is satisfied, but the persistent trend has been for prices to rise. Even chewing gum, with a long history of 5 cents per pack, is now more than twice that amount. It must be recognized that prices are set not by some abstract demand but by people in a position to do so. Galbraith (1975), who has advocated price controls for a long time, blames the producers, business people, and unions for the wage-price spiral. To those who piously argue that price controls will not work, Galbraith replies that they worked during World War II and would work again if governments simply decided to make them work. Any temporary price control measures would not work because the price fixers would simply wait for the lifting of controls. Galbraith would have permanent controls over prices of at least major products. For psychologists the question becomes, Why do the owners of supplies and services raise their prices or fees? Why does everyone want more money? On the purchasers' side, too, the desire to get more goods or services for less money operates in a parallel fashion. Everyone wants more of what might be called the good things of life, and as these are usually available only at a price, for money. Everyone appears to want more money. Why?

The common—perhaps *vulgar* would be the better word—answer is that everyone is greedy. The word *greed* appears in countless accounts by newspaper pundits. Unfortunateely, psychologists are unable to deal with abstract terms and adjectives as causal agents. There is no such thing as greed and, therefore, no way to study it. Yet the term seems to refer to something, namely, the common tendency for most people to strive to improve their lot, to acquire money by one means or another, to hustle and hassle, to value money. How does psychology explains such preoccupation or concern with money? Why does nearly everyone want more money? Why do the extremely rich continue to pursue more wealth? The answer does not come from attributing greed and avarice to people. It is a perfectly natural, that is, human, function to want more of the good things of life. To begin with, it is natural for needs and expenses to rise as a human grows from infancy to adulthood. A baby can be fed relatively cheaply; the growing child and later the adult need more. Babies do not go to college, but adolescents do, and expenses mount. With each additional child more expenses are involved. Clearly, costs increase as a function of living. People need larger houses, larger cars, more furniture, more of everything. A small fixed income does not suffice, and therefore more money is required. Most people's needs increase until middle age.

But more directly to the point, people learn to want money. In earlier discussions it was pointed out that people do what they do because they are reinforced for doing so. Direct rewards or primary reinforcers such as food satisfy physiological needs. No one can survive without primary reinforcers such as food and water, appropriate warmth, and rest. But at the same time as the occurrence of a primary reinforcement, other stimuli will be present—the sights and sounds related to the appearance of food, for example. These other stimuli will soon acquire the properties of secondary reinforcers (see chapter 1) and will, in Mowrer's analysis, arouse a preliminary positive emotional reaction that we can call feeling better. Mowrer called it hope. Thus the sound of "Come and get it" around dinner time will in itself make the hungry person feel better. The cat that hears the can opener working comes to the kitchen, presumably feeling better, or hopeful. In time these secondary reinforcers acquire the capacity for maintaining the behvior involved in attaining primary reinforcers. Thus the cat can be made to come to the kitchen time after time at the sound of the can opener even if it is not fed on each occasion. On the human level words that accompany primary reinforcers also acquire reinforcing capacity. The mother feeding the baby can hardly restrain herself from saying, "Good." "Good" is heard thousands of times and becomes a secondary reinforcer that will last a lifetime. In the course of growing up, a child will see and hear about money being exchanged for primary reinforcers, and money will become a powerful secondary reinforcer in its own right. The sight and mention of money will arouse the feeling better or hope reaction and, depending upon the situation, will lead to approach behavior, that is, activity related to the acquisition or appearance of money. Other stimuli related to money will also acquire positive values, so that they too will arouse hope. Thus black ink in the ledger will arouse hope; red ink will arouse the opposite, fear or anxiety. So long as money can be spent—that is, followed by more primary satisfiers, at least occasionally—it will maintain its secondary reinforcing function. Under normal conditions in the economic world, money will have that capacity, and consequently there will be no satiatition point. One can never extinguish the value of a secondary reinforcer so long as it is occasionally followed by a primary reinforcer. Thus, even if "you can't take it with you," the human being for whom money is a secondary reinforcer will continue to do whatever a situation calls for (assuming the ability to do it) if money is mentioned, hinted at, or suggested in any way. Wealthy tennis players ("who don't need the money") will appear on television advertising anything at all that they think will not demean them. Politicians and wealthy actors will do the same. Of course, some people will have scruples, which can be overcome only by greater and greater amounts of money, but only a few will have such strong scruples as to avoid situations where money might be suggested.

During most people's lifetime there will be losses, setbacks, failures in connection with money, and these negative experiences will result in fears of additional or future losses in relation to conditioned stimuli associated with the losses. Again, people will appear to be greedy or grasping, money-hungry when in fact they are merely anxious under certain circumstances.

The fact that prices are always rising would present no great problem so long as income also rose to meet the new levels. This has been happening to a degree, with prices normally staying one jump ahead. The $3,000 per year college professor of the 1940s is now paid $60,000, but in 1988 was not any better off, because the $1,000 car costs $16,000, and the $8,000 house costs $75,000, with other costs in proportion. The wage-price spiral becomes a chart for economists to study.

The serious problem that is inherent in rising prices is that of savings. Savings banks pay interest on savings, but the interest may not be equal to the rate of inflation, and people with ordinary savings accounts find themselves poorer with each passing day. If they have enough money to play the banking game, they can get interest rates somewhat higher than the rate of inflation and preserve their savings. Higher interest rates, however, involve tying up money for various periods during which inflation may again exceed the interest rate. The poor cannot save, and without saving they cannot plan for future expenses, down payments on cars, houses, children's education, or their own old age. Even social security income is threatened with legislation against COLAs (cost of living adjustments), and those dependent upon such income for survival may have to survive at a lower level. Inflation makes planning for the future risky, if not impossible. People who have saved all their lives find their nest eggs worth far less than they had imagined they would be when they started saving. The eggs may even be rotten.

There is no solution to the inflation problem that would keep prices at a fixed level for any great length of time. *The New York Times* once asked 20 economists to give their solutions to inflation and found 20 different opinions,[1] most of which were unrelated to or contradictory to other opinions. So long as everybody wants more of the available wealth, prices will continue to rise, Legislators will legislate raises in their salaries, taxes will be raised to pay them, employed taxpayers will demand more compensation for their alleged contributions to the total wealth production process, employers will raise prices to meet rising expenses, and the vicious cycle will continue.

Inflation is a problem of human nature in that secondary reinforcing stimuli are almost constantly present, arousing positive-approach responses. It is not a problem that other creatures face unless they are owned by humans. But it is a problem that people cannot help facing if they are to remain human, and consequently it is a problem without a solution. What might modify the situation is a program of legislation that would require governmental approval for any rise (not a drop) in prices. With normal red tape and bureaucracy, the approval could be long in coming and prices could stay put for longer periods and might not be raised as arbitrarily as they are now. The rise would have to be justified. Currently so-called public utility commissions operate in this fashion and keep prices stable for a year or so at a time, always granting a little less than requested (the requests are always for more than is expected). Banks too could be forced to pay the same amount of interest on all monies in savings and other accounts regardless of amount and regardless of time to be held. Again, a measure of stability could be introduced, the poor depositor at least getting the same interest as the wealthy one. The absence of such legislation simply demonstrates the basic principle that everyone wants more. We can conclude by warning anyone planning a saving program for income 50 years later should think in terms of ten times as much as she currently thinks she might want to have.

INTEREST AND DEFICITS

The practice of borrowing money and paying interest on loans is as old as civilization. The Bible and the Koran inveigh against the practice, as did Polonius in his advice to his son. We do not know if Shakespeare himself ever borrowed, but his Shylock suggests that he did not look upon borrowing with any favor. It might be noted that some Arab rulers who borrowed money when the price of oil was high suddenly recalled that the Koran proscribes interest and, as reborn Moslems, decided that paying it was contrary to their religion. Today it is considered almost natural that one should pay interest on borrowed money, although there is nothing natural about it. Many loans among friends are interest free. One does not think of charging a friend a fee for the use of $10.00 "till payday." If the loan is not repaid, the money is considered lost along with the friendship. It is when money is loaned to strangers that the subject of interest arises. In that context the notion of collateral is commonly introduced along with such questions as the stature of the borrower as a credit risk.

Because friends are not commonly in a position to lend large sums, people who think they need to borrow go to banks or to loan sharks or buy on credit with plastic cards issued by banks, retail stores, or other organizations.

The idea that someone should make money by lending money to others is an invention that has a broad appeal to lenders in that only a minimal amount of physical energy need be expended for profitable returns. Banks are so eager to indulge in this money-making operation that they even pay interest to depositors for their savings to obtain money for loans. How much interest lenders charge depends on the desperation of the borrower and the generally agreed-upon rates of banking houses. Loan sharks are the last resort of borrowers whose credit rating is questionble. Loan sharks are not concerned with collateral—threats of broken kneecaps are usually sufficient to assure returns.

Why do people borrow money? Like lending, borrowing has an equally broad appeal. It permits instant gratification. Obviously, people borrow because they want to buy something that costs more than they have on hand. They could, of course, save their money until they could pay in full and avoid the additional cost of the interest, but many people cannot wait to enjoy the dubious pleasures of home ownership, the luxury of a power boat, car, or whatever they cannot buy out of available funds. They prefer to borrow on the "fly now, pay later" principle. There are always potential dangers in lending and borrowing. The borrower may not be able to meet the payments because of changes in circumstances. Debts are not canceled by loss of job, ill health, or other personal difficulties. Buyers of stocks commonly borrow money to pay for shares, which may later fall in value. Some farmers borrow money for seed, planning to repay in the fall; a disastrous crop year puts them behind, often forever. They are worse off than if they had not borrowed.

The common complaint about interest rates is that they are too high. No one ever raises the point that *any* interest rate may be too high. The concept of interest as a proper way of conducting business is never questioned. It has become a way of life and will continue to be a problem society has created for itself, a problem that has the same kinds of advantage and disadvantage as any form of gambling. Though bankers, as pillars of the community, might frown on gambling, they fail to recognize that they themselves are the most obvious proponents of gambling. They even lend to gambling casino operators who want to expand their enterprises. Of course, they are lending to business people, not gamblers.

Governments are the biggest borrowers. Through the medium of bonds sold to investors, they acquire funds for extensive projects that are paid for over long periods from taxes. The taxes, of course, have to go up to pay interest to the bond buyers. Governments, of course, need not be concerned about the interest rates since they can always raise taxes or run deficits, which can be paid off by printing money. Why governments could not save from taxes and pay for projects out of savings is never considered. That people survived for thousands of years without a particular project never seems to occur to anyone. Many projects will be paid for by grandchildren's taxes after the projects are no longer meaningful. New housing projects are often deserted and eventually blown up to make way for newer projects before the old ones are paid off.

When governments borrow from other governments, problems can be expected. Only governments that have not been able to manage themselves need to borrow, and these governments are not especially good risks even for gamblers. At present many governments are expending money from their own taxes to pay foreign governments or bankers interest instead of improving their own countries. In some cases over half the income of a government goes to paying off foreign debts. The simple invention of interest has created some of the worst problems the human race has ever had.

Our principles do not suggest any remedies for the problems created by interest except the elimination of charging it. Psychologists were not consulted when the practice of charging interest arose. Obviously, they would have raised the questions of why anyone should borrow in the first place and why money should earn money in the second place. Because the only reason for borrowing is instant satisfaction, it is clear that the only remedy is delayed gratification. A young married couple need not buy a brand-new house with all of the latest appliances. They could easily live in a one-room cabin until they save enough for a two-room cabin, and so on. With so many people engaged in lending money for profit via interest, it appears an unlikely step. In some communities, for example, the Amish, the community itself builds accommodations for newlyweds, and no one borrows or lends anything except time. Someday it may be recognized that time is time and not money. Some business people, of course, equate the two, but the relationship is a trade-off created by human beings. An immediate, small reward may apear more desirble or practical than a larger, delayed reward depending upon a variety of circumstances.

The practice of lending money at interest has no justification in nature and is unknown except among "civilized" tribes. On the other hand, the practice of giving gifts or interest-free loans is common enough even among "uncivilized" societies. Dowries were the ancient answer to setting up a new household, and even today many parents help their newly married children with their downpayment with no expectation that the money will ever be repaid—however, there may be parents who expect interest on loans, and they may have their reasons. All that is accomplished by money borrowed at interest could be accomplished by simply extending the principles of investment in stocks. Buying shares in any new project, like any gambling operation, amounts to taking a chance that there will be some kind of profit. The profit need not be in monetary terms. Parents providing money for their marrying children are investing in the future happiness of the new couple. It may not be a wise investment if the marriage proves unsuccessful, and the parents should take their gambling losses with a smile. Bankers staking a farmer to his seed should, in effect, be gambling that he succeeds, and the banker should share in the profits, if any, and share the losses equally. There should be no thought of foreclosures on the farmer if bad weather or poor markets result in a catastrophe. It might be argued that bankers would not cooperate in such ventures. They would rather foreclose and acquire properties. Perhaps bankers might better change their function to one of merely storing and safeguarding other people's savings at some small charge. They could be custodians of safety deposit boxes.

Governments might stop selling bonds. They already have the ultimate weapon in taxes. Any debt generated by a government leads only to deficits and inflation, a cheapening of the medium of exchange, along with the inevitable corruption involved in any project. The government can save money for any project of relatively permanent benefit to all of the people now paying taxes.

When bankers lend money to a foreign government, they are lending other people's money (not their own) to people who are unable to run a country efficiently and who will be unable to repay the loans. The bankers rely on their own government to bail them out, compounding the difficulties. It might be wiser to invest in the borrowing country and by-pass the government since officials have a way of syphoning off funds before they are applied to projects for which the money was borrowed.

The abolition of interest would result in the slowing down of the processes that provide instant gratification, if only for a while, and this slowing down might result in considerable benefits all around. We need only remind ourselves that if something does not exist, it has not existed for a very long time—for millions of years, in fact—and another million years may not be too long to wait for it.

DEATH AND TAXES

Death and taxes are regarded as the two inevitable facts of life. Most people try to avoid both, but only some succeed in avoiding the latter. Though taxes have been collected from prebiblical times, no one bothered to explain them prior to Thomas Hobbes, who, in his *Leviathan* (1651), first spelled out in English the notion of a social contract. According to Hobbes, societies (Leviathans) were formed by people agreeing to delegate powers to some authority or representative, the sovereign, who in exchange for their support would protect them from an ever present fear of death, an insecurity Hobbes thought of as a natural fact of human existence. In Hobbes's world, people would work for a king, support him, do battle for him, in exchange for his protection. How much protection they would receive from a king, who might well have their heads removed was never spelled out. The alleged contract never did exist—no citizen was ever consulted or signed a document pledging his support of a monarch,[2] and monarchs traditionally proclaimed only their own rights—and the obligations of the people. The rights of the people emerged only after the power of monarchs had been diminished.

Even in democracies such as the United States, immigrants desiring to become citizens swear a one-sided oath that describes their duties and says nothing about their rights. The rights are interpreted from other documents, such as the Constitution. Native citizens do not have to take an oath, nor do they sign a social contract. Their duties are imposed from above by the authorities.

The basic duty of all citizens is to pay taxes, and authorities busy themselves devising measures by which these duties can be collected with the least difficulty. True, some authorities find taxes irksome or in conflict with economic growth and try to reduce them, but it is commonly recognized that a social structure cannot be preserved or remain effective if some kind of tax is not imposed and collected. Because taxes have always been with us, they are expected, if not accepted, burdens. Those who pay them, however reluctantly, sometimes recognize that by adding their tax contributions to those of others, useful or desirable things can be accomplished, however wastefully. Roads, bridges, schools, parks, and museums can be built and maintained. Armies can be supported, along with governmental administrators, who, because of their public duties, cannot support themselves.

As with the question of wages, no one has yet discovered how much tax anyone should pay. A tax law is always the result of a power struggle among politicians, who have one eye on their constituents and another on their financial supporters. Some politicians regard a tax law as a means of correcting what they regard as social ills and inequities. Because of the differences among people in the amounts of money they possess, any effort to tax everyone at the same rate is easily regarded as unfair. Poor people approve of a "soak the rich" policy, and rich people see no good reason why they should pay more than anyone else. Politicians know that there are more poor people than rich, and in the United States in 1913, a progressive income tax law was enacted that, on paper, obliged people with higher incomes to pay proportionally higher taxes. In the 1980s some steps were taken to approach a flat tax, but the basic question of how much tax anyone should be obliged to pay is never addressed because there appears to be no answer. There is no way the question can be answered on a scientific basis. Animals in the field, forest, or jungle do not pay taxes. For human beings to pay taxes, some kind of power structure must exist through which taxes can be imposed on what must be an arbitrary basis. The taxpayers will resist and complain, and pay if they have no recourse. Those who make the decisions on how much people must pay must reckon on public resistance and their own anxiety about staying in power. If should be noted that, no matter what form the government may take (socialist, capitalist), taxes will be collected. The process may take various forms, for example, sales taxes, duty (as on alcohol and cigarettes), income tax, and social security. In socialist economies a formal tax structure does not even need to exist: the government simply raises prices of consumer goods or does not pay its workers as much as they might earn in other systems—the difference is simply skimmed off at the top. Other forms of taxation include licensing fees for people—barbers, butchers, taxi drivers—and professional people of all varieties. Taxi drivers (in 1987) pay $100,000 in New York City for the privilege of cruising the streets. Whatever form taxes take, they cannot be escaped. Only the forms are changed from time to time.

Tax collectors have two kinds of problem. There is a large underworld of economic activity (prostitution, gambling, drugs, assorted crimes against property) that cannot be taxed. The underworld imposes its own taxes on people who borrow money from loan sharks and on merchants who must pay for protection. Gangsters have no problem with reluctant taxpayers. They have their methods. Some governments try to compete with the underworld and license prostitution, for example, as in Nevada, so that taxes can be collected. Some states operate lotteries to compete with numbers games. Legalizing drugs would bring enormous tax benefits, but some governments are reluctant to take that step and prefer less effective methods of controlling the use of illicit drugs.

The other problem is more of a psychological nature. Because of the nature of tax laws, with their loopholes and deductions, and because of differences in income and expenses, computing taxes in what can be described as a fair way becomes rather complicted for some people. Even taxpayers who pretend to be honest tend to "forget" various items of income, pad expenses, and make errors in simple arithmetic, commonly in their own favor. Those who do not pretend to be honest take chances that their tax cheating will not be discovered. I mentioned earlier that it is improbable that there are many people who are completely honest with regard to money matters. People are often reluctant to reveal how much they earn, even to friends, and a distant or remote government is less likely to be the recipient of confidences of such a nature. Any number of rationalizations can be developed to justify taking liberties with tax forms. When extremely wealthy people and rich corporations pay no taxes at all for perfectly legal reasons, the taxpayer without legal excuses finds illegal ones.

One possible way to avoid dishonest returns, even on the part of gangsters, thieves, and other tax cheats, is to impose higher sales taxes (expenditure taxes) and forget about income taxes. If all taxes were collected on outgo instead of income (with certain products excluded, for example, cheap food, cheap clothing, cheap housing), then those who spend money on luxuries and expensive items such as yachts, Picassos, and limousines would have to pay sales taxes that could match the current income on income taxes. These taxes could be progressive, with proportionately higher taxes on more costly items. If we can trust the judgment of Thorstein Veblen (1899) in his *Theory of the Leisure Class*, the wealthy people in any country could take pride in being able to pay the high taxes involved in their conspicuous consumption. Even gangsters and stock exchange presidents would have to pay taxes in such a system.

NOTES

1. *New York Times, Sunday Magazine*, Dec. 30, 1979.
2. The Magna Carta applied only to nobles.

10
Ideologies

The term *capitalism*, frequently expressed in the phrase *capitalist system*, suggests that there actually exists something worthy of the name. If it does exist, no one has yet seen it. The term *system* implies an organized structure or arrangement that has some kind of order to it, with parts interacting, and is related to some purpose. If we look for anything of the sort in the economic operations that go on in capitalist countries, they are not to be found. What is allegedly a system is an unorganized collection of practices based on slogans like *laissez-faire* and *free enterprise*, which in themselves deny any order or system. To engage in free enterprise means to do whatever you want without interference from any source. This, of course, is not the case anywhere in the world.

What is termed capitalism amounts to the largely unregulated operations of individuals engaged in the accumulation and exchange of goods. A suitable example might be horse trading between individuals or haggling in a bazaar. Such activities have gone on presumably from our caveman days. Inherent in such activities is the notion of profit, in that people are not inclined by nature to do anything that is not to their advantage in some way. I have already indicated that there is no natural drive to work and that our earliest ancestors worked only to survive. In that process it became useful to stake out some territory, protect one's kill, and put something aside for rainy or otherwise impossible days. Though there is no serious evidence about the proclivity of human beings for territoriality, there does appear to be a general tendency to assert possession of useful items. Children have to be taught to share. As humans began to develop social relationships, problems arose about more and less desirable locations, (living space), personal accumultions (property), and who would do what. Inevitably some people, because they were bigger, stronger, or more cunning, began to acquire advantages over others. The inevitable trend was for "the rich to get richer and the poor to get poorer," at least relatively. Death, too, caused problems of disposal of accumulations, and various patterns or customs of inheritance arose. Different practices developed in different parts of the world, but some people were able to begin adult life with greater advantages than others. The rationalization of "from shirtsleeves to shirtsleeves in three genertions" may have had occasional support, but in general, some groupings (families, for example, the Fords, Duponts, and Rockefellers) managed to acquire more and more, so that in any country or social grouping, a majority of the wealth was usually acquired and controlled by a minority of the inhabitants.

In the course of human social evolution, then, some people acquired more property (or its equivalent, money) than they could use immediately for personal satisfactions. In such a situation, something had to be done with the excess, and various choices became available with human inventiveness. One could simply hoard the wealth, like a miser; one could give it away (not an attractive outlet); one could lend it to others eager to improve their situation; or one could invest it either in developing a new enterprise alone or in shares or stocks offered by others who appeared to the investor as having some chance of success. Anyone who owns stocks is a capitalist. Capital usually is defined as assets that can be used to further the production of goods. Such assets include money, land, buildings, tools, and so forth. As soon as money or other assets could be used to make more money either through interest, dividends, or appreciation in stock values, one could say that capitalism had come into being. But capitalism is not a system—it is merely a collection of processes in which one can try to acquire additional assets in a rather uncontrolled and chaotic environment where investors are at some risk of losing their investment. Some economists, for example, Milton Friedman, look back over history and try to impose an order or system upon the practices that have developed. At best they produce a theory about how a system might work—the practices, however, go on without respect to the theory. For example, Friedman advocates free trade between nations, but real capitalists, for example, owners of cotton mills, want the government to impose tariffs on cotton goods. The practioners do not follow the principles of any theory; they are concerned only about profits. But so is the Soviet Union.

Because everyone involved is pursuing the same goal of increments of income, a general background of what is called competition is said to exist. How much actual competition prevails varies with the alleged competitors. A powerful investor or group of investors (cooperators, in a sense) can easily eliminate weaker ones. At times a group of investors (producers) can get together and create a monopoly, as the "oil extorting countries" did in the 1970s and 1980s and raise prices and wreak havoc with the economies of consuming countries. In any case competitiveness appears to be a genuinely significant feature of human behavior in that when there is a limited supply of necessities, real or fancied, there are usually more people trying to get some for themselves. They may have no notion of competing with anyone—they may just be trying to get all that they need—and they may very well, as individuals, be glad to have others get all they want, so long as they themselves have as much as or more than they want. Competition becomes an abstract term to describe a situation rather than a personal motivating force. Inevitably, if there is not enough to go around, there will be winners and losers.

After certain practices develop and persist for any length of time, those who benefit from them will have occasion to defend their position and status against complaints and accusations from those less satisfied. The wealthy will develop a number of beliefs, rationalizations, or position statements to justify the disparity in the distribution of wealth or income. They will speak of free enterprise as a God-given or heavenly-approved right; they will proclaim the right of anyone to equal opportunity they will talk about the right to fail, as Milton Friedman does so eloquently; they will argue that there are no classes in a free economy—anyone can go first class if she works hard and saves her money. They will even argue that "what is good for General Motors is good for the country," and they will want to get "the government off our backs" so that everyone can become wealthy. President John F. Kennedy proclaimed, "A rising tide raises all boats." Such beliefs do not constitute a system of any kind; they merely apologize for the lack of a system.

It should be noted that in countries characterized as capitalist, it is possible for some people to rise in economic status from virtual poverty or modest circumstances. None of the presidents of the United States since Franklin D. Roosevelt, except John Kennedy, was a wealthy man in his early adulthood. They all became millionaires. One was a haberdasher, one a soldier, one a lawyer, one a grade school teacher, one a peanut farmer, one a sportscaster. Wall Street millionaires sometimes, if rarely, come from relatively impoverished homes. A strong element of chance operates in economic affairs, and many people are inclined to gamble, especially in lotteries, and some win. The fact that some win motivates millions of others to persist in their efforts to improve their lot one way or another and to endorse the practices that prevail.

It should also be noted that the governments in capitalist countries are in large measure supported by and in turn support the free enterprise enthusiasts by providing munitions contracts, tariff walls, and other forms of support and by facilitating the building of roads and canals, providing police protection, and otherwise safeguarding the property rights so carefully spelled out in the Constitution. Capitalist governments can subsidize enterprises and buy up surpluses to keep up prices. Of course, in the process of facilitating free enterprise, governments also are required to provide internal peace and to try to keep the unemployed from creating problems thrugh unemployment insurance, welfare, social security, grants-in-aid, and the like. The cost of such measures has to be met by taxation, which the free entrepreneur resents and tries to avoid by lobbying the government to develop loopholes in tax laws.

From a psychological viewpoint capitalism is not a system of any kind; it is merely the outgrowth of normal human nature, a normal "first come, first served" pattern where *first* means stronger (in many ways) or luckier, a pattern sometimes enhanced by additional efforts that are presumably acquired dispositions. It is to a considerable degree a manifestation of the doctrine of the survival of the fittest, and since it is not designed in any way, it is obviously not designed to result in equality and comfort for all. It is a process that is considerably complicated by other factors in human social development arising from human interactions that fostered the growth of religious and emotional attachments that tended to promote interest in support of members of groups. The slogan "If we don't hang together, we shall all hang separately" perhaps expresses the origin of the concern of some humans for the welfare of others. Such altruistic tendencies as we observe may have their origin in what is often considered selfishness. In any case altruism, to the extent that it appears, is one of the contradictions of capitalism that prevents its systematization. Capitalism is not a system, a theory, or an idea. It is a way of life that has charcterized humanity since the earliest human beings met one another.

Critics of capitalism attack what they consider a system on several fronts. They point to the disparity of wealth among individuals, where some are billionaires and others paupers, as if the maldistribution of wealth were somehow a function of a system instead of the machination of individuals exploiting one another at all levels, a few exploiters being more effective than the rest. Exploitation appears to be a common human characteristic even among children: Tom Sawyer managed to exploit his acquaintances by his cunning. Exploited slaves in the Old South exploited their masters, if John Dollard's (1937) observations about how some poor blacks pretended to be incompetent are correct. In *Class and Caste in a Southern Town,* Dollard recognized the eternal pattern of mutual exploitation on all sides. Some exploiters are simply more successful than others. In totalitarian countries that espouse either capitalism or communism, the disparities in income among individuals may be enormous. Leonid Brezhnev collected foreign cars and enjoyed a hunting lodge, among other privileges. Politburo members live well. In more democratic countries voters manage to elect some officials who, in turn, manage to legislate some amelioration for lower-income citizens in terms of welfare, housing, food stamps, medical care, labor laws permitting strikes, unions, and collective bargaining. Exploitation is not exclusively capitalist.

Another front of attack amounts to pointing out the ups and downs of a capitalist economy in the recurring periods of depressions and relative prosperity. Karl Marx saw the business cycles as becoming more and more serious and expected a final cataclysmic depression that would destroy capitalism. Again, depressions are not exclusive to capitalism. There are good and bad times in socialist countries as well, with periods of inflation, shortages, and dislocation of production. In both kinds of economy governments try to mitigate miseries. Franklin D. Roosevelt is sometimes given credit for saving capitalism by his make-work legislation. His efforts were similar to those of an earlier president, Theodore Roosevelt, who introduced laws against "trusts" and for conservation. Such governmental efforts to control the economy are numerous and widespread, with governments regulating transportation, interstate commerce, and banking, and allowing some businesses to fail while propping up others with guaranteed loans, tariffs, quotas on imports, and even ownership of some businesses and industries. The Tennessee Valley Authority, for example, is a government-owned (socialist) power producer. The notion of free enterprise is more a slogan than a reality. Anyone trying to start a business faces a host of obstacles (social security payments, licenses, safety regulations, minimum wage stipulations, and the like). Capitalist governments keep trying to keep the economy stable, and through various agencies like the Federal Reserve Board they try to anticipate depressions or recessions and take steps to prevent them. The catastrophic downfall of capitalism foreseen by Marx in 1848 has still not occurred and shows no sign of doing so.

The weaknesses, sins, or evils of capitalism are features not so much of a system as of human beings. It is true that in a capitalist country cultural activities are encouraged to support the slogans of free enterprise in the schools, veteran's organizations, charities, the press, and in the entertainment world. People are urged to support the system and to fear, resent, or distrust any other system. How well the operations work will be a function of the reinforcements that people attain; if more and more people find the reinforcements diminishing or disappearing, they will start to distrust the supporters and start one form or another of resistance or revolt.

In totalitarian countries the educational and disciplinary systems similarly are geared to produce compliance from the citizenry, and, again, these will work to the extent that they supply appropriate reinforcers. People such as Aldous Huxley (1958) and Czeslaw Milosz (1955) worry that given sufficient time, a country such as the Soviet Union could condition or educate generations of new citizens to be ardent admirers and supporters of the regime. Huxley and Milosz forgot to reckon with the factor of extinction. People can be conditioned to believe anything so long as the beliefs are suitably reinforced. If the reinforcement is withheld or otherwise fails to be provided, the beliefs will also disappear in favor of other beliefs. In both capitalist and socialist countries defectors or refuseniks are individuals who are not reinforced appropriately. Neither capitalism nor socialism has any guarantees of success. People are people and will continue to look out for themselves regardless of any systematic efforts to control them by anything short of physical abuse, incarceration, or other forms of restraint.

COMMUNISM

Communism is no more a system than is capitalism. It is a vague idea or statement that property should not belong to anyone as a private possession but should be owned by all and available to anyone who might need it. The old village green, where anyone could pasture cows, might be an approximation. Ownership of the cows might be questionable. One might say that where everyone owns everything, no one owns anything. Communism is not a system or theory in the sense of consisting of a series of definite, specific statements in an organized or presumably orderly structure. Mikhail Gorbachev (Gorbachev, 1987, p. 163) himself says, "The classics of Marxism-Leninism left us with a definition of the essential characteristics of socialism. They did not give us a detailed picture of socialism." It is not in any sense a reality as something one can point to and has no existence anywhere on earth as operative in any country. Even the Communists in the Soviet Union admit that they do not have communism, yet. Communism is supposed to come into existence when "states wither away," and the state of the Soviet Union appears to be in no mood to start withering. What goes on in the Soviet Union, and in various patterns in other "welfare states," for example, Sweden, Great Britain, and Cuba, is more or less what is called socialism which, in turn, refers to the practice of the state ownership of some of the major means of production and distribution of goods. This normally would mean that the state, that is, some group of people, would declare itself the owner of factories, mines, mills, farms, the land in general, and everything that is on the land, but nowadays it also refers to services such as transportation, communications (mail, telephone, television), education, the press, medical care, orchestras, ballet companies, motion pictures, restaurants, night clubs, and so on. In Britain, for example, the government owns the mines, medical services (to a large degree), airlines, automobile plants, and other industries (railroads). Britain, of course, is considered a capitalist country largely because that is where industrialization began and many of the money-makes-money practices developed. It is also the country where Karl Marx and Friedrich Engels (two Germans) collaborated to spell out the theory of communism.

Communism is not a Marxist invention. Since ancient times there have been individuals and small groups of people who have proclaimed some of the propositions that describe communism, such as that all property should be mutually owned and that all should have access to as much of it as they need. The sporadic early attempts of some small groups to practice a communist form of life had varying degrees of success, but they frequently were based on additional, more dominant principles of a religious nature that had nothing to do with economic viability. Such groups could be found all over the world, and the United States has seen the rise and fall of many of them. Robert Owen, a British factory owner, started one such community in the United States in Indiana in 1825. The Shakers (1774) and the Oneida Community (1847–1879) were other such early groups. The Commune of Paris in 1871 was another effort, and the current Israeli kibbutzim are still others. The latest such communes developed from the proposals of B. F. Skinner in his popular novel *Walden II* (1948), wherein he described a community that was based on the single principle of reinforcement. Many college students were inspired by that work to set up little communities that were variants on the communist theme.

What Karl Marx invented was Marxism, and it is Marxism that is alleged to be the goal of rulers in some countries, for example, China, Ethiopia, Nicaragua, Cuba, and, of course, the Soviet Union, where Marxism is modified to include some of the proposals of Lenin, so that it is a Marxist-Leninist theory that is supposed to be the guide of the present rulers of these countries. The Marxist theory is at best a supernatural theory—it could be called a religion—in that it rests on a metaphysical belief that the social evolution of humanity has a goal, that is, that eventually, sooner or later, society will evolve in such a way that there will be no private ownership of property, that all property will belong to all of the earth's inhabitants, that there will be no states or separate countries. It should be recognized that this is supposed to happen whether anyone does anything about it or not, that is, it is just in the nature of society to go through stages such as feudalism, industrialized capitalism, socialism, and finally communism. Some activities such as organized workers' demands for better conditions may hasten the development, and other activities such as repressive or reform measures taken by states may delay the coming, but just as the Messiah is looked for and will come, so will communism.

Both Marx and Engels were prodigious writers and produced a considerable amount of literature, some of which contained credible facts from history, but they, like all historians, selected facts they considered worthy in relation to preconceived notions derived from Hegel's philosophy. Hegel, an idealist, in his *Philosophy of History* saw the unfolding of history as a preordained course of the development of what he called the absolute idea. All history was merely the result of the dynamic idea; great heroes and leaders were merely the instruments of the unfolding of historical necessity to its eventual purpose. It is not clear what such a purpose might be. To account for historical changes, Hegel propounded the notion of a dialectic, which amounted to saying that virtually every condition has its opposite. A present condition was called a thesis, the opposite the antithesis, and the two were in conflict, the resolution of the conflict would result in a synthesis, or new condition, which would in turn develop its antithesis and result in a new synthesis, and so on indefinitely. Marx saw bourgeois capitalism as the synthesis of the conflict between feudalism and all the developing forces (religions, peasantry, tradesmen, artisans) that opposed it. Now capitalism would see its antithesis in the developing proletarian (industrial worker) population, and the new synthesis would be socialism, which would in turn develop into communism as the final flower of social evolution. Why communism would not inspire an antithesis was never considered. By selection of historical facts, it is possible to find various kinds of supporting evidence for some of Marx's statements. Because he wrote so much, there is a considerable stock of Marxist lore that is right, wrong, and irrelevant. He frequently changed his views while still maintaining the dialectical formula, and he is the dominant saint of the Soviet empire to the extent that the rulers there can impose the official views on the population.

If we try to find out what socialism is, we can at present do no better than look at the Soviet Union, which is the largest officially organized socialist country. The state, in the Soviet Union, owns and controls all or most of the means of production and distribution of goods and services. Private property or personal possessions are restricted to such things as clothing and furnishings of one's state-owned living quarters. All officially recognized employment is controlled by the state, and virtually anyone who wants a job can have one (unless he is considered one form or other of an undesirable). There are no unemployment statistics in the Soviet Union. It is illegal to be unemployed. Everyone is expected to work—"from each according to his abilities," as if this assumption had any merit. The state as the official owner of everything has the responsibility of running everything; to do this the members of the government engage in planning and develop plans for varying periods of time—five-year plans, 25-year plans, and so on. The planning is what makes a system in that hypothetically nothing is left to chance (weather and natural disasters, of course, must be considered). Plans can be worked out so that, again hypothetically, everything will occur as designed—trains will run on time, delivering goods to factories, production will amount to a certain amount, and so on. The planners allocate the appropriate resources to each sector of the economy and start developing new plans. The implementation of the plans, of course, is left to bureaucrats, hired managers, whose job it is to see that the plans are fulfilled. Other bureaucrats provide the help (employees) and see to it that raw materials are provided where needed.

Note that in capitalist countries the owners or capitalists (the stockholders) in large corporations do not personally run the activities; they hire management to conduct the business of the corporation. These managers are not different from Soviet bureaucrats in their function except for their basic instructions, which amount to "Make a profit," whereas those of Soviet bureaucrats are "Produce x amount of goods."

The major problem that socialist economy faces is that it is a latecomer—it can come into being only at a stage in history when a vast historical accumulation of nonsocialist manners, morals, and mores has already existed for a long time, many of which are not compatible with the imposition of a new economic structure onto the existing society with its background of customs, heroes, literature, music, nationalism, chauvinism of various kinds, and traditions. To the degree that such matters are not disturbed, many of the inhabitants will go along with the new ownership arrangements because they do not change most of the important daily activities—people who have been used to working for one employer can adjust to working for another (it happens frequently in capitalist countries). If people, for example, small farmers, have been working for themselves, there will be resistance. If central planners decide to shift populations about because workers are needed 1,000 miles away, there will again be resistance. In fact, central planning is likely to lose much in the translation when the planning finally impinges on individuals who had nothing to do with it. This is equally true in capitalist economies. If, as in the Soviet Union, religion is proclaimed "the opiate of the masses" and is officially restricted, more turmoil can be expected. The intrusion of noneconomic factors into the daily lives of the actual work force used to implement plans can only disturb the fulfillment of the plans.

Some restrictions on the work of artists, poets and other writers, musicians, clergy, even scientists, have been introduced in the Soviet Union on the grounds of the Marxist belief that all culture is an expression of the means of production and distribution, in short, of economic operations.

In France and Central America many Catholic worker priests have tried to reconcile religion and socialism in defiance of the "opiate of the people" doctrine of Marx. They look to biblical statements of Jesus to support socialist principles and find some. In the United States, fundamentalist preachers find biblical statements to support an anticommunist view. It may be that cultural processes determine economic activities as much as vice versa. In any case, neither communism nor capitalism tolerates open opposition if that opposition begins to show signs of strength. In the United States, for example, a strike by airport controllers was put down by governmental dismissal of the controllers. Other less serious strikes can be tolerated for a time, but troops can always be sent in to run mines or railroads if the government finds it desirable. Laws are passed that make strikes by certain groups, for example, teachers, illegal. Some teachers strike anyhow, and nothing much is done about it because education is only indirectly related to the economic structure.

Socialism, then, is distinguished from capitalism only in that the economy is planned from the central headquarters of the rulers (politicians, leaders), some of whom may be competent but many of whom may not be too cognizant of the factors involved in producing materials and services in the amounts required to keep the economy functioning. The political leaders have to function like executive boards of les complicated single industrial enterprises—their closest analogues are the executive boards of multinational conglomerates, which, too, have their problems. Like the occupants of executive suites, they will form a new class, as Djilas (1959) described in his book of that name. As members of a privileged class, they will avail themselves of the privileges. Current members of the Soviet ruling class can expect the best available in the way of housing, vacations, personal adornments, and the like. It has been argued that a socialist system is more likely to divide society into classes than a capitalist one. In either case, some individuals will rise to power and exercise their prerogatives, for example, seeing to it that their children, relatives, and friends get the best available privileges in such areas as education, jobs, and living quarters.

For the most part, the workers will not be worse off than workers under capitalism—Soviet workers are said to enjoy 5-day, 40-hour weeks but are alleged to work less efficiently or industriously than American workers. This may or may not be true—examples of "goofing off" are readily observed in both the United States and the Soviet Union. Incentive systems of positive and negative kinds can be introduced in socialist economies without violating the basic principles of state ownership. To a considerable extent the welfare of workers depends on the presocialist standards to which they were accustomed. In some cases workers are better off. Those who were wealthy before may find the new system intolerable. A Hungarian countess who became a refugee in the United States complained about how hard it was to live without servants. Her former servants may be better off than before.

CAPITALISM VERSUS COMMUNISM

All communists and some capitalists perceive a conflict between the two ideologies. According to Marx and his followers, capitalism will eventually crumble because of its own inherent conflicts and contradictions—it is only a matter of time. In the United States some communists would like to hasten the process and urge "the workers" to unite (unionize) and agitate for changes in conditions that would somehow lead to socialism. Members of the Socialist party hope to achieve socialism by democratic means (elections) and urge reform, public takeovers, governmental ownership of key industries such as transportation and communications, increased public support in such matters as health (socialized medicine) and day-care. Some revolutionary minded groups, for example, the Socialist Labor party, object to any measures that they think will keep capitalism alive and scorn all reforms as tactics that delay the revolution.

Marxist theory predicts that the course of capitalism amounts to an inevitable decrease in the number of capitalists as the more powerful swallow the less powerful through takeovers and mergers. As the number decreases, the wealth of the remainder increases. At the same time the middle class dwindles and adds to the increasing lower class. The workers, now abetted by the dispossessed middle class, will then revolt and establish socialism as the only practical and responsible method of running a society whose existence depends on a steady growth of productivity to match the growing population.

Communists are somewhat embarrassed by the occurrence of socialist revolutions in relatively backward countries, where the classical patterns of capitalist development has not taken place. Revolutions have occurred in countries that were more feudal than capitalist, for example, China, Mexico, Cuba, and Ethiopia. True enough, there was the presumed necessary disparity of wealth, with a small owning and ruling class and an impoverished peasantry or proletriat, as in Russia. In none of these cases, however, was there anything like a revolt of the masses. Revolutions have been the product of small organized groups that took advantage of circumstances such as military defeats (China, Russia) or the failures of dictators (Batista in Cuba, Somoza in Nicaragua) to maintain their control over dissatisfied citizenry. Edmund Wilson (1972) describes in *To the Finland Station* how Lenin and his followers took over a revolution that had already taken place in a country where the vast majority of the population had no notion of what was going on.

In the United States the Marxist predictions might be supported to a degree (though at a snail's pace) by the growing percentage of people who have fallen below the poverty line (in 1986 an income of about

$10,000 for a family of four). The monetary definition is arbitrary, and the growth of the impoverished may not be proceeding at a rate that threatens the economy as a whole. On the rich-get-richer side of the argument, there is, also, an increasing disparity in the distribution of wealth. In the 12 years between 1969 and 1982, for example, the lowest 10 percent of the people had 1 percent of the income whereas the highest 10 percent saw their incomes increase from 29 to 33 percent. The middle class correspondingly lost out to the upper class. According to Thurow (1986), "the richest 20% of all households have 11 times as much income as the poorest 20% in the United States." Such figures describe only current income. When total accumulated wealth is considered, the disparities between the rich and the poor are much greater.

In further support of Marxist views, the growth of conglomerates and takeovers speaks to the point of fewer and fewer people owning or controlling more and more of the productive capacity. How far this trend will go is undeterminable at any time, and some entrepreneurs divest themselves of some acquired properties for various reasons.

As I mentioned earlier, however, capitalists are not free "to do their thing" as they might wish, and procedures are introduced by governments to prevent or lessen economic collapses and to ease the problems of both workers and unemployed people. Thus social security, unemploymnent insurance, welfare, the minimum wage, public works, military contracts, help keep money in circulation and ensure that the poor get enough to survive. Unions too, although they have ups and downs, put some restraints on capital.

The course of economic evolution cannot be predicted any more than the fluctuations in the stock market, whose activity seems to follow no meaningful correlates. The predictions of stock market experts range from strongly positive to strongly negative, and few display any consistent accuracy over a period of time.

What is of greater interest is that socialist economies are not especially successful in their planned operations. Both China and the Soviet Union have been forced to allow some capitalism, that is, free enterprise, to function in their countries, perhaps following the example of Hungary. In the Soviet Union in 1986, for example, people were allowed too engage in some forms of private business (appliance and auto repair, for example) so long as they kept their regular jobs and did not employ people outside the family. The operation of black markets has long been tolerated in all socialist countries to provide enough food and other goods to meet the needs of the population. Gorbachev (1977, p. 23) stated that "on the whole, society was becoming increasingly unmanagable," and, a few pages later, that "things could not go on like this much longer."

How the economic problems of the world will be solved cannot be predicted. Psychologists can only say that people will react to their circumstances in terms of the reinforcements that appear as a conse- quence of their behavior. If an economy does not provide adequate reinforcements, that is, economic goods, it will not succeed. Those who want to shape the nature of an economy must take the problem of reinforcement into serious account. The alternative to positive reinforce- ment is aversive control, and it must be admitted that dictatorships with military support have frequently controlled populations for long periods. One problem then is that controllers appear to desire not only support but adoration from those they control—witness the penchant of com- munist dictators for having statues and huge portraits of themselves adorning their cities. Big Brother apparently wants to be thought of as brotherly or, better, fatherly. Aversive control necessarily breeds re- sentment and, like fear, leads to avoidance, escape, and, if necessary, aggression or revolt. Given the facts of human nature, it is most probable that no kind of economy can be satisfactory to any majority.

Robert L. Heilbroner (1970), in discussing the differences between capitalism and socialism, says of the latter, "If there is a single identi- ficatory mark of socialism, it is not immediately visible on the surface." The same could be said of capitalism. Heilbroner charactarizes socialism as an ideology featuring planning but finds that aspect varying in time and place with the appearance of technological innovations and changes in the ecology, international relations, and the market milieu. In the several socialist economies now extant, central planning has surrendered to varying kinds of individual enterprise activity.

The ideology of socialism is best described as a hope for some sort of classless society, but Heilbroner, again, sees variations in income and status as inevitably emerging because of different kinds of skills, abilities, and levels of education required for different kinds of work. An almost necessary elitism appears inevitable. The ideology of socialism rests on psychological assumptions about human nature for which modern West- ern psychology can find no support in that socialists appear to deny that there is such a thing as human nature, whatever that may turn out to be. For socialists humans are purely creatures of environment and its institutions. Change the institutions and you change the infinitely plastic human. Such a view ignores any biological constraints or imperatives, but humans, like other creatures, remain biological organisms that strive to survive, mate, and protect themselves against real or fancied dangers. Their hopes and fears, while largely environmentally determined, de- termine their approaches and avoidances, their aggressions, as well as any benovelent responses. Socialists must explain the paradox revealed in the observation that some people in socialist environments behave like capitalists and some people in capitalist environments yearn for socialism. In neither case do the institutions or environment, educational system, and propaganda have the officially desired effect. When only coercive and aversive procedures result in conformity of behavior, something about human nature has been left out of the psychology. Gorbachev appears to recognize this when he states (1987, p. 86) that "the best satisfaction of consumer demands and employees' income must strictly depend on end production results, on profits."

THE CONFLICT BETWEEN THE UNITED STATES AND THE SOVIET UNION

For the last 70 years, except for a brief period during World War II when the two countries were allies, there has been a cold war between the governments of the United States and the Soviet Union. During the 60s, 70s, and 80s, both governments, in expressing their foreign policies, indicated that they were seriously at odds and displeased with each other. Each allegedly feared that the other would launch an all-out nuclear attack on the other. How broadly and seriously the citizens of the two countries agreed with their leaders is not really known, but it appears that the mass of the citizenry in each country is more fearful than eager to take up arms. Why does the conflict exist?

The mass of ordinary citizens in either country probably is not concerned about how the economy is run—as long as a worker's personal and immediate needs are satisfied, she may be indifferent to or even support the kinds of economic practice that prevail. In each case there will be times of grumbling and disaffection—periods of inflation, inability to satisfy certain needs, long lines to purchase some products (for example, gasoline in the United States for a period during the 70s). There are some extraneous aspects that may bother some people in both countries—the Soviet Union is officially an atheist state, although some people do observe religious practices, whereas the United States has no state policy other than freedom of religion. For those to whom it is a matter of concern in the United States, the atheism of the Soviet Union may arouse negative attitudes. Beyond the atheism, people in the United States may prefer their own system of justice and find Soviet judicial practices disturbing. It appears that sending people to *gulags* is somehow less civilized than sending them to prisons. Reports of nocturnal knocks on doors and the disappearance of Soviet citizens as well as the diagnosis of insanity of dissidents are additionally disturbing to Americans. But none of these extraneous factors appears to be a reason for anything more than dislike. What appears to be the operative factor in the confrontational policy of both countries is the belief that each is ready to engage in some kind of imperialist adventure to gain or control more territory. The Soviet Union accuses the United States of imperialism because of its activities in the Near East and its efforts to control the oil supply. The Soviet Union also sees the United States attacking revolutionary efforts in Vietnam, Grenada, and Nicaragua and defending regimes in countries where something like a social revolution might be in the making (for example, El Salvador, the Philippines, Chile, and South Africa).

On the American side, the Soviet Union is considered imperialist in its efforts at controlling Eastern European countries as well as its ready support of apparent signs of social disturbance in any part of the world and its provision of arms to rebellious groups. The Soviet invasion of Afghanistan is an obvious example of Soviet territorial ambitions.

The Soviet imperialist policy is sometimes traced back to the czarist policy of expansionism and the search for warm-water ports, but its present efforts might be traced more directly to the policies announced by Lenin and by Trotsky when he was a close partner of Lenin. Trotsky emphasized the view that socialism or communism could not succeed if only one country tried to develop it—socialism had to be worldwide. Stalin opposed this policy on the grounds that the Soviet Union and first to build up its own industrial strength, it seemed appropriate to the government under Leonid Brezhnev to announce the policy of supporting any revolutionary attempt anywhere in the world. The Soviet Union proceeded to do just that, with the resulting confrontation with what U.S. governments consider vital interests of the United States. The conflict, then, is not between Soviet people and American people but between governments who find interests threatened. As President Ronald Reagan stated, "people do not make wars; governments do." Whether these interests are serious or not, the simple fact is that both sides are armed with powerful arsenals of destruction that could be brought into action by accident or a misunderstanding or even some trivial incident involving an allied country.

THE NUCLEAR THREAT

Peace marchers throughout the world (except in the Soviet Union and its satellites) demand the elimination of nuclear arms. It might be argued by some that death from a nuclear explosion is no different from death from an arrow or slingshot pellet, but the argument falls flat when it is obvious that residents in countries not involved in a war would also be killed from the spread of the effects of nuclear weapons, whereas they could remain unconcerned about nonnuclear weapons aimed at combatants. Both the United States and the Soviet Union, which possess most of the nuclear weapons, agree that each side has more than enough and might even agree to reduce the number. It is unlikely that the Soviet Union or the United States would agree to reduce the number to zero because:

1. The Soviet Union has a long border with China and may forsee

some conflict with that country with its billion inhabitants, who could probably do considerable damage to conventional Soviet forces through sheer numbers. The Chinese, fearing Soviet nuclear missiles, are developing their own similar arsenal. The United States appears to view Chinese nuclear weapons as irrelevant.

2. Missiles pointed at China could still be re-aimed at the United States, an impasse is created thereby.

3. The Soviets fear (and cite past experience of) an invasion by West Germany. The West German population is not yet ready to accept its separation from East Germany and its loss of territory tht now makes up half of Poland. The possible attempt to reunite Germany is a strong concern of the Soviet Union and Polish governments. U.S. secretary of state described the division of Germany as "unnatural and inhuman" (Dec. 19, 1985). A statement of that kind can only support the Soviets' view that they are in danger. Any invasion from the West could be prevented easily by conventional arms, at present, but military planners work in terms of decades, with unknown future developments.

4. Western Europe, with its relatively meager land forces, fears an encroachment if not an invasion by the Soviets with conventional forces and cannot afford to give up a nuclear deterrent. The official position of the Soviets is one of international supremacy (communism is the world's destiny), and such a fear cannot be dismissed.

In view of the above, the best that can be hoped for is a reduction to a level of just enough nuclear weapons to destroy the earth: at present there are more than 12 times enough, and the surplus could be sacrificed.

Psychology has no suggestions for how the nuclear threat can be reduced, to say nothing of eliminted. Other countries and territories either already have nuclear bombs or can acquire them. The fact that wars have been occurring throughout history suggests that they will continue. The simple existence of nations with disparate living standards appears to provide a constant goad for military adventures. To expect nationalism to disappear amounts to romantic speculation.

In pre-twentieth-century times when monarchs had some power to control their own populations, they frequently arranged alliances with other countries, potential enemies, by marrying off their children to children of other monarchs. Such alliances could persist over a period of years, even generations. It was awkward to make war on one's own relatives, although it was done in World War I. Such royal intermarriages amounted to a simple "peace corps." The United States has created a Peace Corps of another kind whereby a few individuals are sent to other countries to serve as teachers, advisors, experts of one kind or another. Such a Peace Corps may be worthy of support for various reasons except that it is not a peace-preserving operation. To serve actually as a peace corps, it would have to be considerably expanded and include the children of those members of the government who are in a position to foster or declare war against another country. It is doubtful that the United States would launch an attack against a country where the spouses, parents, and children of all the members of Congress, the Joint Chiefs of Staff, the president, and the cabinet were visiting. If something more than a token number of relatives could be exchanged as visitors or temporary residents between countries where hostilities were possible, there could be a reduction in the level of belligerence. Relatives of policy makers could be genuine ambassadors for peace. Frequent replacement of these peace corps members would amount to a serious cultural exchange and perhaps curtail military adventures. Of course, the Soviets would have to send spouses and children of important government officials to the United States in equal numbers for such a peace corps to work. The peace corps members might be considered benign hostages, but hostages whose presence fostered tranquility instead of terror. The exchange of tourists or students if of little help—they are not in a position to declare war and could even provoke it. Cultural exchanges (for example, the Bolshoi Ballet for an American rock group) are inadequate. Ballet dncers and rock singers are expendable.

As I stated earlier, psychology has nothing to offer by way of a hopeful resolution of the nuclear confrontation. Both countries have powerful military-industrial complexes, and governmental leaders in both countries are fully aware of the possibilities of mutual destruction. They are also aware that there would be no gain in a first strike in that the destroyed country would be of no value to the conqueror and in fact might be a source of problems (the "nuclear winter"). Both countries are almost bound to a deterrent or détente policy. If the détente lasts long enough, the possibility of some kind of meaningful defense being developed will increase. The real danger lies in the possibility of accidental attacks, and both countries could encourage each other in accident prevention by exchanges of information on how accidents could be forestalled.

It may turn out that the development of superweapons will actually be the only way in which major international conflicts can be prevented. Minor wars can be expected to continue as they have throughout history.

From the discussion above it may properly be inferred that psychlogists do not have much to say about how nuclear wars (or any other kinds) might be prevented. In a long article on the subject, James G. Blight (1987) faults psychologists who have been greatly concerned about nuclear holocausts for their failure to take account of realistic national interest. According to Blight the real danger lies in how the crises that arise quite frequently are handled. The arms race itself may no longer be the problem. Blight cites Hoffman (1986), who suggests that the arms buildup of the last few decades may have actually reduced the risk of a nuclear attack by either side by the rather secure knowledge that the overwhelming supplies of nuclear weapons on both sides preclude victory by either. Neither side can prevent a retaliatory attack.

Perhaps the real danger lies in the development of nuclear arsenals by other countries whose enemies do not have a sufficient deterrent arsenal. The so-called superpowers may well have to start paying attention to nuclear aspirants while their own economic and social problems evolve toward closer commonalities that might reduce the level of animosity.

11

"The Law Is a Ass, a Idiot."

One commonly speaks of "the law" as if it were a thing, something permanent, with an independent existence, out there somewhere, which is supposed to guide or control our behavior. Actually there is no law but rather thousands of laws, which amount to statements written in law books or in documents prepared by legislative bodies. New laws are written every day. What was not the law yesterday is the law today. Some laws are repealed and are no longer part of the law. Sometimes laws are merely proclaimed by a new dictator who has not had time or bothered with the formality of having the statement written in legalese, the language spoken by lawyers. Laws, then, are rules made by people who may or may not have the power to enforce them. Commonly a mechanism or bureaucracy is set up for enforcement purposes, with a police force, courts, a judiciary, and so on. The enforcement machinery may be corrupt, indolent, or very active. Because there are so many laws, there is rarely sufficient staff available to enforce all of them to the letter, and the consequence is that many laws are broken with no consequence. Most lawbreakers are not caught, and if they are, they may escape the consequences stipulated by the law in question in various ways. Compared to the number of lawbreakers, the actual number of those who go to jail, for example, is miniscule. Authorities may proclaim that prisons are overcrowded, but this may only mean that they are too small or too few. The percentage of the population behind bars is less than one-half of 1 percent. Actually, the number of crimes that are perpetrated is not known because not all are reported. Many cases of rape, child abuse, extortion, and vandalism are never brought to the attention of authorities because the victims may be embarrassed, have no confi dence that anything will be done, or have their own ways of dealing with the perpetrators. Despite major raids, crackdowns, and arrests of drug rings, the illicit trade in drugs only grows in scope. The law, at best, is only partially functional.

Despite the thousands and thousands of laws on the books—so many that no one can know them all—authorities proclaim that all laws must be obeyed and that ignorance of the law is no excuse for a transgression. This assumption is clearly fatuous, but it is only one of several underlying the law that are at variance with human nature. In Charles Dickens' *Oliver Twist* (chapter 51), Mr. Bumble is informed that the law supposes that Mrs. Bumble acts at his direction. Whereupon Mr. Bumble remarks that if the law supposes that, "the law is a ass, a idiot." What Mr. Bumble appears not to have appreciated is that some legislators had decided, guided by their beliefs about human nature, that wives were or should be obedient servants of their husbands. Whenever legislators make such decisions, they are practicing psychology without a license. But such decisions are trivial compared with the basic assumption underlying all of the law, both civil and criminal, namely that people are responsible for their behavior.

Before we consider this basic assumption of responsibility, we must note that some form of law must have existed from the earliest days of human existence. As soon as people began to live in groups, in proximity to one another, there must have been occasions where one individual or group annoyed, disturbed, or got in the way of another. These occasions could lead to disputes, possible violence, and aggressive acts and would frequently call for others and step in to arrange for peaceful coexistence. In time, usage, custom, tradition, and mores would become established that would foster less troublesome existence. Sometimes the customs would be embellished with religious accoutrements, as in the case of the Ten Commandments that Moses brought down from the mountain. The Ten Commandments were very simply stated as a series of "thou shalts" and "thou shalt nots," with no mention of penalties for infractions and no definition of terms. "Thou shalt not kill" was clear and simple. No degrees of manslaughter or homicide were specified. No mitigating circumstances were suggested. Apparently the Ten Commandments were not enough, and it was not long before amendments began. Punishments were introduced—the *lex talionis*, or law of retaliation, whereby culprits were punished by equating the damage done by them with damage done to them; thus the "eye for an eye" principle. This principle would not work for some crimes, for example, adultery, and thousands of years later Gilbert and Sullivan had their Mikado still searching for a punishment to fit the crime. The practice of punishment was probably operating long before any laws were spoken or written. Monkeys, the great apes, and cats and dogs cuff one another around for various transgressions, and it is little wonder that human beings likewise defend their possessions, food supplies, "their turf," and infringe upon their fellows in one way or another. The intruder or annoyer is regarded negatively, as the obvious cause of the annoyance, and therefore as the person responsible.

The term *responsible* as just used is equated with causation in the sense that what causes something is responsible for it. There are other meanings of *responsible* in the dictionary—as, for example, being responsible for the care of funds or children, being answerable to parents or to a constituency—and these usages are innocent enough. It is when the term *responsible* is introduced into legal thinking that the difficulty with it arises. In law *responsible* is supposed to mean that a human being is a rational individual possessed of something called a mind, an intellect, and a free will and can reflect upon future actions, arrive at a decision, and implement that decision; it is also supposed to mean that a human being could have arrived at a different decision or refrained from carrying out the act on some presumed moral imperative that would have identified the prospective action as wrong.

The concept of responsibility in law, in short, is identified with what is called the *mens rea*, or "state of mind," of any individual alleged to be involved in a crime, or for that matter, any activity related to law. To establish criminal liability it has been considered necessary to show that the perpetrator of an act was in a state of mind that included something called intent, that is, that the person chose the action. Anyone who was not in a state of mind that could harbor an intent could not be subject to any legal process. In 1582 in England, it was considered proper for William Lombard to ask if the accused was a man, a natural fool, a lunatic, or a child. Presumably natural fools, lunatics, and children could not have a *mens rea* of any meaningful sort and should not be treated as criminals. Over the centuries since then we have added other considerations that incapacitate a *mens rea*. Thus drunkeness or being drugged, being emotionally disturbed (crimes of passion), being victim of a faulty environment (poor, uneducated), and in the case of members of Congress, among others, entrapment. These additions may not allow a criminal to get off completely, but they determine the kind and degree of criminal charges. Leaving the scene of an accident while driving while drunk is considered more excusable than leaving the scene sober. The victim is just as dead, but the rules of law have always been worked out in terms of the criminal and not the victim.

Returning to *mens rea*, we run into difficulties because the confidence of courts (judges, juries) in the nature of intent has been undermined at an accelerating pace over the last two centuries with the development of psychiatry and psychology. It is as if the idea that "to know all is to forgive all" were actually operative in human affairs and, with psychiatrists and psychologists pretending to know all, we find ourselves not blaming criminals, finding causes or reasons for their behavior; and understanding the behavior, we find it possible to excuse, if not forgive. Thus, if crime rises with economic bad times, we accept the correlation and do nothing about it. The all-forgiving citizens say, "Don't build more jails—eliminate poverty." Get at the roots of crime. Though the correlation between poverty and crime may be real, correlations, it should be clearly understood, do not imply causation. There is no direct evidence that poverty causes crime or anything else. Poverty is a financial status or lack thereof. Certainly most poor people do not commit crimes; they are far more likely to be victims. Certainly poverty does not account for crimes by members of the New York Stock Exchange.

The *mens rea* becomes awkward with juvenile crime. For no clear reason courts got around to declaring people under 16[1] unsuitable for trial in standard legal settings and established children's or family courts where lawbreakers below that age would be examined and disposed of, sometimes by being sent to reformatories, wherefrom they would be released on becoming 18 or 21 or whatever age had been arbitrarily designated by the state. What is the rationale? What reason can there be for different treatment? Is there some age when one becomes old enough to intend? One's mental age does rise till the chronological age of 15 or so, according to test inventors, but that may be due only to their weakness as inventors. Are not infants capable of intent? Do they not reject certain foods? Do they know what is good for them? When do you get to know right from wrong?

Intent is, of course, only one aspect that is considered in juvenile courts. Some courts distinguish between juvenile "delinquents" and "persons in need of supervision." The delinquents have done something that, if done by an adult, would be a crime, whereas persons in need of supervision are young people who, for their own good and protection, are petitioned to the courts for undesirable behavior such as truancy, incorrigibility, running away, or promiscuity. Such behavior is considered not so much unlawful as harmful to the individual. Improper parenting may be the basis rather than some intent to do wrong. Certainly, with normal growth and development, we appear to acquire some capacity to restrain ourselves. This retraint might be called frustration tolerance. To delay gratification might appear synonymous with intent, but when frustration appears unlikely to disappear, our capacity for delay may also diminish.

We go back to the principle of determinism. From the viewpoint of psychology there is no meaning to the concept of choice at any age, at any educational or any socioeconomic level. We always do what we have to do. We respond to the more attractive or less threatening of whatever alternatives face us. Normally what we do, we do quickly, directly, without hesitation. It is only when we cannot act immediately, when we are forced to wait, when circumstances require a pause of any length, that the question of choice, or freedom thereof, arises. A simple restaurant menu offers a variety of choices, but what each diner will choose has been decided long before, perhaps years before the diner enters that restaurant. If there are ten entrées, some of them are not even choices in that there is no chance they will be chosen. The diner does not like fish, turkey, kidneys, pork, or squid. He is a red-meat-and-potatoes man and his choice has been made. Another person may even have the habit of eating something new and different everytime she goes to a restaurant. Her choices are systematically reduced. Similarly for any other situation—what appear to be alternatives from some objective viewpoint are not alternatives to the one who chooses. This is not to say that people do not make choices. It is to say that the nature of the choice is subject to the chooser's history. Thus a juror may listen to evidence with an open mind—he might state, in fact, that he is not yet convinced of the guilt or innocence of the accused, but as he goes over the evidence in the jury room and listens to other jurors, what he will finally come to believe is determined by what kind of person he is, what his previous experiences have been, what kind of argument impresses him, and so on. Determinism does not suggest that this juror will vote one way or the other prior to a trial and jury room considerations. It only states that what a person will agree with, find true, or approve is a result of his history. He cannot approve what he does not approve.

The law itself and common public opinion accept determinism to a considerable degree even if sometimes denying it. Thus the public or lawyers will stress mitigating circumstances, meaning excuses, in many kinds of crime. A husband who shoots his adulterous wife is not treated in the same way as the robber who shoots a liquor store owner's wife. The husband was justified and really only did the natural thing that all betrayed husbands are expected to do.

Murdering presidents or other rulers has been a common practice throughout the ages. When a South American, African, Asian, or other colonel or sergeant gets rid of an incumbent ruler by murder, exile, or imprisonment, it is called a coup. If the attempt is unsuccessful, it is called treason and punished. When Irish terrorists from either side blow up a theater full of people, it is called a revolutionary or political act of freedom fighters by supporters of the terrorists and a horrible, heinous crime by supporters of the victims. In any case, the terrorists did what they had to do as determined by their past. They could not help themselves. When teenagers kick an old man to death, they may not even search him for money. They get their kicks out of the act they could not help performing. They cannot be blamed, because they were obviously not responsible. In general, the more heinous the crime, the crazier the criminal.

The attempt on the life of President Reagan was followed by a trial of the perpetrator, John W. Hinkley, Jr., who was fortunate enough to have wealthy parents who could afford a team of psychiatrists. These worthies, aided by District of Columbia law, were able to get a jury that declared Hinkley innocent by virtue of insanity. The verdict aroused a lot of heated discussion throughout the country by people who wanted Hinkley dead or imprisoned forever. Clearly Hinkley was guilty of shooting the President and several others. Certainly he was reponsible in the causative sense. By the rules of the legal game, he was not even asked if he shot the president. Instead, the trial was based on the question, Is Hinkley sane? The local rules required that the prosecution prove that he was sane, a virtually impossible task, for no one can prove anyone sane beyond a reasonable doubt. How could sanity be proved? By a vote of 100 psychiatrists? There is no way to prove sanity. Insane people (those so labeled by a judge) do most of the same things that sane people do. That someone has not yet done something that insane people do means nothing. The person might do it tomorrow. To prove insanity might be a little easier—it would be necessary only to prove that someone did something that other insane people have done. That might convince a jury, but not the all-knowing, all-understanding, all-forgiving psychiatrists and psychologists, especially if they were being paid by someone interested in the judgment.

It is common belief that anyone who commits a heinous crime is insane. *Insane* is a legal term and has no recognized medical status. Psychiatrists prefer to talk about psychotics, neurotics, mentally disturbed people, and the like. The lay person calls some people crazy, nuts, bonkers, or by other colorful terms that have no objective correspondence with anything except undesirable behavior. Thomas Szasz (1974), a rather idiosyncratic psychiatrist, prefers to talk only about undesirable behavior—for him there is no such thing as mental illness. But undesirable behavior varies with different people, times, places, and consequences. The young woman who attempted to shoot President Ford was not declared insane and was jailed. Was she less insane than Hinkley? Or just a poorer shot? Since President Ford was not hurt, the undesirable behavior in this case was less serious or important than in Hinkley's case. The terrorist who shot the pope in 1981 did not present a defense of insanity. As far as he was concerned, he was a political prisoner. Other terrorists will probably kidnap someone and demand the release of the pope's assailant as ransom. After all, political activists should not be jailed.

The question of sanity and insanity has become a legal issue on the grounds of *mens rea*. It is not a psychiatric question, for psychiatrists do not worry about questions of right and wrong—for them such questions relate to the outcome of some behavior. Behavior itself cannot be right or wrong. Is it right to apply a lighted match to some combustible material? If it is to start a campfire, yes, to start a fire at an orphanage, no. The psychiatrist is concerned only with the question of why the match was struck, not in terms of intent, but in terms of causes. Was the match striker an only child? Educated? Frustrated? Did she need help? Toward what end? To become a non–match striker? To adjust to her environment? In situations where psychiatrists get involved, someone is acting in a way to displease himself or someone else, be that a single person or a group, or the rest of the world's population. If the psychiatrist has the support of the authorities, she can get the misbehaver into a hospital or her office and proceed to treat him for his mental illness. In the Soviet Union, where the psychiatrist works for the authorities, she can declare anyone who opposes the government mentally ill and have him placed in a hospital for perhaps some different kind of treatment. In either cse the treatments are unlikely to be related to the behavior.

NOTE

1. The age varies in different states. In some states children over 13 can be tried as adults for designated felonies.

12

Crimes and the Law

Psychologists don't know much about crime. It is not an easy area to study considering the kinds of people involved, the places where some kinds of crime predominate (slums and dark streets), and the very definition of crime. Psychologists have left the subject to criminologists, who gather statistics and issue statements such as "Most crime is committed by teenagers" with the implication that once they leave their teens, they also abandon crime.

What constitutes a crime depends on legislative enactments. Breaking a law is a crime, but the same behavior may not be criminal the next day if the law is repealed or amended. The great volume and variety of laws makes a lot of behavior criminal, but criminals commonly take at least minimal precautions about being observed, and psychological study depends upon observation. The only practical method for psychologists to study criminal behavior is *ex post facto* observation of criminals who have been apprehended (a small minority), and such subjects are not inclined to cooperate with psychologists in truth-revealing sessions. Psychologists then proceed to test them and inquire into their parentage. They find that most are below average in intelligence (IQ about 90) and that there is some relationship between crimes committed by parents and crimes committed by their children. Identical twins, for example, are rather more likely to be arrested, at different times, than fraternal twins, and children who are adopted are more likely to be criminals if their biological parents are criminals than if they are not. But such data are not very helpful. The data have been used by James Wilson and Richard Herrnstein (1985) to argue that inherited temperament is related to crime to some extent, and if this is true, one would be left with the problem of determining the temperament of all newborn children and trying to arrange the circumstances of their lives in such a way that the temperament would not be channeled into crime, a rather unlikely enterprise. One can imagine the outrage of parents who are told that their offspring are potential criminals. The fact that we are all potential criminals does not reduce the outrage of any individual singled out as "more likely." Wilson and Herrnstein's finding about IQ might suggest that their sample is limited to those not quite intelligent enough to avoid capture. The number of crimes far outnumbers the number of arrests, to say nothing of convictions, which run about 2 percent of arrests.

Psychologists' difficulties are increased by the fact that prisons include all kinds of criminals sentenced to various lengths of stay. What might be more suitable would be to have specialized prisons, one for those convicted of premeditated murders, one for rapists, one for burglars, and so on. In that way a reasonable sample of current malefactors might be available, for crimes perpetrated years before may have been influenced by factors that are no longer viable. The problem is, of course, that no two crimes are alike although they are classified as the same. A murder during the holdup where the victim tries to take some kind of defensive action is different from a wife slowly poisoning her husband or a husband killing his wife in a drunken rage. True, homicides are classified in various ways, but people who oppose executions, for example, on the grounds that they do not deter murders do not know how many murders might be prevented if executions were restricted to those who planned their killings. No one has statistics of this kind.

THE CAUSES OF CRIME

With so many different kinds of behavior qualifying as crimes, infractions, misdemeanors, and felonies of various degrees, the notion that there are common causes of crime becomes rather amorphous. One might as well look for common causes of accidents. No two crimes or accidents are exactly the same. Despite the lack of evidence, crime is normally associated with poverty, although most poor people do not commit crimes for which they are arrested. Some poor people do commit some kinds of crime, but so do rich people, including stock exchange presidents. The frequency of teenage crime as studied by Wilson and Hernstein cannot lead to any serious conclusion about either teenagers or crime. We have no idea how many teenagers actually commit crimes. Those who are not caught cannot be studied. As I noted above, age has little to do with crime, although one might be safe in concluding that few people over the age of 80 are arrested with any frequency. Age, however, is not a factor that can lead those concerned with crime to any action.

Some attempts at broad classification divide crimes into those that involve violence and those that do not. Some crimes are labeled white-collar; others are victimless. Such labels are less than helpful. If behavior is to be studied, it must be identified by some measurable parameters, and the color of a collar is probably not a relevant feature of criminal behavior. The possibility of a victimless crime is probably whimsical prose because the propriety of legal action where no one is hurt should be questioned. Recreational drug users support drug pushers who provide addicts with life-destroying materials.

In the United States, with 50 separate legislatures deciding upon what is criminal, one should expect problems. Motorists who do not fasten seat belts are lawbreakers in some states but not in others. In some states children of 11 can be tried for murder; in others they are sent home to mommy or become wards of the state. In Nevada, prostitution is merely good business. The psychologists who would study crime must recognize that there is no such thing as crime. There are only crimes of different kinds and levels of disturbance of the peace, and each kind must be analyzed as to such factors as when, where, what, who, to whom, and why. To these questions one might add such queries as how often a given individual has been involved and whether the crime could be repeated. The practice of letting off first offenders should be questioned since it is probably as misnomer that should be translated into "first arrests." With such background information one could then proceed to query parentage, economic bckground, education, intelligence, temperament, and so forth. the variety of answers from such an inquiry would force the psychologist into increasingly specific probing. As an example, we might suggest that running a stop sign, for example, would probably force multiple inquiries such that a psychologist who hoped to get some meaningful information might have to select a specific stop sign in a specific city, a specific hour of the day, specific vehicles—for example, trucks of a certain tonnage—drivers of specific age groups and sex, hours driven, hours to be driven, driving, history, and perhaps some other variables. There is no single cause of a crime. The causes are as multiple as the behaviors and the perpetrators.

WHO ARE THE CRIMINALS?

The public in general appears to think that there are certain people who are criminals and others who are not. From this viewpoint all that needs to be done is to eliminate, in one way or another, the criminal groups, and thereby put a stop to crime. The problem, of course, is with the identifiction of criminal classes. In earlier times, some criminologists, for example, Cesare Lombroso, hoped to find some kinds of physical stigmata, such as large ears, that would mark the criminal type. More recent suggestions link possession of two y chromosomes in males with criminal tendencies. This would not account for female criminals. Most recently Wilson and Herrnstein have suggested that inherited temperament, linked with low IQ, would account for much of teenage crime. Wilson and Herrnstein (1985), of course, recognize the importance of environmental factors, economic status, and education, which merely complicates the problem. Their basic assumption of the inheritance of temperament (aggressiveness) may be valid, but only by a stretch of the imagination can one describe all crime as aggressive. Much crime is just ordinary business such as some state governors engage in without a trace of aggression in any biological sense. The probability is, of course, that inherited aggressiveness is normally distributed, and much aggressiveness has other outlets. It is more likely that everyone is a potential criminal. Certainly it is possible for almost anyone to strike terror in the hearts of others on occasion, and we may all be potential terrorists, given appropriate circumstances. In most cases people do not have the need to express their basic temperamental characteristics in criminal ways. Some of us do not sense the need to be agressive because our needs are met more effectively by noncriminal actions.

Over 60 years ago, Hartshorne and May (1927) reported on a series of *Studies of Deceit* done with schoolchildren. The conclusions they arrived at were that most children would lie, cheat, or steal, given the opportunity and the expectation of getting away with it. Not all children would do all of these things, but most would do one or another. Smart children might not need to cheat on tests, and wealthy children might not need to steal pennies, but there was enough of such petty crime among the children for the authors to imply that given the appropriate opportunities and conditions, everyone is a potential malefactor.

Humans do differ in their genetic equipment, and their environments range across wide extremes, but the notion that criminality is confined to some special segment of the population that could be identified at birth or from some kinds of test scores is at best naive. When we find crime among the pillars of society ranging from members of Congress, cabinet secretaries, governors, managers of huge financial empires, stock exchange members, and chiefs of state such as Stalin, Hitler, and Idi Amin to just about every other profession and social class including clergymen, judges, doctors, lawyers, and college professors, we might as well cease the search for the criminal type: ordinary husbands and wives kill each other and their babies. The girl next door cannot be trusted to baby-sit with 100 percent confidence. Radio announcers rob banks and business people rip off their customers while the customers try to do the same. Shopkeepers cannot trust employees, who supplement their wages by walking off with the merchandise.

Ignoring for the moment the notion that anyone might commit a crime under some circumstances, some crime prevention experts believe that much crime is committed by a relatively small populatioin of professional criminals whose daily business it is to operate in a criminal fashion. Such a population includes what is called organized crime and so-called hardened criminals who regularly and routinely engage in holdups, burglaries and other kinds of robbery, peddle drugs, run prostitution rings, and so on. One burglar might, for example, break into dozens, if not hundreds of homes or business establishements before being caught. He would then be charged with the crime for which he was arrested and might be treated lightly for a first offense. If such professional criminals could be apprehended and hailed, a great proportion of crime might be prevented. Some police authorities urge concentration on such repeaters as the more effective road to crime prevention, and they may be correct. It is also the case tht professional criminals are usually careful about their operations and make the task of arresting and jailing them very difficult. They and their lawyers take every precaution against failure.

It is also a fact that most crime reported to the police is perpetrated by teenagers. The teenages, however, grow up, push drugs, pimp, and steal, and some become specialists in burglary, loan sharking, or any of the vast panorama of criminal behavior. The only people who do not commit crimes are those who do not need to, are afraid to, or have acquired some strong moral code that excludes such behavior. But even among this last group, circumstances may change enough to justify to some the perpetration of "righteous" crimes, or unrighteous ones, for that matter. Some television evangelists have been exposed in unsavory relationships. The Holocaust in Germany is just an illustration of what fine, ordinary, law-abiding, industrious, educated, and cultured people can do. Hitler loved children and Wagner. Other Nazis loved children, Bach, and Beethoven.

PUNISHMENT

Reference has been made above to the prevalence of punishment in both the general animal kingdom and the human realm. Punishment is so common as to be familiar to everyone. Punishment is administered by parents, teachers, peers, governments—and by strangers, as in the countless muggings, assaults, rapes, and threatening letters from lawyers or the IRS. "Spare the rod and spoil the child" is hardly ever questioned. Punishment takes many forms, from inflicting bodily pain, to isolating people (putting them someplace where they do not want to be), depriving them of worldly goods or privileges, even loud noises in the form of verbal abuse. Even the threat of punishment is a form of punishment. In general, punishment amounts to some form of aversive treatment. Punishment of criminals only follows punishment their victims received.

When punishment is administered by the law we may well wonder why, and why it takes the forms that it does. The commonly cited reasons for punishment cover a broad range of motives, and when someone is punished legally, different people can take some satisfaction from the punishment for different reasons. Among the motives for punishment, we have the three Rs of Revenge, Retaliation, and Rehabilitation. Revenge is a personal motive arising from some personal philosophy of getting even. Retaliation may appear to be the same, but it may have some loftier philosophical or religious origin based in some belief that something like justice exists somewhere (perhaps as a goddess), which requires a balance among things—thus a wrong must be corrected by a right or there will be some kind of earthly imbalance. People who have not been personally affected by a crime may feel that a criminal deserves punishment because of what she did. She benefited, therefore she must pay. Rehabilitation or reform is a higher aspiration of some people who believe that a period of time in detention will result in some kind of change. The prisoner can ponder her evil ways and arrive at new decisions. She may be helped by counselors, teachers, productive labor, and so on. Actually, the rehabilitation view is no longer held strongly by criminologists, who take account of the high level of recidivism. Many prisoners have been in prison before and are likely to return. Whatever else they may learn, they may also lezrn new methods of becoming more successful criminals, new ways to avoid capture, new kinds of criminal behavior, and acquire new, and necessarily criminal friends. Hardly anyone today believes that criminals will emerge from prison as somehow better citizens.

A commonsense motive for punishment of any kind is the assumption that the punished person will stop doing whatever he is being punished for. The motive here might be labeled prevention. Putting someone in jail does prevent him from committing some kinds of crime. He can hardly steal women's purses or rob banks.

Prevention of repetition of some behavior can also be thought of as deterrence.[1] Certainly the one being punished is being deterred from repeating the crime if the punishment is effective or at least while the punishment is being applied. Washing a child's mouth with soapy water may very well prevent or deter him from using dirty language while the mouth is full of water. Skinner takes a dim view of the effectiveness of such preventive practices. Children whose mouths are washed out are not necesarily going to use only polite language in the future. In the laboratory, rats that are shocked after pressing levers that previously provided food pellets will also stop pressing the lever for a while. Sooner or later, however, they return, and, if the pressing is no longer punished, they keep on pressing as if the shock incident never happened. Skinner argues that punishment in this form is meaningless and ineffective. On the human level punishment (aversive treatment) will also led to unpleasant social relations between punisher and punished—children can come to hate punitive parents, for example. Criminals are unlikely to have any respect for the law or its representatives.

The prevention motive has been extrapolated by some into a more general deterrent function. It is argued that punishment provides examples that warn the rest of us to behave ourselves or we'll get the same punishment. Opponents of capital punishment argue that such deterrence does not really work, that just as many murders are committed whether there is capital punishment or not. The statistics in such arguments are usually rather sketchy and perhaps not suitably evaluated. Many muruders occur in the home, the most popular locus for murder, and are the consequence of emotional disturbances, drunken assaults, violent actions where murder was not necessarily the object but only the unfortunate consequence. No one should expect that murders resulting from strong emotional disturbance could be deterred—in such cases murder is not necessarily the intent. Executing a wife murderer may have no deterrent effect on others. Murders committed during other crimes might well be reduced if the criminals involved considered the possibility of execution if caught. In any case, the argument that punishment of some does not deter others cannot be evaluated. No one knows how many people have not committed some kinds of crime out of fear of apprehension and punishment. Certainly automobile drivers slow down on the highway when they see another motorist flagged down by the police or even if they see a police officer. With an adequate police force patrolling all possible crime areas, deterrence could be very potent. Do we want a policeman on every corner?

If the motive for punishment is revenge or retaliation, one can hardly argue that punishment doesn't work. It may not satisfy some injured party completely if the criminal is sentenced to four years instead of life, but to the extent that any punishment is given, it obviously works. Some vengeance has been attained.

The theory of general deterrence, as I suggested above, has rather dubious support. One has to assume that the example of others being punished will be effective on those who have not been treated in the same way. Examples, however, abound on the other side, where criminals who are guilty get off through legal tricks, as when a truck driver who is carrying a load of drugs is stopped on suspicion and a search of the truck is delayed for some reason. Lawyers can cite the delay as improper police procedure and find a judge who will agree and dismiss the charge, even though the truck was loaded with drugs. Obviously guilty criminals can be released if they have not been read their rights. Wealthy or otherwise powerful criminals frequently get off with little or no punishment and serve as counter examples for the deterrence function. The problem with the deterrence hypothesis is that it cannot be evaluated. Most people do not commit crimes. Is it because they are deterred by knowledge of what happened to others? How many people would rob a bank if they thought they could get away with it? Do people stop at traffic lights because of some fear of arrest, or do they stop because they have come to appreciate that it is probably wiser to stop than risk a collision? In the latter case, there is also a kind of deterrence operating that is not in the nature of a legal deterrent.

Whatever the motive for punishment, it is clearly a common practice in all cultures to impose consequences on those who violate mores, morals, or laws from disapproval to execution or exile. The costs involved in carrying out programs of punishment are often enormous—if the punishment involves sending someone to a prison where the annual expenses are greater than those involved in sending a student to Harvard. The subject bears examination. We might best reexamine the various motives.

Revenge or retaliation amounts to an aggression generated by frustration. When someone interferes with our lives by presenting obstacles to our freedom of movement and going about our business, it is apparently quite natural for us to be annoyed. The more important our goals and the stronger the obstacles, the greater our annoyance, from mild disapproval to explosive anger. If we are unable to remove the obstacle (the frustrator), we call upon additional help (friends, family, police) and want something done about the frustrator. If we have been trained to follow Old Testament advice, we might demand an eye for an eye. We might want the frustrator to suffer as we did, at least. We want to get even. The origin of the common desire to get even is obscure, but its prevalence is readily acknowledged. In the clan warfare of the Kentucky hills, "if they shoot one of ours, we shoot one of theirs." Getting even is another form of trying to restore our own balance, recouping our losses, getting back to where we were before we were frustrated. This is sometimes quite impossible. How can a girl who is raped get even with the rapist? She can't rape him. The getting even then takes other forms, but no form can actually fit the crime. Whatever form the punishment takes, it will have to be other than even. Over long periods of time social forces have established that where compensation cannot be even and direct, the criminal should be removed from the scene, incarcerated in some building (now euphemiustically called a correctional institution) for some length of time. Whatever the time, it cannot possible be "even." Many violations of federal law carry the punishment of a year in prison, the only rational explation being that a year is a recognized unit of time. Different people react to the notion of a year in jail differently, and for some even a day in jail or the simple exposure to the public of the fact that one is a criminal might cause far more suffering than that undergone by some victim. In the case of federal crimes, such as income tax cheating, the victim can hardly be said to suffer at all, for there is no individual victim, and the cost of the crime is spread over millions of people in an unnoticeable way in the case of any one cheater. The average taxpaying citizen is unaware of any pain from the crime and can hardly be said to be compensated by the imprisonment.

In any case there is nothing natural about punishment as a function of someone's frustration. The aggression generated by frustration is not naturally accompanied by any desire for revenge—it is normally a blind hitting out at the obstacle, an effort to remove the obstacle, an immediate, uncontrolled reaction, and any subsequent explanations of why one wants someone else punished is a function of individual training. In some religions people are urged to turn the other cheek, to forgive their frustrators, to be patient, even to suffer quietly. Revenge must be put down as a rationalization based on acquired beliefs about how one gets along in this world.

The rehabilitation motive has suffered a loss of support over the years because of the high rates of recidivism. As I suggested earlier, people do learn new things in prison, to be sure, and they are frequently alleged to become better criminals. In some cases prisoners do get some additional noncriminal education, even college degrees, and some may avoid future conflicts with the law. If some people have not managed to get an education before prison, there might be that justifiction for prison. One would want to be sure they were there long enough to get a useful education. People who are already educated might not be good candidates for prisons in any sense.

We come back to deterrence, but only from the point of view of the criminal. A person in jail is not in a position to commit a lot of crimes; there are still criminal opportunities in jail, but they involve other inmates and are not generally of interest to the public. Prison does deter the criminals who are in prison, and the longer they are there, the longer they are deterred. The question is, then, Is imprisonment the best, most cost-effective way of preventing crime?

Note that prisons, reformatories, and similar places of detention are relatively new, only a few centuries old. It is true that kings and other nobles had dungeons in their castles or sent undesirables "to the tower," but these were only temporary storage places for captives for whom ransom was to be demanded or for whom no final disposition had been decided. Russia always had Siberia as a reception center for criminals; France had Devil's Island; Britain had Australia. William Penn, in establishing Pennsylvania, also established penitentiaries, where transgressors could be sent to meditate upon their sins and do penance of some sort. Penn's prisoners were sinners who had to come to see the light. The practice of building establishments to warehouse criminals, then, is not something that has been around as long as humanity and must be recognized as an attempt at solving the problem that is very costly, not very efficient, and not especially effective. There are not even any standard rules of what should be done with people who are incarcerated. Some prisons are like country clubs; others are unpleasant and miserable places. No one knows what prisoners are entitled to, how they should be treated, or what can be done to them. Different prisons have different rules.[2] Some allow conjugal visits, some permit homosexuals to share cells, some permit work leaves of various kinds. Others favor isolation, few visits, and censored mail. To prisoners it makes a big difference where they are sent. Probably all would favor being sent to the federal prison that once housed a former attorney general.

I note in passing that some countries have little use for prisons and prefer other means of deterrence. In Moslem countries, for example, a pickpocket may have his hand cut off. That appears to be a rather direct form of deterrence for that kind of crime. Flogging, the stocks, fines, or civic duties are alternatives that have been and are practiced. In any case, prisons are not a natural and necessary form of handling criminals, and alternatives could be explored.

From the viewpoint of psychology there is no question that crimes do occur—that is, some people inflict damage on the body or property, including the reputation, of others. Over the centuries a body of law— that is, statements defining such damage as criminal, intolerable, and to be compensated for—has emerged. People who perpetrate criminal acts, if apprehended and found guilty according to society's rules, are to be labeled as criminals, and something must be done to or with them. The question is, What?

Clearly, the question of what to do with criminals has never been answered in any logical way and certainly not in any way consistent with what psychology might endorse. To send someone to a place of incarceration for either a fixed period or for some indeterminate time has no justification whatsoever and represents only a failure to arrive at a meaningful answer. It will be recalled that in earlier times people who could not pay their debts were also sent to prison, where their inability to pay only increased. Obviously, if someone is either to pay his debts or to compensate a victim, he should not be locked up in some place where he cannot acquire funds or have opportunities to provide compensation. He is sometimes said to be paying his debt to society by doing time, but in most cases it was not society that he injured but some individual, who is not compensated in any way by the time done. In some communities convicted criminals are forced to do some kind of community service. If they sweep the streets or cut grass in public parks, they may be paying society. It would, of course, be more proper for them to work for the victim (without receiving any wage) until the financial loss was made up. If the loss is not financial but of a different nature, for example, rape, the problem of translating the loss into work hours or money would have to be faced.

In ordinary child rearing a lot of punishment is perpetrated on children who displease parents, frequently for quite accidental acts. The presumed purpose of the punishment is deterrence, that is, an attempt to prevent recurrence of the behavior. Sometimes, of course, the punishment occurs from distraction, anger, or other negative origins, and nothing much can be done about such punishment behavior on the part of incompetent parents. If the purpose is to prevent repetition, the approch that is taken by safety engineers with respect to accidents may offer some leads. When automobile accidents occur frequently at an intersection, traffic signals and speed limits are set up and help in the reduction of such accidents. In factories where accidents happen involving machines, the machines are frequently redesigned so that the particular accident cannot happen. Thus, if the operator must place both hands on controls for a machine to operate, she cannot have her hands in some undesirable locus. So with any undesirable behavior: to prevent undesirable behavior, conditions must be arranged so that the behavior cannot occur. This is not always easy or possible, but a child (or adult for that matter) cannot steal money if there is no money around. Women who carry purses slung over one arm can end up purseless. Placing the strap over the opposite shoulder at least increases the difficulty for a purse snatcher. Carrying credit cards instead of money saves one immediate cash losses. Leaving garage doors open is an invitation for visits. What to do about crimes like rape might be a little more difficult. It would be easy enough to prevent future rapes if cruel and unusual punishment were not forbidden by the constitution. Whatever remedies or punishments are devised, they should at least try to ensure that "it can't happen again."

THE LAW AND LAWYERS

Whereas the Ten Commandments have been ascribed to God and some of them have been integrated into the body of written laws in some countries, the laws that are assumed to apply to the citizens of any country are human statements produced by legislators who operate on their own psychologies of human nature. Laws amount to lists of do's and don'ts, but as these lists develop, the legislators have great difficulty in finding just the right words in which to phrase the laws because they recognize ambiguities, mitigating circumstances, contradictory laws previously enacted, and conflicting interests.

In New York State, for example, many people, perhaps a majority, are opposed to something called pornography and feel it should be outlawed, that is, that laws should be passed prohibiting pornography. There are of course some people, perhaps a sizable minority, who do not want to outlaw pornography. Some make a living out of producing it. Others enjoy it. Those who produce it challenge the opponents to define pornography and confront them with a difficult task since the essence of pornography amounts to subjective revulsion at what individuals find indecent, lewd, prurient, objectionable, and the like. The promoters of magazines, films, videocassettes, and other materials that feature explicit sexual activities choose to describe these as artistic or educational or as having some social value. The result is that laws are passed prohibiting pornography, but pornographers continue in business because judges and juries cannot resolve the question of whether something is artistic or indecent.

The complex collections of laws provide many safeguards for presumably innocent people. In the United States anyone accused of anything is presumed innocent until proven guilty beyond a reasonable doubt. In other countries, for example, France, an accused is presumed guilty until proven innocent. With the safeguards (having a lawyer, choice of judge or jury, change of venue, postponements and delays until witnesses die or disappear, among others) many legal actions drag on for long periods, sometimes for years. A murder trial may not begin for years after a suspect is accused. Rules of evidence must be rigorously obeyed, and sometimes obvious criminals are released because some infraction of the law occurred in the process of arrest, arraignment, or trial. Even if there were a precise, agreed-upon definition of pornography, to return to the earlier example, an accused could continue in business for years before anything resembling a final disposition occurred.

In many countries at some point in time some people in a position to do so attempt to spell out the legal philosophy that should prevail. They write a constitution that embodies that philosophy. Any constitution hsa to be rather generally stated because anybody with enough wit to write one also realizes that times change and not every contingency can be foreseen. The result is that a constitution will contain general statements that may make some immediate sense to the framers but decades or centuries later may be open to dispute or interpretation. Again, in some constitutions provision is made to have someone serve as an interpreter. In the United States this function is served by the Supreme Court. The Supreme Court members are appointed by the president, who selects people who he presumes, will follow his own inclinations. Whether or not they will is never known at the time of the appointment. In any case, the Supreme Court does not operate in a vacuum—it listens to lawyers who argue for one interpretation or another. What the court decides then becomes the law.

As an example of how laws are interpreted we can cite the first amendment to the U.S. Constitution. It provides for freedom of religion, speech, and press. The framers were presumably concerned about political freedoms, the right to express opinions on political subjects. By the 1970s, however, some women began to earn their living by standing on bars in taverns and swinging their nude breasts about for the entertainment of the patrons. When some outraged citizens were offended and demanded the arrest of these women, a defense was presented based on the first amendment, which was now alleged to guarantee the right of expression—the breast-swinging dancers were merely expressing themselves artistically, it was asserted, and had every constitutional right to do so. The founding fathers would have been disturbed. This example is chosen to demonstrate that all laws are subject to interpretation and that the business of interpretation is assigned to allotted to, or claimed by lawyers. Lawyers are only people who claim some expertise in the interpretation of the law and who have been licensed to practice this art by governmental agencies. To practice their art, the lawyers must learn the rules incorporated into the law by history, tradition, or custom. In every case that comes before a court, we find, then, an adversarial contest, quite factually a game played by two sides, with lawyers representing the sides whether the case be a criminal one or a civil one. One side is the defendant, or the accused, and the other the plaintiff, or the accuser. The contest begins with a judge (the referee) opening the case and inviting the opposing lawyers to do their best for their side. It should be noted that a lawyer for a defendant or plaintiff need not be concerned with the merits of the case. Her job is to do the best she can for her client. In a criminal case, the lawyer is not concerned with whether or not her client is guilty. She is there to be sure that her client gets a fair trial, that every legal nicety is observed, even if it means the release of an actually guilty client.

In a 1985 case a murderer was tape recorded threatening the victim, who had turned on the recorder when the murderer entered his office. Pistols shots and comments establishing the murderer's guilt were heard. Defense lawyers argued that the evidence was inadmissible because there was a law that forbade tape recording a conversation without informing all participants. In such a case, obviously, the murderer should be found guilty and the victim could also be tried for breaking the recording law. The fact that he was head would not deter some lawyers from both defending and prosecuting him.

Evidence is often excluded because it was obtained illegally. Somehow it has not occurred to lawmakers to pass laws allowing the evidence but punishing the collectors of the evidence if they too behaved illegally. People should not be allowed to get away with a crime if they are actually guilty. If they do, the law loses effectiveness. Every criminal is entitled to the best defense possible, and if convicted can even appeal his case on the grounds that his lawyer was incompetent. In a 1985 case one lawyer appealed a lost case on the grounds that at the time of the trial he was under the influence of drugs and did not handle his client's interests competently. Note that the guilt of the client was not the question. Lawyers are champions fighting for their clients according to certain rules. Since most legislators are lawyers, the rules are written largely by lawyers, and so we have lawyers engaged in a game of their own devising.

At a 1984 American Bar Association meeting, it was decided that lawyers had no responsibility other than that of defending their clients and could not even warn the public of any wrongdoing contemplated by a client unless the act under consideration would result in bodily harm. Lawyers were not obligated to report any other kind of contemplated crime *unless they were not paid*. If paid, they had to keep their mouths shut.

The remarks above were intended to demonstrate only that the laws that people live by are made by people, are sometimes not too clearly understood by many, are subject to interpretation, especially with the passage of time, and in no way represent any kind of appreciation of the nature of human beings based on any scientific observation. As such they should be recognized as verbalizations of those with the power to make such verbalizations about how affairs should be conducted. It is obvious, also, that laws will always be framed to benefit the lawmakers or their clients and supporters, that they will not automatically be accepted or endorsed by everyone and that, in effect, they are made to be broken—otherwise there would be no need for lawyers. Even a law requiring automobile riders to fasten seat belts is not universally approved. Some oppose it because they believe that seat belts do not actually protect people in some kinds of accident; others oppose it because it interferes with their personal liberty. The fact that there is a law about anything indicates that somebody is behaving in a manner someone else does not approve of, or the law would never have been enacted. Some, probably most, legal systems contain provisions that permit the law to be changed by repeal or amendment. These operations take considerable time and effort, but the very existence of legal methods for changing the law suggests that the law is not Holy Writ and should never be regarded as such. For the game of life to be played without undue stress, rules must be established for any community. As in any other game, for example, football, there must be rules or there could be no game. There might be exercise, but no spectators, and the exercise might be rather chaotic. Whenever there are rules, there must be some kind of arbitrator, referee, umpire, judge. In the game of life, in any settled society, one gradually comes to know the rules, and most people observe them or at least want others to observe them. Laws, regardless of how they come into being (dictator's whims, legislators' enactments, town meeting decisions) are usually written statements that are made public in one way or another. With the passage of time some are forgotten but remain on the books unless a "sunset" provision is included. Whatever the law may be, it can be expected that someone will break it, or there would be no point to the law in the first place. What to do with those who break the law becomes the question. In a football game the referee can eject a player for unsportsmanlike conduct if he decides that the player is guilty. In the game of life we encounter problems about who should be the referee, what constitutes guilt, and most importantly, what to do about the guilty ones. They cannot be ejected from that game without a lot of difficulty.

In many communities the question of guilt is decided simply on the basis of an accusation or of a confession extracted by torture. In some crimes, for example, rape, no witnesses may be available since it is in most cases committed in circumstances deliberately chosen to avoid observation. A woman can accuse man of rape or sexual harassment and he may be unable to prove innocence. In one case a woman stated that she accused the wrong man after the man spent seven years in prison. Clearly, in his case, if one assumes that the woman was telling the truth on the second occasion, prison was the wrong punishment. In all cases the question of punishment is a separate issue. The first and perhaps the only function of law might be to establishg guilt. What should be done with a guilty person could then be considered separately as a completely different matter to be decided by others selected for the task. Who these others might be and what their qualifications might be are serious questions that the human race has not yet been able to answer in any meaningful way.

NOTES

1. Legal writers distinguish between specific and general deterrence. The latter refers to deterrence of others who might be tempted to do the same thing.

2. Courts have been trying to establish minimal constitutional standards for prisoners, but there are great differences from state to state.

13

Rights and Civil Liberties

Over 200 years ago, Thomas Jefferson penned the words, "We hold these Truths to be self-evident, that all Men are created equal, that they are endowed by their Creator with certain unalienable Rights, that among these are Life, Liberty, and the Pursuit of Happiness." These resounding words have served to encourage many people not only to assert these rights but also to spell out and specify what they might encompass. The truths mentioned by Jefferson may not appear so self-evident to many others whose objectives are to deny life, liberty, and other pursuits to anyone but themselves. Jefferson himself did not deem it proper to include "all women" or to mention slaves, whom he himself owned. Women and slaves were obviously not men.[1]

It is probably self-evident today that all babies are not born free and equal, nor are they necessarily endowed with any rights at all. Jefferson did mention that the endowment was by their Creator, but many babies around the world die in the process of being born, and some are born with defects or deficiencies, so that any happiness they might pursue and enjoy is dubious. To present-day biologists and psychologists, no babies appear to be born with any rights whatsoever, although some parents are affluent enough to pay for certain priviledges in the care and treatment of their offspring. Other babies are aborted by their mothers, who apparently are exercising some rights to their bodies. Many babies are abandoned in garbage cans or public toilets, and some of these are saved and turned over to social service agencies, which have certain responsibilities.

In the above paragraph the term baby refers to a newborn living individual. Legal arguments have developed over the question of when biological tissue becomes a person. A person is deemed to have constitutional rights, for example, the issuance of a birth certificate. Simply emerging from a mother's body does not create personhood. The product could be called a fetus if aborted or premature. Congress and the courts are still undecided about when a fetus becomes a person or a baby.

Despite Jefferson's words, it appears that George III did not agree with them and sent an army over the ocean to deny the proclaimed rights. American colonists then fought off the Redcoats, and the rights became theirs. It appears to be the same with any matter of rights. One has those rights that one is powerful enough to exercise.

In the United States some people are elected to serve as lawmakers and declare what is legal and what is not legal, that is, what is a right and what is not a right. In times of peace, for example, no American citizen has the right to kill another citizen or even an illegal immigrant.[2] In other countries and at other times, monarchs, dictators, or *Führers* had the right to cut off heads of wives or anyone else they thought merited such treatment or to send thousands, even millions of people to gas chambers. At least nobody stopped them from such deeds, and so they must be presumed to have had the right to do what they did.

At the present time in many countries, some people are kidnapped, tortured, killed, or sent into one form or another of slave labor. Other people are bombed or otherwise killed by terrorists, who call themselves freedom fighters or revolutionaries. The perpetrators of these acts insist on their right to inflict any kind of injury on their victims, who apparently do not have any rights; at most the right to resist is the only one left, even if their ability to resist is effectively zero. When President Carter framed his foreign policy, he made it a point to have no dealings with countries that did not demonstrate that they honored human rights. These rights were never spelled out by the president, but they could be assumed to be such as are enjoyed by the citizens of the United States. Rulers of other countries took the position that no one had the right to tell them how their countries should be ruled, and not much came of the policy. Certainly human rights throughout the world have not increased.

What are human rights? As I stated earlier, rights are only legally recognized powers or privileges that have been enacted by legislators and are more or less accepted by the citizenry of a country. In Iran women have the right to wear black gowns and more or less stay out of sight. Similarly in Saudi Arabia, women have the right to stay indoors and keep their faces covered when men are around. Girls growing up in such countries presumably get used to certain practices and behave in accordance with the rules that govern them. Some of the women probably approve of their status and would resist interference with what has become tradition (a tradition with a power behind it that would enforce it if needed).

In the United States the word *right* has become a shibboleth for anything anyone happens to want. Unemployed people demand, as a right, support (rent, food, utilities) from the government. In the United States this right has been recognized by the states with different degrees of generosity. Some people, for reasons of religion or other beliefs, demand the right of fetuses to be carried to full term and to be born. Some women demand the right to abort unwanted babies. Hunters demand the right to shoot animals, and farmers demand the right to post land to prevent trespassing. Both rights exist as a matter of law. Bird lovers demand the right to protect eagles, and conservationists demand the right to protect plants, fish, forests, and so on. Some of these rights become encted into law and can be said to exist as legal rights. Societies are formed to create rights for animals, children, the retarded, and the sick, among others. The kinds of rights vary from the right of children not to be spanked to the right of high school students not to be searched or have their lockers searched for weapons or drugs, even though the schools are operating in loco parentis and are trying to protect the rights of other students. In 1984 the Supreme court ruled that school authorities have the right to search students if they have reasonable grounds.

Laws in general are two-edged: they grant privileges or rights to some and prohibit some kinds of activity that legislators regard as not in the public interest. Thus a driver's license gives one the right to drive a car, but laws against speeding or parking in certain places deny certain desires. Not all human activity has been legislated for or against, although that situation is approaching. In New York, for example, some 900 new laws are enacted every year. Laws tell saloon keepers how long they can stay open and whether or not they can give free drinks or serve drinks at lower prices during certain hours. At the rate of 900 laws a year, one can anticipate that someday laws will define just about everything a human may do.

CIVIL LIBERTIES

At the present time some activities are not subject to legal control. No laws tell one when one must be in bed (although in the military and prisons even this activity is controlled). No laws tell us to shave or not to shave, to get a haircut, or to drink tomato juice every morning. Where no laws have been established, a person may behave in certain ways without any restriction, but not necessarily without disapproval from some. In short, in the United States, and presumably everywhere else, some behaviors are not, as yet, legislated against or proscribed. These behaviors come under the heading of civil liberties.

Before the late 1980s people who smoked tobacco did so almost anywhere they chose to do so. Occasional "No Smoking" signs might inhibit some smokers. Smoking was a civil liberty. As the decade drew to a close, various local and state officials passed laws prohibiting smoking in some public places. Smoking was no longer a broad civil liberty. It had become a non-civil right in some areas. Similar efforts are being developed to restrict drinking of alcoholic beverages at football games. Drinkers are to be segregated from certain sections in a stadium.

With a permit, Ku Klux Klansmen may parade through a city—that is a civil right. People not in sympathy can practice whatever civil liberties they enjoy to protest, boo, and harass the paraders short of inflicting bodily harm. Civil rights and civil liberties thus can come into conflict and lead to more legislation.

No psychological investigation has demonstrated that anyone has any rights at all as a function of birth. On the contrary, the human child is by nature restricted by its weakness, small size, lack of experience, and general incapacity, is kept under the control of adults for many years, in most cases through the teens, and begins to get some rights only at age 18 or 21.

Children have been endowed by courts and legislators with the right to be treated as children in cases where they have committed crimes, including murder and arson. Up to the age of 16 in many states a child can get way with almost any crime, including murder, with minimum punitive action. After 16 he loses those rights and becomes subject to other people's rights to try him as an adult. At 18 a child can vote in federal elections even though he may be illiterate and has no conception of what the election is all about. He has the right to vote. At 18 also, he is subject to the draft in cases of national emergency if a draft procedure is enacted. Some states allow an 18-year-old to purchase alcohol. Others say 19, and still others deny anyone the right to purchase alcohol. Note that the right to drink is usually not involved. That is a matter of civil liberties of children and parents.

When there are no facts, biological or otherwise, to support verbal statements, any concept of rights becomes merely a matter of verbal statements some of which become enacted into law and become civil rights. But even then the behaviors involved only amount to what can be enforced by one's own power, aided, if legal, by police forces should they choose to participate. One has the right, if one cares to exercise it, to walk the streets of any city at night unless there is a curfew. So with any other right. At any moment what has been a right can be taken away by legislators. The civil liberty of driving a car without strapping oneself in with a seat belt has become a non–civil right in some states that have enacted laws gainst such motorists.[3] Rights are simply a matter of power and people interested in certain rights must concern themselves about how to get them enacted into law and then about enforcement.

What one country has to say about human rights in other countries is basically reduced to what power the asserting country has over the other. Obviously, if one country is dependent upon another, its legislature will enact appeasing laws. How they will be enforced is another question. Some groups, including psychological associations, try to exert pressure on states to enact laws relating to womens' rights by not holding conventions in states that do not cooperate. State legislatures do not appear to be too concerned over such tactics unsupported by more effective power. In some countries, including the United States, the slogan "Might makes right" has occasionally been announced. Though the slogan may be offensive to some, it happens to be as true as any statement that could be made about behavior.

As an illustration of the problem of rights, consider the conflict now raging in the United States about abortion, currently a legal right. The conflict is actually about a right to privacy, not a right to abort. The war of words goes on between suporters of abortion (the prochoice or free-choice group) and those opposed to it (the prolife group).

The sociologist Kristin Luker (1986) analyzes the conflict between prolife groups and free-choice groups as a difference between those women who enter the job market (for whatever reason) and those who do not. The latter stay home and raise their children, well or poorly, and place a value on motherhood. Without that value they allegedly would feel useless, worthless, little more than kept women. The working woman cannot afford to have children interfering with her economic progress. All other arguments advanced by either group in support of their position are irrelevant, immaterial, and inconsequential rationalizations. Luker does not appear to appreciate the importance of religious beliefs, which motivate many prolife supporters.

Orginally the abortion question was raised by doctors who wanted to get rid of quacks and midwives who were cutting into what the doctors felt was medical practice. Abortions were legal if performed to save the prospective mother's life or for other therapeutic reasons. These reasons were later expanded to include mental stress resulting from the prospective birth of a deformed child; Ronald Reagan, as governor, signed the California law permitting such abortions, and there was a 2000 percent increase in therapeutic abortions in California after 1967. Doctors were in the lead in increasing the abortion business until the number of abortions grew so great as to become socially noticeable. In 1973 the Supreme court decided that fetuses were not persons and therefore not under the protection of the fourteenth amendment, and abortions became available upon demand.

Luker points out that the prochoice group does not consist of welfare recipients or unwed teenagers who might have a practical interest in abortion and who do account for a large percentage of abortions. It consists of upper-middle-class women who have embarked on what formerly were masculine careers. The prochoice spokeswomen are largely those who are concerned about social and economic equality with men. To acquire and preserve such equality, they cannot be hampered by unwanted pregnancies. (With their obvious intellectual gifts, such women should be able to practice effective birth control.) According to Luker, prolife women are largely lower-middle-class housewives with husbands in less than professional jobs—for them abortion is an affront to their dignity and responsibility, their very worth as individuals, "indeed, the only resource on which they can confidently trade in their relations with their husbands and the outside world." "If motherhood is no longer sacred, then their lives are effectively worthless."[4]

The companion issue to abortion is that of capital punishment. Consistency might require that those who are opposed to abortion also oppose executions. this is not always the case and, again, a variety of rationalizations can be developed to bolster one's stand.

The question of the worth of Luker's findings may well be raised. Obviously, prolifers will not read the book and would only be offended if they did. Career women are too busy to read it, and unwed welfare mothers couldn't care less about sociological findings. The point is that nothing is done about undesired pregnancies by those who get into such a state except for abortions, legal or illegal, competent or incompetent. Birth control measures may be undertaken by governments such as that of China, which currently approves only of one-child families to stem its overwhelming population. What form punitive measures may take remains to be seen. Males and females will continue to engage in sexual practices as they have done from the beginning of human existence. The outcome of these practices will create social problems for some countries, although the social problems are primarily economic ones.

Underlying the prochoice-prolife debate is the weightier question of why people have children. For a long time in human development it must have been the case that there was no awareness of the biological facts of life. Sexual intercourse was presumably a matter of drives. The arrival of children must have been a deep mystery. When appreciation of the consequences of intercourse did develop, so did new questions. What to do about pregnant women whose condition put restrictions on their activities? What to do with the offspring? Observation of animals in a similar condition might have led to some analogous caring behavior. The long infancy period created other problems. The usefulness of children in helping out around the cave might have been considered as a plus. The eventual development of the concept of immortality through one's progeny might have played some role. Reluctance to part with one's property on the "you can't take it with you" rationalization may have been a consideration. The ancient Egyptian kings tried to take it with them, but tomb robbers foiled them in most cases. In time it became accepted custom for some men to control some women long enough to acquire a collection of children and to pride themselves on their progeny. The development of monogamy and stable marriages eventually led to relatively smaller families (as the medical problems of infant survival were solved) so that in some cultures, as in the United States, it became customary for young men to marry young women and expect to have a family in due course. Homosexuals of either sex avoided these family problems, and some of both sexes did not marry for various reasons. In any case, once marriage is undertaken, the question of whether or not to have children arises, and no obvious reasons can support or refute the decision made, if it is indeed raised as a question. Many children are accidents in the sense that the question was never raised prior to intercourse, which may have taken place in a drunken stupor, as a result of inflamed passions, as rape, or as seduction.

Once pregnancy is established, the question of allowing it to continue can be raised by those who recognize that it is a terminable condition. Since the outcome includes a variety of unknowns (What sex will it be? Will it be normal? Will it be smart? Will it be talented?), the question is not trivial. What about the ability of the mother (age, strength, financial position) to care for the child? Will there be a father around to help with expenses, care, education? In some countries the question of legitimacy may have to be considered. In some marriages the question of who the father is may also come into question, for not all wives are faithful.

Eventually the decision is always made by the prospective mother in terms of the forces, pressures, and reinforcement history she has undergone. Because each pregnancy is an individual affair, no general rules, laws, programs, propaganda, education, or anything else will be universally effective, for each reinforcement history is different. Psychologists cannot help. In short, there is no solution to the problem of women becoming pregnant and probably no scientific solution to whether or not one should allow the pregnancy to continue to its natural conclusion. There is not even an answer to whether one should try to have children or not. Homosexuals have a built-in answer. Heterosexuals do not.

NOTES

1. Slaves were considered 3/5 of a person for purposes of enumeration for representation.

2. Except for executioners. Police officers must prove they were in mortal danger, as do citizens pleading self-defense if they kill someone.

3. The issue becomes complicated by licensing procedures, which make driving a car a privilege instead of a right.

4. Paul Robinson, *New York Times Book Review*, May 6, 1984.

14

Schools and Learning

From the "whining school-boy, with his satchel, . . . creeping like snail unwillingly to school," to the secretary of education, we hear complaints about education. Pundits, parents, and pupils all complain—they find fault with schools, teachers, courses, and educational programs. Such complaints are not new—Socrates complained about the youths of his day, and educational reformers and critics have always been with us. In modern, more democratic times, everyone is supposed to get educated, and if some do not turn out knowledgeable, sophisticated, financially successful, and socially respectable, we find fault with their upbringing, their education, their teachers. Most commonly education is identified with what is supposed to go on in the public schools. One does not hear much about possible weaknesses or problems in private schools or expensive prep schools. Nor do we hear many complaints about specialized schools such as secretarial or barber colleges. It is the public schools tht take the great brunt of the criticism.

Ever since the Soviets launched their Sputnik into the skies, great concern has been voiced bout weaknesses in the educational system of the United States. Suddenly it appeared that Johnny could not read, write, or do arithmetic, that high school gradutes could not fill out job applications, and that college basketball players who could not make it as professionals were illiterate and unqualified for other vocations. Newspaper pundits demanded that something be done. "Back to basics" became a rallying cry, and teachers began to lose what little respect they might once have enjoyed. No one queried the pundits on how they became so smart. Were they not products of the public schools? Well, yes, but schools had changed—deteriorated, fallen apart—somehow.

By the late 1980s criticism of the schools extended to high schools and colleges. Not only were American youths illiterate and incompetent in mathematics, but they were also abysmally ignorant. They did not know when the Civil War was fought or even that there had been one. Eric Hirsch (1987) and Allan Bloom (1987) became national best-sellers by castigating the educational system that was producing ignoramuses. Hirsch demonstrated that large percentages of students were ignorant of events, names, and words that were necessary background information for comprehending almost any written matter, to say nothing of classical literature. Students might be able to read, that is, pronounce words that appear in print, but they could not appreciate what they were reading. Bloom found his students no longer interested in pursuing the truth or how to lead the "good life." They were victims of a moral disease he identifies with relativism. Interestingly enough, Bloom does not tell us what the "Absolute Goods" are, although he knows that some things are better than others. This might be somewhat difficult to prove. Bloom merely asserts it. Whether or not schools have actually diminished in quality may be difficult to establish. When the pundits went to school, their classmates were pretty much like them—members of the middle or upper middle class. They were not upper-class, or they would not have to be pundits. In the 1930s and 1940s very few young-sters went to high school, and the great northward migration of rural families of the South had not taken place. The invasions by Puerto Ricans and Mexicans with little or no education were yet to come, and the public schools were humdrum processing establishments wherein a teacher's frown was enough to maintain discipline; parents inquired about and helped with homework.

Slowly and apparently imperceptibly the population of students be-gan to change. More and more children were attending school and going on to high school and college. Whether all who were enrolled were qualified to participate in programs such as were the norm in the 1920s, 1930s, and 1940s was not seriously questioned. Difficulties began to appear. Scores in the basic subjects began to fall (Zajonc, 1986) and there was a 15-year progressive drop in SAT scores. High school students began to drop out in increasing numbers and came to be counted as unemployed instead of being placed in some other kind of facility where they might develop some skills that might make them employable.

To learn about what is wrong with the schools, we must look at several aspects of our educational system. What is the purpose of sending children to school in the first place? How is this purpose being approached, that is, what are the means being employed to im-plement the goals? What is the role of teachers? And finally, what are the results?

THE PURPOSE OF EDUCATION

The purpose of education, as any parent will tell you, is to prepare a child for adult life, which will include, for most children, an occupation, a job, some form of employment. Immediately a problem arises: what should *this child* be trained for? Doctor, lawyer, merchant, thief? Unfortunately, no parent is in position to make such a decision on any rational basis. If the father is a farmer or a small businessman, he may hope the child will take over the business; if he is himself unhappily employed, he may want something better for his children; but what? Does the child have any special talents? If so, what are they? How would the average parent know? Let the child become whatever she is good (best) at, but what is that? The problem is that no one knows what the future will bring. Even the son of a king cannot plan on succeeding his father. Witness the Shah of Iran. In the 20 or so years tht it takes to educate a child, many of today's occuptions will no longer exist and new ones may come into being. It is an arrogant parent who will decide a child's future. One may decide that her child will be an Olympic class swimmer and start swimming lessons at age two; another will opt for a Wimbledon winner and have the child on the courts every day from age four. Some may be successful in such ambitions, but the world will decide who will be the stars of the future. The chances of very talented young pianists becoming concert soloists are but one in thousands. Deciding that your child will be a medical doctor depends on the fancies of a medical school admission committee. The simple fact of life is that you don't always get what you want. Problems are sure to follow upon early decisions about careers.

It was not always thus. In ancient times education was designed to prepare the sons of the wealthy for happiness, as Aristotle opined. Happiness would amount to contemplating such matters as the nature of truth and virtue. In John Locke's time, education was a matter of training young men to become gentlemen, and only sons of gentlemen were supposed to undergo such training. Young women need not apply—they could get their education at home because all they had to know could be learned there.

In modern times people have settled for a kind of "let's see what happens" view and hope that if they send their children to school, things will work out for the best. Somehow the child will grow up and find herself, and she will settle for something that will be better than the parents enjoyed.

One other purpose cannot be overlooked. Parents, in general, are commonly too busy earning a living to be able to attend to the education of their children by themselves. It does happen, but rarely, that some parents keep their children out of school and try to teach them all they think they should know. There are legal obstacles to such actions, and most parents do not feel qualified to attend to the business of teaching. They may also see other values in schools, such as socialization, development of friendships, participation in group activities, and so on. But, because of the demands of employment—and this now applies also to many mothers—schools have become not merely convenient but necessary sanctuaries for child care while the parents are working. Some parents are only too happy to get their children out of the house and dread the coming of holidays and vacations. The notion that parents are making use of schools as baby-sitters will be hotly denied by many parents, but the obvious value of such socially acceptable child-care facilities cannot be rejected. Parents who can afford to send their children away from home to a distant college often rationalize the action by claims that the experience is necessary or helpful in developing independence and maturity, when the truth is that they are only too pleased to be relieved of the burden of controlling teenagers. Young mothers cannot wait to place their children in nursery schools on the unfounded rationalization that they will get a head start in a competitive world. Such head starts are probably valuable where children live in poverty or neglect, but psychological evidence seems to weight rather heavily on the side of the argument that it does not make much difference whether children start school at three, four, or even nine. The real issue of importance is that of how the child is nurtured. If the parents are inadequate, some schools may be better caretakers; others may compound the problem.

Whatever reason parents have for sending children to school, it matters greatly what goes on in schools. The reasons and the means may not be in the ideal relationship.

THE SCHOOLS

For whatever historical reasons, most, if not all, schools are operated like factories or business establishments. They receive materials (the pupils or students) and turn out graduates on a time schedule that includes minutes, hours, days, and finally, years. The expression "K–12" covers the educational process from kindergarten through high school. A college curriculum is designed for a four-year program upon the completion of which students are defined as educated regardless of what they have actually learned. The hours of a school day are controlled to some extent by prents, who want their children home "on time." The school week appears to have no use for weekends, and the school year must include vacations. It has been asserted that originally summer vacations were instituted to release children for work on the farm, but that hardly justifies vacations for urban children. State legisltors provide funds for a certain number of school days for students in public schools, and local school systems see to it that only that number of days will be dedicated to education. Economic issues cannot be separated from educational policy. Schools clearly illustrate the adage "you get what you pay for."

The Concept of Classes

When King Phillip of Macedonia desired to have his son, the future Alexander the Great, educated, he hired Aristotle to be his tutor. Presumably there was no finer teacher to be found, and Aristotle taught the young Alexander all he needed to know. Similarily King George VI, facing the problem of educating Princess Elizabeth to become a proper queen, hired tutors for his daughter—different tutors for horsemanship, music, art, French, and other areas suitable for a queen to be educated in. The French tutor was a French Canadian so that the queen would speak French like a Canadian and not like Parisienne. The results can be pronounced admirable since Queen Elizabeth has been an undoubtedly successful monarch. But average parents cannot hire tutors for their children. They send them to school. In school the child finds herself immediately surrounded by other children of about her own age—she is a member of a class. The simple reason for classes is an economic one. Taxpayers will not provide enough funds to engage tutors for individual children. Instead they pay only enough to provide one teacher for a group. The size of the group depends on the size of the school budget and can vary from 5 or 6 handicapped children to 25, 30, or more children assigned to one teacher. Each techer may be responsible for four or five such groups per day, and the business of education becomes inefficient as far as learning is concerned. It has been estimated by B. F. Skinner (1968) and others, that the learning efficiency in schools is about 25 percent of what could be learned by other methods, for example, the use of teaching machines. Studies in Chicago schools suggest that children in groups of 12 in half-day kindergartens learn twice as much as children in groups of 26 learn in full-day kindergartens. That suggests that one can learn about twice as much in half the time if one receives more individual attention.

One of the troubles with schools, then, is the grouping of children in classes. The reason children in groups do not achieve as much as they might if taught individually is twofold: the presence of other children is distracting and interferes with learning; and a teacher working with a class tries to teach a class—an abstract entity. The teacher tries to aim at some hypothetical average child, who does not exist, and so does not provide for the more able children to move ahead and cannot help those who fall behind. The general result is that at the end of the term there is a normal distribution of achievement, with some far ahead and others far behind. Because of other (social) considerations the whole class is passed on to the next grading unit, with those who fell behind now less prepared to go on with advanced work.

The root of the problem is the assumption that all children of the sme age are equally ready to be taught the same material. In short, the children are graded whereas the learning material should be graded. What should be done, and has never been done to any great extent, for any subject matter is to define subject content and arrange it in steps. The subject matter in a course should be subdivided into sections or units, starting with material that is easy to master. As each unit is learned, the student is allowed to proceed to the next unit, which he learns at his own rate. At any given time in any subject area, some students will be at the beginning or early phases while others will be well advanced. Such is the program suggested by Fred Keller (1969) in his Personalized Instruction System. In this system the learners are not graded; the subject matter is. No one proceeds to a later unit before mastering prior units.

In the public schools children are routinely advanced from grade to grade whether they have achieved reasonable amounts of mastery or not. Some are held back (in New York State they may be held back once in the first six grades and once in the seventh or eighth grade). This sets the average age of graduating from the eighth grade at about 14. Compulsory education legally ends at age 16 in most states, which means that many will drop out with one or two years of high school and start being counted as unemployed. With 22 the average age of graduation from college, it might be questioned why 16-year-old dropouts should be counted as unemployed. Who would want to employ someone who probably found the first two years of high school difficult to handle— except for low-paying manual labor? The unemployment rate could be meaningfully reduced if compulsory eduction were extended to 18 or 20. With the explosion of information and technological developments of the last century, it is doubtful that anyone can be seriously educted with even four years of college. The college program could well be increased to eight years if one is to get a meaningful education.

Class Time

For purely administrative reasons classes in schools are arranged to last 50 minutes. To presume tht any specific allotment of time is appropriate for any kind of learning is a gross miscalculation. Studies of laboratory learning have established beyond any question that different people learn in different amounts of time, and providing some fixed interval clearly means that some may have more than enough time while others are still in an earlier stage of mastery. Teachers do attempt to arrange lesson plans so that they will finish in the allotted time, but the question really is, Did the students finish along with the teacher?

The time factor has to be looked at more directly. It takes a certain amount of time for anyone to learn anything, and if insufficient time is allowed, the learning will be incomplete. To set some limit on an exercise—say, a piano lesson that lasts one hour—is simply inane. A lesson should last long enough for some units to be learned. When one considers the number of units involved in acquiring a skill, for example, learning to play tennis, it has been estimated that about 5,000 hours are required for reasonable mastery. No one should be asked to listen to a pianist who has not practiced for at least 5,000 hours unless one is the teacher. To listen seriously to a psychologist who has not put in at least 5,000 hours of study is to hear some rather unqualified opinions. The reference here to 5,000 hours is not meant to be rigid or specific. Individual differences have to be taken into account, but the point might not be made if it was stated simply that one has to study long enough to master a certain unit of material or certain aspects of a skill. No one can spell out the time required for any specific individual. If there are to be classes, they should last as long as necessary for everyone to know all that is expected, whether for five minutes or three hours. No administration would permit such a logical arrangement.

THE EDUCATIONAL MYSTIQUE

It was argued erlier that no one really knows what children should learn or study in schools. On the contrary, it is assumed for no good reason that if one goes to school, everything will work out somehow. When we consider specifics, however, we have to recognize that the greatest flaw in education is that no student ever knows what she is supposed to know or learn or how good she should be at it, whatever it is. Typically the teacher has some idea of what is to be presented. The teacher may have a syllabus and lesson plans. The problem is that the student does not. In some college courses the instructors may distribute some semblance of a syllabus describing the course, but the syllabus is usually not sufficiently detailed for students to discover precisely what they are supposed to know. At the grade school and high school level, such a practice is relatively unheard of. In many college courses the instructor may have no fixed program and may present what occurs to him at the moment.

Two examples of a more appropriate educational procedure are in order. In New York and other states, a person may wish to obtain a license to operate a motor vehicle. She applies at an office and is handed a manual that contains the questions she may be asked in a written test.

The manual also contains the answers. She will also be required to take a road test, and the maneuvers involved in the road test will also be described. In short, the candidate is told precisely what she has to know. Furthermore, she is privileged to take the test as often as necessary to pass. A newspaper story told of a woman in England who took the test 123 times. It may not be a true story but it makes the point. People should be allowed to take a test as often as needed—she might have to pay for extra opportunities. In the case of driving license tests, she has to pay for all opportunities.

Another example comes from the Boy Scouts. To become a tenderfoot a boy must, among other things, tie nine specific knots. Not ten or eight or seven, but nine. He can find the knots described in his manual and can seek all the help he needs, but he must tie those nine knots or he cannot become a tenderfoot. Similarly with the other grades in scouting. The requirements for each merit badge are detailed, and suitable sources are provided. A boy knows what he has to know. In the schools, however, students gather that they are supposed to know something about geography and arithmetic, but never exactly what. Teachers and administrators defend themselves by arguing that if pupils knew what they had to know, they would learn only that much and not reach out beyond what was required. They do not appear to recognize that more can be required as each unit is mastered. It will be gathered from the above discussion that somehow going through school under the guidance of teachers will result in an education. Teachers, in general, are regarded as those who know something and will pass on this knowledge, somehow. It is this *somehow* that we must now examine.

THE TEACHERS

Who are the teachers to whom youngsters are entrusted? In most states they are people who have gone through some sort of program in a school of education, where they passed courses that were designed to prepare them to teach. Whether such courses actually have any value or not has never been determined. There are literally no criteria by which teacher effectiveness can be appraised. Pundits cry for better teachers and propose merit raises or salary adjustments for the better teachers, but teachers themselves oppose such programs—they know, if no one else does, that there are no meaningful yardsticks by which the quality of a teacher can be measured. If anyone is singled out as better, the rest must accept the impl* iction that they are worse or at least not as good. Such appraisals are not welcome in any field. It is a recognized fact that students who elect education courses in college are not generally the highest scorers on college aptitude tests. The critics keep proposing that better students be selected as potential teachers. This would only mean that we would then have poorer students in engineering, medicine, law, and so forth. There is no evidence that even poor graduates of education courses are necessarily poor teachers. The problem is not with the teachers; it is with what teachers do. It is time to examine the function of teachers.

The Role of Teachers

We can ignore the many nonteaching aspects of a teacher's job, such as standing guard in a bathroom, trying to maintain discipline in a classroom, looking out for the welfare of unhappy children, and look at teachers only when they are teaching. What do they do? They talk, more or less endlessly. They ask questions. They write on blackboards, and they sometimes demonstrate something. Some of them assign homework. It is highly likely that only this last activity results in anything like learning. When a student does homework, she is at least by herself, not in a group of distractors. She may have help from parents or friends, but if she does seek help, it is for a specific purpose. She is trying to get an answer to some question or problem. If she is merely listening to a teacher talk, she may hear something stated, usually once, although some teachers do repeat and force students to repeat some things, but she may or may not be interested in what the teacher is saying. She may be interested in how the teacher is saying it or acting at the time. Talking or lecturing is not a very effective teaching method.

With the advent of radio and, later, television, some people had high hopes that great teachers would be able to teach millions at a time. Today it is unlikely that anyone would assert that anything like that has happened. True, children watching television may learn how to commit crimes (not too precisely), but television lectures or educational programs that do not repeat some small units of material often enough to be learned are at best entertainment. They may interest someone in a subject so that they then proceeds to study, but they do not teach much of anything. If a television watcher could stop the lecturer as often as he liked and review what was said, that would be help. A recorded lecture is far better than a live one in that respect. One can go over it as often as one likes. Without the replay, a lecture is like a football game. We may know who won, but we may not know much about what went on. The replay of football action on television is indeed a great help in following the game. We then know the outcome of a play and can go back and find out how it was achieved. Again, we know what to look for. A week later we will not remember much—perhaps the score, and an outstanding play that was replayed from several angles.

What else do teachers do? They give tests. Tests deserve a careful look.

The Practice of Testing

Testing, if done correctly, is a desirable practice. It suggests that we have a way of finding out how much someone knows, and this is often useful. The actual practice of testing, however, suggests something else. Except where state or district authorities develop tests for special purposes, tests are usually devised by teachers. The teacher can make the test passable by all or none. Whatever the difficulty level, there are some caveats about testing that should be universally maintained. A test should be *reliable,* that is, known to result in the same score every time (allowing for some benefits from repetition) and be *valid,* that is, actually bear on the issue involved. A test in history, for example, should test for historical knowledge and not mathematics or literature or spelling. Before a test can be given legitimately, it should be tested itself for both reliability and validity. If this is not done, no one should be asked to take it. Newspapers and magazines commonly feature tests of marital happiness or personality. They have only amusement value because no one has ascertained their reliability or validity. The statistical methods for developing measures of reliability and validity need not detain us. The point is that students graduating from the eighth grade, high school, or college may well not have taken a meaningful test throughout their educational career.

In short, teachers should not be testers. They can easily pass a class along to the next unfortunate teacher with no one having learned anything. Testing should be done by testers. If we are to have schools at all, there should be a special office for administering tests. Furthermore, a student should have the privilege of taking a test whenever she feels ready for it and as often as she likes. Multiple forms of a test can be devised if that is deemed useful, but the general rule could be simply to state what a student is supposed to know or be able to do and leave it at that. In spelling, for example, one could list all the words a person should be able to spell before he would be recognized as a speller. The words could be arranged in groups or units of 10, 100, or whatever proved to be efficient; they could be grouped according to frequency of usage, difficulty, or some other criterion. A candidate for a spelling certificate or merit badge could then take appropriate tests after having had access to the words on which the test would be based. She should not take the test until she feels ready; tests should never be sprung on students as a disciplinary measure. That only violates the usefulness of tests.

The Proper Function of Teachers

From what has been stated above, it might be inferred that teachers are engaged in a rather impossible sets of tasks, and they are. They are supposed to handle groups of students, teach them all, maintain some level of order, attend to a variety of needs, pronounce students fit to go on to higher levels, or at least as having met some (undefined) standards. In addition to these obligations they are also supposed to assist students in other aspects of becoming civilized: to be honest, unprejudiced, peaceful, and whatever school authorities think appropriate. Some teachers may be good at some or many of these aspects of the job, but there are no bases for evaluation of many of these. Instead, some school systems introduce tests for teachers that presumably measure their literacy and familiarity with mathematics. Such tests may have some modest utility in weeding out gross incompetents, but they do not have much merit for assessing competence in handling specific subject matter or for evaluating a teacher for what a teacher (tutor) really should be doing, namely supervising the learning progress of specific individuals in carefully prepared and serially arranged programs of content in specific areas.

The Curriculum

In the introductory comments on education, it was stated that no one could forecast the future and plan an appropriate education for every individual, that what a given student gets around to learning was left to chance. In the elementry grades there is general agreement that everyone should be exposed to the three R's, but beyond that there appears to be no general agreement. It is assumed rather generally that school systems have spelled out an appropriate arrangement of courses of study, but no two school systems are alike in what is required of students. In some countries, for example, France, it is said that the educational system is so strictly organized that it can be assumed that throughout the country, at 11 o'clock on Tuesday every child at the same grade level will be in a class devoted to the same subject, studying the same lessons. This is hardly likely, but one can be sure that in the United States no more than 30 students in the country will be engaged in the same activity at 11 o'clock on Tuesday or any other day. Teachers, like anyone else, believe they know what is best for their charges and, within limits, decide what they will have their students do, even in gym classes.

Underlying the educational mystique is a vague notion that everyone should "fulfill his potential," become a jack-of-all-trades, a well-rounded person, whatever that may mean. To make students well rounded the schools keep adding to their programs by introducing new courses without recognizing that given the fixed duration of the school day, something has to be subtracted. The subtraction is accomplished by reducing the time devoted to other, already established parts of a curriculum. If students are to study sex education, they will have less time for arithmetic or other subjects. Once a number of additions are introduced, students are often given a choice of electives. Nowhere does this become more obvious than at the college level, where some students can graduate without ever taking a required course. College faculties are the most guilty of introducing electives because such courses are commonly merely expressions of a particular instructor's interests. College faculties, having committed the error, gather in committee sessions and argue that students *ought* to be required to take courses in the arts, social and natural sciences, languages, mathematics, and so on. But when they finish their deliberations, they find that they have merely "required" any of a number of electives with, most likely, some new courses added to an already heady catalogue. Except where professional schools insist on required courses, the programs of colleges allow such variation that no one becomes well rounded—a student may have a wide variety of elementary courses on her record or a grossly one-sided concentration that leaves her not even marginally educated except for her major or specialty. Engineering and medical schools then complain that their graduates are not really educated, neither scholars nor gentlemen. The problem with curricula in elementary or high schools, of course, is that educators are concerned both with the unpredictable future and, worse yet, with contemporary problems such as teenage sex, and it becomes impossible for any local group to devise a program of studies that will meet general satisfaction and endorsement by the local community, to say nothing of a broader, national public.

It is not being suggested here that there is any set or fixed amount of knowledge that anyone should be exposed to—the arena of what should be learned or known is full of opinionated combatants; no teacher is willing to sacrifice his own field of presumed competence. Gym teachers will insist that physical training is vital; Latin teachers will extol the virtues of familiarity with the classics; scientists will bewail the ignorance of the average citizen about physics and chemistry. Legislators in some states will insist that every child should know the history of that state at the expense of studying the history of medieval Europe. The arguments will continue as new interests are created in the passage of time. We can already see the result of the lack of systematic programs in the activities of industrial, business, and military establishments that have introduced their own training programs for new employees. Specialized education will become a function of employers, who will have to hire graduates of schools on the basis of criteria other than what they have learned in the schools.

It should be recognized, of course, that with the constant changes in curricula, the introduction of many electives, and the explosion of information in the development of new discoveries and new theories, no one who graduates from an educational program can consider that her education will have any real equivalence with the education of those who come after or those who went before. What passed for a B.A. degree in 1950 will not represent the same kind of educational content as the B.A. of 1990. Neither degree may mean much even in its own time. Courses in physics or chemistry, for example, vary from year to year in their content, and teachers offering Psychology 101 in 1985 were not even nearly covering the material they offered in Psychology 101 in 1970. The same is true even in such courses as French 101, which varies in content not only from school to school but also from year to year, some students spending their time listening to tapes, others studying grammar, others reading stories, and still others conversing.

The remarks above are not new observations. It has always been thus with education and presumably will continue to be. The doctors of the eighteenth century learned by apprenticeship, later doctors-to-be went to school for one year, then two, then four, and now they have internships and residencies added to their program before they are allowed to practice. They specialize to the point of knowing much about some area of medicine but little about others. The case is the same with lawyers and engineers and auto mechanics. With new electronically controlled automobiles, many former auto mechanics suddenly became incompetent and had to be reeducated if they were to stay in business. The chaos in education is only a reflection of the unpredictability of human affairs, and nothing much can be done about it. When the various disgruntled sections of the public demand that schools teach automobile driving, creationism, and birth control, as well as allowing time for prayer, somebody has to develop plans for extending the school day and year.

The curriculum is only one problem. Regardless of what is offered in the schools, only a little will be learned because, though schools may be teaching institutions, they are not necessarily learning institutions. To appreciate the difference we must take cognizance of the nature of learning.

15

The Nature of Learning

To make the job of teaching meaningful, it is first necessry to understand the nature of learning. In the first instance it is necessary to recognize that only individuals learn. Classes do not learn—as I noted earlier, a class is a label for a group of children, no two of whom are alike. Children differ in intelligence, attention, motivation, background, energy, and countless other ways. If a teacher has 30 students and a class hour of 50 minutes, the teacher can interact with any given student for about 2 minutes per class period. At that rate a student with five classes per day may enjoy 10 minutes of educational attention per day. In those 10 minutes the teacher might be able to ask a question, correct an eroneous answer, point out a shortcut, or otherwise help a student; the remainder of the time may be wasted unless the student himself goes about the process of learning by himself. This is what happened in the old one-room schoolhouse, where children differed in the additional factors of aged and background. Such schoolhouses were effective and many people acquired meaningful amounts of knowledge because all that a teacher could do in such situations was *not* talk to a class but to assign work to individuals and supervise their progress. If a student needed help, he could ask a question more or less privately and return to the business of studying or learning.

Though the nature of learning is not fully agreed upon by students of the subject, it is rather generally recognized tht learning is a personal matter, one that involves a learner in facing a problem or question and trying to arrive at an answer. If a series of questions is arranged in a logical manner, the student can progress from one question to another as answers are developed. This is the basic principle underlying B. F.

Skinner's (1968) teaching machines. It was up to the student to look at a question, think about it, try to answer it, and get on to the next question. Implicit in this arrangement is that the student was working alone, at her own level of difficulty, without distraction from other students. Implicit too, is that the student goes along at her own pace, free to stop at any time and to resume whenever she chooses. Of course, it is necessary that the student arrive at the machine (or book, lesson, exercise, or whatever the form in which the program is arranged) and work at it. This is sometimes considered to be a matter of motivation.

MOTIVATION

Some authorities argue that motivation is necessary for learning; this is only partially or indirectly true. All that has to happen for learning to occur is for someone to look at a question or to experience some event and respond to the issue in some way. The only role of motivation is to bring the learner into a learning situation. She does not have to be concerned over the importance of the matter; she need not want to learn; all she needs to do is to react to a question. If she reacts in a correct way, she will learn to some extent, what amounts to a correct response; if she reacts in some incorrect way, she will learn that to some extent. For this reason Skinner emphasized the importance of providing correct answers or arranging a program in such a way as almost to assure the arrival at a correct answer. For a long time psychologists worried over the function of correct answers. Some considered them to be rewards and believed that rewards were necessary for learning to be somehow strengthened. It has since been fairly well established that rewards re irrelevant (Bugelski, 1978). What is important is that the response be made. It is of the greatest importance that the response be made to some specific stimulus and not to some extraneous, distracting stimulus.

It is also necessary that an appropriate amount of time be allowed for the neural underpinnings of the association to be formed. If material is presented or answers attempted at too rapid a rate, the resulting associations will be so intermingled that no clear association will remain. It is also important to repeat the stimulus-response pattern often enough to assure some reasonable or desirable retention. Some things can be remembered for a long time even though there has been only a single pairing. Other materials require more than one or a few pairings. The repetitions amount to extending the time for association formation.

Assuming that the nature of learning has been described meaningfully above, we can return to the business of describing what a teacher should be doing. Teachers should first ascertain what a given student already knows about a subject that is going to be studied. The next duty of the teacher is to show or tell the learner what he is supposed to learn as the next assignment. The student is then required to start working at that task, getting answers for himself. The teacher can be called upon for help if the student is unable to arrive at a correct answer. No questions or tasks should be assigned that are beyond the possibilities of a particular student; if some background is required, that must be supplied. At any time, an outside examiner can be called upon to evaluate a student's status, although the teacher, of course, in such teaching conditions, would be well aware of the student's progress.

While a student is working, a teacher could be checking other students' progress and preparing (constructing, revising) future lessons in a given area. That is about all that a teacher should be asked to do. What should be the criteria for selecting teachers? Beyond a mastery of the area to be taught, there are no specific or meaningful standards that can be specified beyond ordinary decency, civility, and productivity in developing lessons or exercises. In a world with a set of complete and perfectly developed programs in all subjects, there would be no need for teachers. There would be only a need for people to provide programs and to get students to work at them. The students could learn at home and go to school for other purposes such as socializing, sports, and other forms of amusement calling for group activities.

It should now be clear that schools are multipurpose institutions where learning is only part of the business. Many schools are doing the job that the taxpayers are paying for. Teachers are not to be singled out as the reason for the poor performance of some students. Some students are simply in the wrong place at the wrong time. Some are unable to make the grade because of inherent limitations. Community and public pressures to pass students along on the basis of age prevent meaningful educational practices. Considering the lack of parental advice and help, especially in one-prent families with latchkey children left to their own devices for much of the day, it is remarkable how well the schools are actually doing. When parents cannot or do not help with homework and see to it that it is done, they should give up great expectations. It has been clear for a long time that educated parents have educated children, just as Catholic parents have Catholic children. With so many lower-income children now going to school, any hope of graduating classes of all genius-level or even literate students is simply absurd. The actual graduates of any school program will be distributed more or less normally, almost randomly by any measure of capacity. Grading students on curves merely aids and abets such a random distribution of attainment. When the lower end of the scale of students is singled out and schools are attacked as ineffective, the wrong target is being blamed. Nowhere is this clearer than in the current concern about illiteracy that is said to characterize so many students. It might be rewarding to look at the subject of reading as a example of what schools cannot accomplish.

While we are examining literacy, it should be remembered that similar remarks could be made about every other subject offered in the schools. We are all abysmally ignorant about something, if not most things.

LITERACY AND ILLITERACY

In recent years the schools have suffered a torrent of criticism because Johnny can't read or write and Mary can't do arithmetic. Much of the criticism has been leveled at reding, various newspaper pundits bewailing the illiteracy of not only grammar school pupils but high school and even college students. The dictionary defines literacy as the ability to read a simple sentence and answer questions about it. That is hardly a serious or satisfactory level, and what the critics talk about is functional literacy, which is never defined precisely but which the White House interprets as something like a fifth-grade reading level. What a fifth-grade level amounts to cannot be considered seriously because publishers adjust the reading difficulty of texts to the demands of school systems. In what may be more practical terms, literacy appears to mean something like being able to fill out a job application. It is alleged that many high school graduates cannot do so. Such a claim is possibly correct in a very small number of cases where someone graduates for social reasons, but most grammar school children have written their names and addresses hundreds of times before they leave the eighth grade, and job applications for low-level jobs rarely require much more.

What is the criticism all about? In 1983 the White House released statistics indicating that 26 million Americans were functionally illiterate. That figure suggests that about 16 percent of Americans were not up to the fifth-grade level. There were no corresponding statistics about how many American had gone through the fifth grade. Nothing was mentioned about immigrants from foreign countries or rural migrants. Percentages for blacks and Hispanics were somewhat higher, but their educational histories were not described. In 1985 the Census Bureau, using a fifth-grade standard, found 13 percent of adult Americans illiterate; of Americans whose native language was English, 9 percent were illiterate.

We may get a clearer picture of the meaning of literacy by looking at the criteria set up by the National Assessment of Educational Progress. That body defines five levels of reading in somewhat practical terms:

1. Rudimentary: read a simple sentence.
2. Basic: read a paragraph of simple sentences.
3. Intermediate: read material at the level of the *New York Daily News.*
4. Adept: read material at the level of the *New York Times.*
5. Advanced: read difficult college texts.

In 1985 the National Assessment of Educational Progress found that about 40 percent of 17-year-olds (presumably in high school) reached level 4, but only 5 percent reached level 5. With 60 percent unable to reach level 4, there may be a problem. It should also be noted that not all 17-year-olds are in school, and the true percentage might be higher. The findings also suggest that about 5 percent of the 17-year-olds should be filling out applications for college. This percentage may not be as bad as is implied. How many peole are really qualified to take college courses?

These figures are looked at with dismay by the pundits. How much functional literacy would satisfy them? If anyone expects a large percentage of Americans or any other nationality to read Shakespeare, Schopenhauer, William Buckley, or a college chemistry text, he is indeed expecting too much. It is probable that no amount of effort could raise literacy levels to such a degree given the normal distribution of intelligence, regardless of what steps were taken to improve literacy. Millions of people hold jobs that require little or no reading—some call for recognition of a limited number of frequently encountered words—not too difficult a problem for most. With modern assembly line and mass production methods, most employees have few occasions to read anything. The argument that illiterates cannot qualify for high-tech jobs may be sound enough, but there are not that many openings for such jobs, and even they are commonly reduced to simple, repetitive functions. With many of the employment opportunities now falling into so-called service occupations, the need to read will decline. The overwhelming influence of television as a source of news, opinion, and entertainment further subtracts from reading requirements. When public libraries provide videocassettes, they are self-defeating as regards promoting literacy.

We appear to have reached a stage in cultural development where the ability to read has become seriously devalued. Actual functional literacy may never have been even as high as it is today, when children are under the legal obligation to go to school and when most of them get to around level 3, as was described above. There are some children, mostly boys, who appear to be slow in picking up reading skills—some have visual problems, and some are just slower than others. Many are hastily diagnosed as having dyslexia when they have problems on encountering print. The problems may have multiple causes including a home environment where no one ever reads anything or reads to a child.

The problem of low literacy levels should be examined, as should the problems associated with any other kind of skill. How much time is devoted to fostering the skill? Can everyone be expected to play Wimbledon levels of tennis? What are the special physical, intellectual, and social attributes required? Are there aspects of literacy that are not being provided? In the case of literacy, we can recognize that at least two factors—vocabulary and reading experience—are vital. Without these, we are all illiterate in some areas. Chemists cannot read treatises in law any better than lawyers can read chemistry. Most college graduates cannot read scientific papers even in their own field without specialization, to say nothing of other fields. Doctors who specialize in gynecology cannot read papers in cancer journals and do not even try.

The critics who attack the schools for failing to teach reading sometimes attack the methiods employed when the methods hardly matter. What matters is to have a teacher at the elbow of every beginning reader, something the critics will not urge anyone to provide. Once a child has made a little progress with either phonics or a whole word method, she will quickly incorporate both methods for herself. The problem is to get her to spend time with books rather than in front of the television set. Most critics of illiteracy were students in the days before television took over the home entertainment role. Given the cultural realities, very few, perhaps 5 percent of children, will ever become serious readers at what might be considered a college textbook level.

The corresponding difficulties concerning the ability to write or do arithmetic have the same sources—the lack of individual instruction, the infrequency of practice, and the ubiquitous individual differences. As with reading, the need for writing has declined. Many cities used to have several newspapers. Nowadays even large cities can support only one paper, and writing staffs have declined. Tape recorders have replaced pencils, and copying machines have eliminated typists. Computers now write letters. In the area of arithmetic the calculator has almost eliminated the need to know how to extract square roots. Logarithms are no longer needed and slide rules are in a class with the ancient abacus. Children can now multiply and divide without knowing what they are doing other than pressing buttons. When everybody goes to school and there are not enough teachers, the critics had better lower their expectations.

SUMMARY

The principles discussed in the first chapters of this book are most clearly evident in our discussion of education. We see the role of conditioning as the basis for education or learning when we recognize that only individuals can learn, and in quiet settings without distraction and with time controlled for the purpose of enabling assocations to be formed. We recognize that any skill or content area is not a matter of one simple assocation and that any meaningful mastery calls for thousands of hours of practice and experience. We see the reward role as one of motivating students to submit to the conditions under which learning can take place. The role of individual differences must be highlighted because it is so greatly overlooked. Given a normal distribution of intelligence, it is inevitable that only a relatively small percentage of people is able to profit from any kind of educational system, especially one that is time-bound, children being herded from class to class and from grade to grade whether they have learned anything or not. Only a small proportion of students will become even passably literate. They may get to the stage of reading advice columns in newspapes but avoid the editorial pages. Most students will learn to follow newspaper accounts of sports activities, but they will ignore the pundits on the op-ed page.

Our principle of determinism is seen at work in the multivariate outcomes of the educational system, where courses are taken on the chance advice of friends or even professional advisors, who differ widely among themselves. What a student becomes is the consequence of chance happenings that impinge upon her.

Finally, our principle of context plays a large role. War, economic circumstances, geographical location, family features, income and education of parents, and manifold other factors impact upon the developing student and shape his experiences, multiplying the differences between him and his contemporaries while, at the same time, forcing upon him similarities that make him a unit of his generation. The rock music and drug practices that prevail in adolescent society bring about a conformity that almost conceals the diversity. Individuals will still be different even in the drugs they prefer and the combos that turn them on. Most importantly, they will become different in what they know and how well they know it. Only a few will become broadly knowledgeable. Nearly everyone will know how to turn on a television set, but even the television repairer may not understand how it works.

Schools and their products could be improved, if only marginally, by steps that probably will not be taken. The school day would have to be lengthened to perhaps eight hours to provide time for "homework"—that is, individualized learning—because parents cannot be relied upon to be either able or willing to supervise such study. The school year would have to be lengthened to about 240 days instead of the customary 180 days in the United States—in Europe and Japan children attend school for 240 or so days. Because of the lengthened year, teachers' salaries would have to be raised, and more teachers would have to be employed to provide the personalized supervision (giving assignments and supervising the learning operation). Examinations and tests would have to be developed on a national scale to provide criteria for evaluation of students and bases for the assessment of accountability. Leaving education under the control of local school boards may result in variety, but it hardly promotes quality.

Better teachers could be attracted to the profession through attractive salaries and through sabbaticals restricted to additional education and up-grading studies. Teachers of strictly academic subjects could be paid more than others whose efforts are directed at fringe interests, and distinctions could even be made among the academicians; for example, math and science teachers could be paid more than others; depending upon their credentials. Degrees in education would have to be more advanced than the bachelor of arts degree and would be based on a major in the subject to be taught.

At upper levels, high school and college, again programs would have to be lengthened—perhaps five years for each instead of the current four. There is simply too much to learn for one to be considered educated in modern times.

Those not qualifying for additional academic development should enter training programs in trades (for example, construction, machine shop work, arts, or whatever taxpayers are inclined to pay for) and remain in these programs until qualified as appropriately skilled. There should be no dropouts. To count 16-year-old academic dropouts as unemployed is a gross absurdity—they are only exploited by employers of low-level talents or turn to crime or life on the dole.

All of the proposals indicated above cost money and will not be supported graciously by taxes on citizens. The support would probably have to be based on income taxes and would require federal instigation and supervision.

16
And in Conclusion

Readers of this book may have been looking for answers to personal problems. The reader may have been searching for answers to the problems described, but no answers have been recommended, although some were implied. It was indicated (chapter 2) in discussing beliefs, that advice is taken only by those who have been conditioned to accept the kinds of advice offered and to reject advice that appears unpromising or otherwise disagreeable. In any case, people are going to do what they are going to do because of the ways they have been conditioned and reinforced. The last statement includes references to three of the principles mentioned in the introductory chapter. Taken with the fourth principle, that of individual differences, they are the reasons for which I wrote this book and for which the reader is reading it. The writer has been reinforced for writing books, the reader for reading them.

If the reader was reinforced in the course of her reading by some of the remarks, she will also have been conditioned to have some new beliefs. The beliefs will not of themselves lead to any new patterns of behavior or actions but will amount to new sets of attitudes, which may alter some of the reader's former inclinations. She will not have any more choices about what she will do than the author had in writing this book.

THE DECLINE OF THE WEST

In the opening chapter I described the views of Mowrer and Skinner insofar as the causes of behavior were concerned. Neither view was especially flattering to the human race, but though similar, they were accompanied by different philosophical orientations. Mowrer was content to accept people for what they are and the world as it is. Because of his own background of conditioning he had a set of values for himself that included a strong Christian (if not religious) ethic—help others, turn the other cheek, walk the extra mile, don't look for credit for good deeds. Mowrer admits to having been strongly influenced by the character in *The Magnificent Obsession* (Douglas, 1927) who secretly helped other people. Mowrer would not find fault with or blame others. They could not help their conditioning.

Skinner, on the other hand, though recognizing and, in fact, insisting on the role of reinforcement in everyone's behavioral history, and specifically emphasizing that no one is to be blamed or praised for what he does, still finds fault with the world, the environment and what has happened to it. He is disturbed by the way mankind has evolved socially and is concerned that unless the environment is restructured, only dire results can follow. Civilization, as we know it in the Western world, has been accompanied by damaging side effects. Skinner (1987) is not suggesting that any other part of the world is even as well off as the West and is perfectly aware of the misery in undeveloped countries. What he is upset about is that if they do develop, it will only be in the direction that the West has taken, at which point the whole world will have gone to pot.

What does Skinner find so disenchanting about the West? The basic flaw in our civilization is that people have acquired habits, practices, and traditions that structure the environment in such a way as to reinforce inactivity rather than activity. What Skinner appears to be saying is that the affluence of Western society has resulted in a situation where most people are alienated from work (be it professional, managerial, or simply humdrum manual or clerical). The simplification of jobs through machinery, technology, computerization, and mass production has made work repetitive and aversive. Skinner appears to want people to enjoy work and get reinforcement from it, as the artisans of old were supposed to. How modern production methods could be altered to produce happy workers Skinner does not say. In our discussion of work it was suggested that work itself is an aversive ctivity except perhaps for workaholics with a history of work ethic conditioning.

Not only does Skinner find that work situtions are intolerable because we are always working under aversive conditions (the threat of losing our jobs, being told what to do, and where, when, and how to do it); but he also finds that we have lost the freedom to adjust, correct our own errors, or discover new solutions to difficulties, in that we are always being *advised* by others or controlled by rules, laws, and regultions. Within this pattern of cultural practices, we even work to help others who could really help themselves, or we overprotect the aged, children, and some of the handicapped, who should instead be encourged to do as much for themselves as possible. Any such assistance means that the reinforcement that might come from performance is lost.

Skinner finds that even pleasant activities (looking at or listening to the performances or products of others) reinforce only the activity of looking or listening. Thus going to football games reinforces only the activity of going to games, and not even playing them. In some way that Skinner does not explain, he finds such pleasant ways of passing the time undesirable. No pundits find the watching of television shows by children commendable, although they themselves watch television programs (only important ones, of course).

From Skinner's complaints one might infer that something like the decline of the West is progressing at a rapid rate. The rest of the world has not yet reached the stage where its people can begin to enjoy life and begin the process of deterioration. "The West", says Skinner (1987), "has lost its inclination to act." People no longer work for themselves, that is, do their own work. The human race is no longer evolving in the world as it used to be—it is now a world made by humans, and they have made a rather poor job of it. Behavior has grown weaker because so much of it amounts to seeking pleasure instead of leading to reinforcement for the consequences of action. Skinner asks, "How much richer would the whole world be if the reinforcers in daily life were more effectively contingent on productive work?"

Thus Skinner, in contrast to Mowrer, cannot accept this as the only possible world. As if forgetting his own principles, he looks for sources of reinforcement that the Western world does not provide. Neither he nor anyone else can turn back the clock, nor can he have anyone raise himself by his own bootstraps or act in any way that has not been reinforcing in his past. One does not have to like this world, with its environmental pollution, its holocausts, its wars, its terrorism, and its threat of atomic annihilation, but one will continue to live in it and continue to do what has been reinforcing in the past. When enough people in the affluent West become bored with watching movies on their video recorders, they may turn to other activities, some of which might change things for the better, whatever that may be.

There is no reason to expect humanity to change in any significant ways for thousands of years to come. The Soviet Union after some 70 years of socialism has failed to produce "the New Soviet Man." Its population still consists of the same types of people the czars governed—workers who do as little work as possible for their employers, bureaucrats who, like those everywhere, hang onto their jobs, secret police who try to put down ethnic rebellions, and dedicted revolutionaries who prefer to imagine utopias that they would find intolerable because they are intellectuals who find ordinary jobs unworthy. Revolutionaries do not work for a living—they prefer to plot and plan, read, write, speak out, and lead others. Like Karl Marx, they permit others to support them if they are not independently wealthy.

Though we cannot anticipate changes in human nature, we can expect the environment to change, probably for the worse, as concrete covers former grassland and natural resources are consumed. Because of probable new inventions all kinds of changes in life-styles will occur as they always have over anyone's lifetime. People have always said, "They don't build them like they used to," "Children no longer respect their parents," "What's happened to our schools?" Freud asked, What do women want? He should have applied the same question to men. In neither case do we have an answer other than that which makes them feel better as individuals, and that may vary with each individual. Despite Skinner's admonitions people will continue to avoid work and seek pleasure. In some instances (writers, artists, musicians, and entertainers in general) they will love their work because the applause and approval of others has come to be their major source of reinforcement, even if long delayed. Others will find reinforcement from bossing other people around in jobs that may be of questionable merit. Though most jobs are rather meaningless so far as strengthening a culture's chances of survival is concerned, many people find pleasure in their work even though their contribution to social evolution would never be missed.

THE IMPLICATIONS OF THE PRINCIPLES

As I indicated at the beginning of this chapter, this book was written because it had to be written. The necessity was accompanied by the hope that the writer could not help having that individual readers, by reflection upon the content would possibly benefit by attitudinal changes. It is time to spell out some of these.

One of the attitudes that the writer hopes has been created by the repeated emphasis on individual differences and determinism is a greater tolerance of others. Such tolerance does not involve greater respect for anyone—just the recognition that we are all different and do what we have to do, whether it is overdosing on drugs, robbing blind cripples, raping children, or contributing to the blood bank and the United Fund. Tolerance of people does not involve tolerance of their behavior. Of course, what one does about somebody's undesirable behavior will again depend upon how one was conditioned and reinforced.

Tolerance of people includes tolerance of oneself. Many people are dissatisfied with their condition or prospects and contrast their situation with that of people who have attained some perceived happiness, satisfaction, or status. It might be useful to recall at this time the views of Thorndike on learning. For Thorndike learning was a matter of effort and luck (trial and error and chance success). Whatever other people have or achieve is due to some (maybe very little) effort and some (maybe a lot of) lock. The luck Thorndike was talking about was not the intervention of some magical force but simply accident, chance, doing the right thing at the right time for no very good reason. One should also be careful about one's judgments of the happiness of other people—they may be spending hours on a psychoanalyst's couch or going through a private hell. Whatever your own status happens to be, it is also a matter of effort and luck. You are who you are and where you are; don't waste your time trying to find yourself or finding out who you *really* are. There is only one of you and you are here.

Another attitude I have tried to promote is a distrust of empty words—not only the empty slogans of propagandists or promoters of one cause or another or the words of advertisers such as "the new and improved . . . ," but of common, everyday words that we all use. The reader must recognize that almost any word means something different to everybody—even a simple word like *mother* means one thing to me and something else to you. Most of the time we can get along and communicate with others; if what we are trying to say seems to be ineffective, we can draw pictures or point at things, but as soon as we introduce any abstract word we may get into trouble.

The abstract words of chief concern here are those that allegedly describe some supposed internal agency or trait such as intelligence, honesty, ambition, and thousands of others that are used to explain behvior. We are always complaining about someone else's stupidity, corruption, or other trait when no one has ever established any basis for believing that such terms describe anything other than behavior we find appropriate or inappropriate. As I emphasized earlier, one of the worst offenders among terms commonly used to apply to traits is *greed*. Greed appears to explain all of the villainy we read about in our newspapers. Greedy doctors, greedy lawyers, greedy politicians, greedy bankers, greedy everybody. The implication is that some people are greedier than others. Unfortunately for those who would explain crime and corruption by citing greed, there is no basis for assuming that anyone possesses such a trait—all animals including the human kind look out for themselves and do what they do because of their reinforcement and conditioning histories. They may try to explain that they do what they think is right, but what they think is right is also a result of their histories. When they behave in a self-sacrificing, generous manner, they are also doing what they think is right and are being just as greedy in looking out for themselves—they have been conditioned to enjoy their self-esteem in that fashion. People just differ in what they're "greedy" about.

In chapter 2, I inveighed against abstract terms applied to groups or organizations of people, such as *corporations, country, and Supreme Court* and titled positions as judge, professor, or doctor. Every day we have a president's press secretry inform reporters about the official viewpoint or what the government thinks, and the press dutifully informs us about our country's interests. The reporters then call at the Soviet Embassy to get the view of the Soviet Union, as if there were such a thing. The acceptance of such abstract terms as actually meaningful is deplorable enough, but when they are used to mask some completely different plan of action, they are doubly dangerous. When a vice president talks about stabilizing prices of oil when he means raising prices, it is worse than misleading. A president who talks about enhancing revenues when he means raising taxes is guilty of something more than corrupting the language.

We must always remember that governments and countries do not talk. Only people talk. An "official" position is always what some officials want us to accept as something beyond the words of people, who often enough do not know what they are talking about or are simply lying.

Besides the attitudes of tolerance and distrust of abstractions I have tried to suggest that the concept of relevance is a relative one. Despite Bloom, no one hs yet established any absolutes, except for a few in physics, and even these depend on conditions. What is relevant at one time may not be relevant at others or to the events. Things get better and things get worse: wars start and wars end; the concerns of today will appear less significant tomorrow. The only sure things today, as always, are death and taxes. A relevant psychology must take them into account. For the average college student these two certainties are largely irrelevnt and she wants answers to what she considers important here and now.

PROBLEMS AND SOLUTIONS

In this book the problems of the here and now have been described as arising from two sourses. Firstly, human beings are human beings and will behave like humans. They are neither saints nor devils but somewhere in between, with some closer to either end but most distributed rather normally along any scale one might contrive. Secondly, people are social—John Donne's "No man is an island" has always been true. Robinson Crusoe was miserable until Friday appeared. But, by living with others, people make problems for themselves, and the solutions are never totally or permanently satisfactory. Most solutions follow a zero-sum pattern; somebody wins and others lose. Perhaps a basic fault in social life is the long, perhaps everlasting, pattern whereby everyone apparently tries to lead not merely a satisfactory life but one that he might regard as better than that of his neighbors. Is this a throwback to the struggle for existence, the survival of the fittest? The "better than" syndrome expresses itself in individual efforts, in our training of our own children, in our local civic pride, our nationalistic chauvinism, in virtually all aspects of sports and entertainment, with the constant award ceremonies, the first-prize manias, and the ubiquitous downgrading of anyone we can feel superior to for any reason, real or imaginary.

The principles I have described in the introductory chapters should be sufficient to convince the reader that there is great merit in the old adage "There, but for the grace of God, go I." Should a consideration of the principles lead to the development of such an attitude, my ambitions will be fulfilled. Once you can accept the view that you are no better than anyone else and that no one is better than you, a great many personal problems disappear and you can go about your business of doing whatever you have to do. You are going to do it anyhow and might as well do it without anxiety.

Although we looked at a great many problems that plague mankind, we hve not touched on a great many others. We have not considered terrorism, for example. Not much can be done about people who want to hasten their arrival in heaven by self-destruction or who believe in the wisdom of their leaders. Problems such as the pollution of the air and water by chemical companies who promise "better things for better living through chemistry" call for action by politicians who vote the way their financial supporters dictate. Atomic reactors pose problems of possible dangerous radiation, but considerations of the need for energy create dilemmas for people.

When scientists, tinkerers, or politicians discover or propose something new, it is often promoted as progress. Most people, if polled, would add progress to motherhood, baseball, and apple pie as their ideals. But progress often appears to involve risks, dangers, unpredictable costs, and undesirable side effects. The invention of television was hailed as a dramatic innovation, and no one could have predicted that much of what appears on television could be correctly described as a vast wasteland. The effect of television on literacy was not anticipated, and its spin-offs in the form of videocassettes may have even more profound effects in many aspects of life besides literacy. The inventions of the steam locomotive, the automobile, and the airplane have cost thousands of lives, but they represent progress, if getting someplace faster is progress.

The invention of the telephone enabled cellar waterproofers who cannot waterproof anything to call and tell you that you have just won a prize. One form of progress has occurred in the United States in the rather weak establishment of legislation that requires studies of environmental impact before another part of the earth is covered with asphalt or concrete. The concrete is poured anyhow, but someone had to think about the propriety of the action. That is progress. Earlier in this work I mentioned that if something has not been done in the last 1,000 years, perhaps we can get along without it for another 1,000 years. The slogan "Don't just do something, stand there" might save a lot of future grief. Before the patent office issues a new patent it might add a requirement that any new device be required to be not only foolproof but "damn foolproof" and pose no danger for anyone.

THE PREDICTABILITY OF BEHAVIOR

The humorist Robert Benchley once said that there are two kinds of people—those who say there are two kinds of people and those who don't. The reader will have long ago inferred that there are all kinds of people, that every person is different from every other person, a product of her own unique genetics and her own personal history of reinforcement. The complex interactions between genetics and reinforcement history produce all sorts of combinations of reactions, largely unpredictable. What a child of three might be expected to do may be readily foreseen by his parents; after that, despite some orderliness in developmental schedules, behavior is largely unpredictable. By the time a person becomes an adult one might well forget about predictability of an individual's behavior. Of course, people are constrained by their habits, their environment, their job, and their immediate family or associates to behave in certain expected ways in certain situations. After 20 centuries of so-called civilization, most people have come to behave in fairly orderly ways in routine situations. On a statistical level some kinds of prediction are fairly accurate. The Gallup polls will tell us who will win an election or if the election will be close. Restaurant owners will expect a certain number of diners on a certain day of the week. The mail will be delivered and the newspaper will be there, most of the time. A certain number of people will be killed in auto accidents on holiday weekends or any other weekends. Of the 5 billion people now on earth, most of them will be orderly and law-abiding most of the time. Nearly everybody drives on the correct side of the road. Practically no one drives through a red traffic signal, even late at night when no one else is on the road.

The story of civilization amounts to a slow process wherein a majority of human beings have learned to adapt to their circumstances and have found it better to follow rules, customs, traditions and common practices. People will take their place in line at a ticket office, and only occasionally will someone try to break into a line ahead of those already there. A certain amount of tolerance of frustration will be acquired by the time one is old enough to buy tickets, even for a rock concert.

The predictability of people in the mass, to the extent that it is feasible, encourages us in the practice of classifying or labeling everyone but oneself as "one of those," whosoever "those" might be. We try to predict the individual behavior of redheads, Irishmen, blacks, Germans, women, short people, fat people, and so on. We are surprised when a German is not neat, orderly, and industrious; we cannot understand a mildly disposed, placid redhead, or an unjolly fat man, or even a gangster who cries at his mother's funeral. Our need to simplify our relationships prompts us to look for easy answers and to explain the behavior of others by convenient labels we pick up from parents, assocites, teachers, and newspapers. It is difficult for anyone to appreciate that not everyone else is crazy, nuts, evil, crooked when they do not happen to like what someone else is doing. The psychiatrist Thomas Szasz likes to provoke his readers by asserting that there is no such thing as mental illness—that people we like to label as being so stricken are only behaving in ways we find inconvenient or undesirable, that the fault really, as Cassius said, "is ourselves."[1] It is so easy to discover in others various traits or charcteristics that explain their evil ways—or their virtuous ones, for that matter.

Our own lack of experience with others forces us to rely on other sources of information about people, and these sources, mostly newspapers, television, our friends and families, will tend to emphasize the interesting, bizarre, strange, and unusual, so that we form opinions— about crime, terrorism, welfare clients, poverty, or any other kind of social problem—that bear little relation to reality. On a percentage basis there are very few criminals in any society—the prisons may be full, but there are not many prisons and not many large ones. The mentally ill are, again, a small percentage of the population—they are not cluttering up the streets of New York or any other city. Not all old people are being warehoused in reprehensible retirement homes. On the contrary, most people are minding their own business, "doing their thing," staying home watching television and thereby discovering what everyone else is doing—shooting, mugging, raping, and pushing drugs to schoolchildren, among other things.

In contrast to the often expressed "people are no damned good" view, one might well consider the opposite position. People in general find much of their reinforcement from meeting with others, participating in joint activities, from the old-fashioned quilting bee to athletics, card games, charity drives, good works, fund-raising groups, choruses, orchestras, political organizations, PTA's, or any of the countless societies, unions, clubs, fraternities, and the like that take up much of the leisure time at most people's disposal. Though there is an undoubted self-interest in many such activities, there is also a recognition that nothing great is likely to result from one's participation as second violin in a community orchestra. People will say that they do it for fun. And the reality is that, for the most part, they are telling the truth. It appears that humans, the only animals known to smile (and that even in a three-day-old infant), like to have fun and devote a great deal of their lives to that pursuit.

The problems we have discussed and those that have been ignored are only today's problems. The future will undoubtedly bring with it a host of new ones. It has been argued here that the principles of determinism, conditioning, reinforcement, and individual differences are helpful in appreciating the nature of the problems. It is assumed that since humanity has not changed noticeably in its physical nature in the last 50,000 years, it will not change much in the next 500 or so and that the same principles will be helpful in the analysis of future problems. Readers are invited to apply the principles to any problems they face now or later. In the meantime the moral of this work is "What's the hurry? Relax and enjoy it."

NOTE

1. William Shakespeare, *Julius Caesar*, 1.2.134.

Bibliography

Albus, J. S. 1976. *Brains, Behavior, and Robotics*. Petersborough, N.H.: BYTE Publications.

Allison, J. 1983. *Behavioral Economics*. New York: Praeger.

Allport, F. 1947. Institutional behavior. In T. Newcomb and E. Hartley (Eds.), *Readings in Social Psychology*. New York: Holt.

Allport, G. 1937. *Personality*. New York: Holt.

Blight, J. G. 1987. Toward a policy-relevant psychology of avoiding nuclear war. *American Psychologist, 42*, 1, 12–29.

Bloom, A. 1987. *The Closing of the American Mind*. New York: Simon and Schuster.

Boorstin, D. J. 1983. *The Discoverers*. New York: Random House.

Brown, J. F. 1936. *Psychology and the Social Order*. New York: McGraw-Hill.

Bugelski, B. R. 1941. The relationship between patterns of ergographic decrement and decrement in other tasks. *Journal of Experimental Psychology, 28*, 389–406.

———. 1944. The analysis of aviation accidents. *Journal of Aviation Medicine*. June issue.

———. 1978. *Principles of Learning and Memory*. New York: Praeger.

———. 1982. Learning and imagery. *Journal of Mental Imagery, 6*, 1–92.

Camus, A. 1956. *The Rebel*. New York: Vintage Books.

Djilas, M. 1957. *The New Class*. New York: Praeger.

Dollard, J. 1937. *Class and Caste in a Southern Town*. New Haven: Yale University Press.

Durant, W., and Durant, A. 1954–1967. *The Story of Civilization*. New York: Simon and Schuster.

Fjermedal, G. 1986. *The Tomorrow Makers*. New York: Macmillan.

Freud, S. 1923. *The Complete Introductory Lectures on Psychoanalysis*. New York: Norton.

Friedman, M. 1980. *Free to Choose*. New York: Harcourt Brace.

Galbraith, J. K. 1975. *Money. Where It Came from and Where It Went*. Boston: Houghton Mifflin.

———. 1986. *A View from the Stands*. Boston: Houghton Mifflin.

———. 1987. *Economics in Perspective*. Boston: Houghton Mifflin.

Gorbachev, M. 1987. *Perestroika*. New York: Harper and Row.

Hammer, A. 1987. *Armand Hammer*. New York: Putnam.

Harlow, H. 1958. The nature of love. *American Psychologist, 13*, 673–85.

Hartshorne, H., and May, M. 1927. *Studies in Deceit*. New York: Macmillan.

Hegel, G. 1857. See any modern edition.

Heilbroner, R. L. 1970. *Between Capitalism and Socialism*. New York: Random House.

Hirsch, E. D., Jr. 1987. *Cultural Literacy*. Boston: Houghton Mifflin.

Hobbes, T. 1651. *Leviathan*. New York: Oxford (1947).

Hoffman, S. 1986. On the political psychology of peace and war. *Political Psychology, 7*, 1–21.

Hull, C. 1943. *Principles of Behavior*. New York: Appleton-Century-Crofts.

Huxley, A. 1968. *Brave New World Revisited*. New York: Harper.

Jensen, A. 1969. How much can we boost the I.Q. and scholastic achievement? *Harvard Educational Review, 39*, 1–123.

Keller, F. 1969. A programmed system of instruction. *Educational Technology Monographs, 2*, 1–27.

Kinsey, A. 1948. *Sexual Behavior in the Human Male*. Philadelphia: Saunders.

Lorenz, K. 1965. *On Aggression*. New York: Harcourt Brace.

Luker, K. 1986. *Abortion and the Politics of Motherhood*. Berkeley: University of California Press.

Marx, K. 1867. *Das Kapital*. See any modern edition.

McLuhan, M. 1967. *The Medium is the Massage*. New York: Bantam.

McGregor, D. M. 1960. *The Human Side of Enterprise*. New York: McGraw-Hill.

Milgram, S. 1974. *Obedience to Authority: An Experimental View*. New York: Harper and Row.

Milosz, C. 1955. *The Captive Mind*. New York: Vintage.

Mowrer, O. H. 1960. *Psychology and the Symbolic Processes*. New York: Wiley.

Pavlov, I. 1927. *Conditioned Reflexes* (G. Anrep, Trans.). London: Oxford University Press.

Robinson, P. 1987. Review of Luker's *Abortion and the Politics of Motherhood*. *New York Times Book Review*, May 6.

Sarason, S. B. 1973. Jewishness, blackishness, and the nature-nuture controversy. *American Psychologist, 28*, 962–71.

Schwartz, B. 1986. *The Battle for Human Nature: Science, Morality, and Modern Life*. New York: Norton.

Skinner, B. F. 1948. *Walden II*. New York: Macmillan.

———. 1968. *The Technology of Teaching*. New York: Appleton-Century-Crofts.

———. 1971. *Beyond Freedom and Dignity*. New York: Knopf.

———. 1986. What is wrong with daily life in the western world. *American Psychologist, 41*, 568–74.

———. 1987. *Upon Further Reflection*. Englewood Cliffs, N.J.: Prentice-Hall.

Smith, A. 1776. *The Wealth of Nations*. See any modern edition.

Smith, V. L. 1978. Relevance of laboratory experiments to testing resource allocation theory. In J. Kmenta and J. Ramsey (Eds.), *Evaluation of Econometric Models*. New York: Academic Press.

Szacz, T. 1974. *The Myth of Mental Illness: Foundation of a Theory of Personal Conduct*. New York: Harper and Row.

Thorndike, E. L. 1932. *The Fundamentals of Learning*. New York: Teachers College, Columbia University.

Thurber, J. 1946. *Men, Women and Dogs*. New York: Bantam Books.

Thurow, L. C. 1985. *The Zero-sum Solution*. New York: Simon and Schuster.

Veblen, T. 1934. *The Theory of the Leisure Class*. New York: Modern Library.

Walberg, H., and Shanahan, T. 1983. High school effects on individual students. *Educational Researchers, 12*, 4–9.

Watson, J. B. 1929. *Psychology from the Standpoint of a Behaviorist*. Philadelphia: Lippincott.

Wilson, E. 1972. *To the Finland Station*. New York: Farrar, Straus and Giroux.

Wilson, E. O. 1975. *Sociobiology*. Cambridge: Harvard University Press.

Wilson, J. Q., and Herrnstein, R. J. 1985. *Crime and Human Nature*. New York: Simon and Schuster.

Zajonc, R. B. 1986. The decline and rise of Scholastic Aptitude scores. A prediction derived from the Confluence model. *American Psychologist, 41*, 862–867.

Index

abortion, 68–69, 173–75
abstract words, 203
advice, 199
aggression, 15, 111, 156, 160–61
aging, 55–60
Albus, James S., 109
Allison, James, 61, 107
Allport, Floyd, 18
Allport, Gordon, 23, 29
Aristophanes, 46
altruism, 21, 69, 130
Aristotle, 179, 181
anticommunism, 85
anti-Semitism, 51
anxiety, 14
assimilation, 55, 72–74
attitudes, 25, 202

behavior, control of, 11; intentional, 15
belief, 26–27
belonging, as a motive, 83
Benchley, Robert, 206
"betterness," concept of, 86–88, 204
Blight, James G., 143
Bloom, Allan, 178
Boorstin, Daniel J., 113
borrowing, 121

bread and circuses, 109
Brezhnev, Leonid, 79, 130, 141
Brown, J. F., 41, 42
Buckley, William, 195
Bugelski, B. R., 10, 27, 107, 192

Camus, Albert, 34, 93
capital, 128
capitalism: as a religion, 85; as an ideology, 127; in communist countries, 138; versus communism, 137
capital punishment, 68–69, 159, 174
carelessness, 22
castes, 85–86
choice, 149
civil liberties, 169–71
classrooms, 181; time in, 182
class membership, 41
classes, socio-economic, 41
committees, 19
communism, 78, 132; as a religion, 133
competition, 128
conditioned reinforcers, 8
conditioned inhibition, 107
conditioning, 5–7; in the environment, 80; and education, 196
conflict, United States vs. Soviet Union, 140–41

context, 16, 30–31, 197
"country," 20, 81–82
crime, 148–53
criminals, 155
cruelty, 68
cultures and subcultures, 70–76
curriculum, 187

Darwin, Charles, 69, 92
decline of the west, 199–200
delinquency, 148
demand, in supply and demand, 99
democracy, 78
desegregation, 53
determinism, 3, 148–49, 197
deterrence, 158–62
Djilas, Milovan, 89, 136
dialectics, 134
Dickens, Charles, 146
dignity, 3, 13–14
dis-ease, 88
divine right of kings, 79
Dollard, John, 130
drive, 10; for rest, 107
drugs, 60–63
Durant, Ariel, 57, 66, 115
Durant, Will, 57, 66, 115

economic problems, 91, 96
economics, 34
educational mystique, 183
education, purpose of, 179
employment, 101; and slavery, 104
Engels, Friedrich, 133
entertainment, 110
evolution, social, 133; and economic
    survival, 92
extinction, 9–10; of beliefs, 70, 131

fear, 6, 14
Fjermedal, Grant, 109
freedom, 3, 13–14
free enterprise, 127; in the Soviet
    Union, 138
Freud, Sigmund, 1, 47, 67, 202
Friedman, Milton, 96, 97, 128, 129
frustration, 160; tolerance of, 148, 206
future orientation, 92–93, 111

Galbraith, John K., 97, 104, 117
Gorbachev, Mikhail, 138, 140
government, 19, 76
Gaunt, John, 11
greed, 20, 117, 203

Hammer, Armand, 95
Harlow, Harry, 7
Hartshorne, H., 156
Hegel, Georg W. F., 134
Heilbroner, R. L., 134
heredity, 18, 87
Herrnstein, R. J., 153–54, 156
Hirsch, E. D., Jr., 178
Hobbes, Thomas, 123
Hoffman, S., 143
Holocaust, 157
homework, 185
homosexuality, 39, 45, 47, 48
hope, 7, 17
Hull, Clark, 107
human rights, 170
Huxley, Aldous, 131
hyphen-Americans, 71

idealism, 134
illiteracy, 194
incest, 45
income, distribution of, 138
individual differences, 4; in educa-
    tion, 197
inflation, 115
insanity, 150
instincts, 18
institutional thinking, 18, 203
intent, 147–48
interest, 120
integration, of races, 53
intelligence tests, 4–5

Jensen, Arthur, 17

Keller, Fred, 189
Kinsey, A. C., 45

labor-management strife, 106
labor-saving machines, 108
laissez-faire policy, 127

Landers, Ann, 45
law and laws, 35, 145
lawyers, 165
leadership, 77
learning, nature of, 191–92
leisure time, 110
Lenin, V. I., 133, 141
lex talionis, 146
literacy, 194
Locke, John, 179
Lombroso, Cesare, 156
Lorenz, Konrad, 111
love, 7
Luker, Kristin, 173–74

McLuhan, Marshall, 19
McGregor, Douglas M., 107
Magna Carta, 123
Malthus, Thomas, 44
management, 135
marriage, 46, 49
Marx, Karl, 78, 97, 131, 133–34, 137, 201
masculinity-femininity, 44–45
May, Mark, 156
melting pot, 72
mens rea, 147–48, 150
Milgram, Stanley, 68
Milosz, Czeslaw, 131
minorities, 71
money, 91–93, 113
morality, 65
motivation, 8, 10; and learning, 192
Mowrer, O. Hobart, 6–7, 9, 15, 89, 115, 199–201

National Assessment of Educational Progress, 194
nationalism, 76
nationality, 41
nature-nurture, 17
New Soviet Man, 201
nuclear threat, 141–42

Oneida community, 133
opinion, 23–24
Owen, Robert, 133

patriotism, 76–79
Pavlov, Ivan, 8
Peace Corps, 142
person, definition of, 170
Personalized Instruction System, 182
politicians, 2, 32, 86
population, 22, 33
pornography, 48, 164
predictability of behavior, 206
prejudice, 28–29
prisons, 162
problem solution, 36–39
prochoice supporters, 173
progress, 205
prolife supporters, 173
prostitution, 47
punishment, 9, 15, 146; and the law, 157–58

race, 40
racism, 50–53
reading, 194
Reagan, Ronald W., 141; on abortion, 173
rebels, 34
recidivism, 158, 161
rehabilitation, 158, 161
reinforcement, 3, 8–9; and drugs, 62; in economic systems, 139; intermittent, 12–13; as motivation, 8; negative, 9; as payment for effort, 10; secondary, 8; vicarious, 139
relief, 14
religion, 65–68
responsibility, 146–47
retaliation, 158, 160
retribution, 158
revenge, 138, 160
revolution, 137
revolutionists, 201
rights, 36, 46, 48, 169–70
Robinson, Paul, 174
rugged individualism, 95

Sarason, Seymour B., 53
schools, criticism of, 177–78; as factories, 180; as multi-purpose institutions, 193

Schwartz, Barry, 13
secondary reinforcement, 3; money
    as, 92
segregation, 53
sex, 43–47
Shakers, 133
Skinner, B. F., 5, 9, 10, 12, 13–15,
    133, 158; on teaching, 181; on val-
    ues, 192
slavery, 95, 102, 104, 169
Smith, Adam, 96
Smith, Vernon, L., 100
sociability, 18, 20
social contract, 123
social evolution, 133
social problems, 65
socialism, 136; and ideology, 139
Socialist Labor party, 137
Socialist party, 137
social security, 58–59
Socrates, 69, 177
Stalin, Joseph, 78
stereotypes, 41
subcultures, 70–76
supply and demand, law of, 61, 98–
    99
surplus value, 97, 106
survival of the fittest, 130, 204
Szasz, Thomas, 150, 207

taxes, 77, 123, 125
teachers, 184, 185; functions of, 187
teaching machines, 196
teen-age pregnancies, 48

temperament, 18, 153
territoriality, 80, 127
tests, in school, 185–86
Thayer, Tiffany, 57
Thoreau, Henry David, 6, 72
Thorndike, Edward L., 94, 202
Thurber, James, 46
Thurow, Lester C., 106, 138
tolerance, 202
Trotsky, Leon, 78, 141

unemployment, 101–5

values, 200
Veblen, Thorstein, 126
Vietnam, 19

wages, 106
Walden II, 133
wars, 33, 84, 141
warlords, 78
WASPS, 29
Watson, John B., 113
welfare, 108
Wilson, Edmund, 137
Wilson, E. O., 21
Wilson, J. Q., 103–54, 157
work, 102–108

Y-chromosomes, 156

Zajonc, Robert B., 178
zero-sum game, 17, 31, 204

ABOUT THE AUTHOR

B. R. BUGELSKI is a Distinguished Professor, Emeritus, at the State University of New York at Buffalo. A Yale Ph.D. (1938), he taught at Antioch College, the University of Toledo, and at Buffalo (1946–1978). During World War II he served with the United States Navy as an Aviation Safety Analyst and from time to time acted as consultant to companies involved in the aviation and space areas. During approximately forty years of teaching and research, he has been consistently concerned with the implications and relevance of theoretical findings as related to practical affairs. In this book he spells out such implications for the common cause.